"Jonathan Parker is a gifted scholar and communicator who has opened fresh pathways for understanding the power of story in cross-cultural apologetics. With clarity and depth, he shows how narratives like C. S. Lewis's *Chronicles of Narnia* can bridge worldviews and invite readers to encounter the beauty and truth of the gospel. This book is both timely and important, offering Christians an imaginative and faithful resource for sharing Christ in a pluralistic age."

—DAVID A. CROTEAU, Dean, Seminary and School of Counseling,
Columbia International University

"In a world filled with competing stories and beliefs, *Other Watchful Dragons* is an essential resource. Parker bridges the worlds of literary imagination and missional urgency, providing a practical tool for missionaries, pastors, and Christians seeking to build authentic connections and share the gospel across cultures. This book offers a thoughtful analysis of Narnia, equipping the church for more thoughtful, creative, and effective witness."

—GREG VRUGGINK, Associate Professor of Old Testament,
Asia Biblical Theological Seminary

"As Jonathan Parker's winsome study shows, when C. S. Lewis in the 1950s shifted from writing apologetics to become the chronicler of Narnia, he didn't leave his Christian apologetics at the wardrobe door. Parker draws on narrative apologetics, comparative worldviews, and cross-cultural evangelism to offer his readers fresh insights into how the Narnia stories dramatize worldviews and woo readers to treasure the beauty, goodness, and truth found in Jesus Christ."

—STEVE BAARENDSE, Professor of English and Humanities,
Columbia International University

"How did Lewis and Tolkien captivate the attention of entire generations? They found that the use of stories is sometimes a more powerful apologetic tool than a logical syllogism. Jonathan Parker's new book on narrative apologetics offers a well-researched, theologically informed, and thoughtfully constructed framework for contextualizing the Christian message in just this way. This is a must have book for any apologist seeking to inspire others to take a stroll through the Shire, navigate their way through Narnia, or eagerly embark on a brand-new journey that builds bridges between the imagination and the truths of the Christian worldview."

—JOSH WALTMAN, Associate Professor of Theological Studies, Liberty Theological Seminary

"Jonathan Parker offers a compelling exploration of how *The Chronicles of Narnia* serves as a rich resource for cross-cultural apologetics. By weaving together narrative and theological insight, this work shows how Lewis's fiction not only communicates Christian truth and beauty but also challenges the coherence of competing belief systems. A vital contribution to both narrative and cross-cultural apologetics, this book reaffirms the enduring power of story in translating faith across cultures."

—BRIAN AUTRY, Executive Director, Southern Baptist Convention of Virginia

Other Watchful Dragons

Other Watchful Dragons

C. S. Lewis's *Chronicles of Narnia*
and Cross-Cultural Apologetics

JONATHAN M. PARKER

Foreword by Daniel J. Janosik

WIPF & STOCK · Eugene, Oregon

OTHER WATCHFUL DRAGONS
C. S. Lewis's *Chronicles of Narnia* and Cross-Cultural Apologetics

Copyright © 2026 Jonathan M. Parker. All rights reserved. Except for brief quotations in critical publications or reviews, no part of this book may be reproduced in any manner without prior written permission from the publisher. Write: Permissions, Wipf and Stock Publishers, 199 W. 8th Ave., Suite 3, Eugene, OR 97401.

Wipf & Stock
An Imprint of Wipf and Stock Publishers
199 W. 8th Ave., Suite 3
Eugene, OR 97401

www.wipfandstock.com

PAPERBACK ISBN: 979-8-3852-3711-1
HARDCOVER ISBN: 979-8-3852-3712-8
EBOOK ISBN: 979-8-3852-3713-5

01/02/26

Scripture quotations are from the ESV® Bible (The Holy Bible, English Standard Version®), © 2001 by Crossway, a publishing ministry of Good News Publishers. ESV text edition: 2025. The ESV text may not be quoted in any publication made available to the public by a Creative Commons license. The ESV may not be translated in whole or in part into any other language. Used by permission. All rights reserved.

Quotations from *Reimagining Apologetics* copyright © Justin Ariel Bailey, 2020. Used by permission of InterVarsity Press, P.O. Box 1400, Downers Grove, IL 60515, USA. www.ivpress.com.

All extracts by C. S. Lewis copyright © C. S. Lewis Pte. Ltd. Reprinted by permission.

Excerpts from *Narrative Apologetics* by Alister E. McGrath copyright © 2019. Used by permission of Baker Books, a division of Baker Publishing Group.

Quotations from *Apologetics and the Christian Imagination: An Integrated Approach to Defending the Faith* copyright © Holly Ordway, 2017. Used by permission of Emmaus Road Publishing.

Quotations from *The Universe Next Door: Sixth Edition* by James W. Sire. Copyright © 2020 by the Estate of James W. Sire. Used by permission of InterVarsity Press, P.O. Box 1400, Downers Grove, IL 60515, USA. www.ivpress.com.

Quotations from J. R. R. Tolkien reprinted by permission of HarperCollins Publishers Ltd.:

The Lord of the Rings © The Trustees of The J. R. R. Tolkien 1967 Settlement 1954/55, 1966.

The Letters of J. R. R. Tolkien © The Tolkien Estate Limited, 1981, 2023.

"On Fairy-stories" © The Tolkien Trust, 1947, 1964, 2008.

Quotations from *Christian Apologetics as Cross-Cultural Dialogue* © Benno van den Toren, 2011. Used by permission of T&T Clark, an imprint of Bloomsbury Publishing Plc.

To Kathryn, in gratitude for your love
and unwavering support (Prov 31:11).

To Kayleigh, Abigail, Kara, Nathan, and Zoe,
I am truly thankful for each of you.

Contents

Foreword by Daniel J. Janosik ... ix
Acknowledgments ... xi
Introduction ... 1

PART ONE | PAST WATCHFUL DRAGONS: EXPLORING NARRATIVE AND CROSS-CULTURAL APOLOGETICS

1. Classic Narrative Apologetics ... 15
2. Contemporary Narrative Apologetics ... 47
3. Cross-Cultural Apologetics ... 72
4. Six Keys for Cross-Cultural Narrative Apologetics ... 92

PART TWO | OTHER WATCHFUL DRAGONS: HOW NARNIA SPEAKS TO DIFFERENT WORLDVIEWS

5. Engaging Islam with *The Lion, the Witch and the Wardrobe* ... 103
6. Engaging Naturalism with *The Voyage of the Dawn Treader* ... 133
7. Engaging the Ontological Argument in *The Silver Chair* ... 153
8. Engaging Eastern Mysticism with *The Magician's Nephew* ... 168
9. Engaging Apatheism with *The Last Battle* ... 194

Conclusion: Building Bridges with Story ... 217
Appendix: Key Terms and Explanations ... 233
Bibliography ... 239
Index ... 261

Foreword

PEOPLE LOVE STORIES. STORIES have a way of slipping in behind our defenses and capturing our hearts. Stories open new worlds and offer fresh visions. No one understood the power of telling stories better than Jesus Christ.

C. S. Lewis, the beloved author of both fiction and nonfiction, clearly understood the power of stories. His fiction has been loved by generations. In particular, his *Chronicles of Narnia* have been translated into over forty-five languages and have sold well over one hundred million copies. The *Chronicles* are one of the bestselling series of all time.

Lewis understood the power of narrative. His *Narnia* tales confront false philosophies and religions in a way that directly engages the heart and captures the imagination of his readers. The truths of his tales have a way of sneaking behind a reader's natural defenses and capturing the mind before these defenses are even raised.

In our time, multiple philosophies and beliefs have raised seemingly impregnable walls against the truths of the gospel. But as a number of scholars have recently noted, the gospel travels most effectively through stories, and these stories can offer insight and conviction that other forms of evangelism cannot match.

A major contribution of Jonathan's book is to demonstrate the importance of narrative apologetics in our worldwide desire to reach every nation, tribe, and language with the gospel of Jesus Christ. His treatment of worldview profiles provides great models of how C. S. Lewis's *Narnia* stories can speak to various cultures and worldviews in a way that is not only disarming and creative, but also transforming. The need for narrative apologetics is greater now than ever before because good stories can better reach a wider range of cultures, with truth that sneaks in through the stories.

Many evangelists, missionaries, theologians, and apologists can greatly benefit from Jonathan's book. In addition, Jonathan's highlighting of the importance of narrative apologetics in our mission to reach the world for Christ will encourage an army of Christian writers to reflect on how their own stories can invite readers to go "further up and further in"![1]

DANIEL J. JANOSIK, PHD
Columbia, South Carolina

---

1. Lewis, *Last Battle*, 1077.

Acknowledgments

MANY MORE DESERVE ACKNOWLEDGMENT, but I will focus on just a few:

To my wife, Kathryn, who has been as supportive as a person can be. She has enriched my life and helped me be faithful to our family and ministry in ways I could not have done alone.

To my children, Kayleigh, Abigail, Kara, Nathan, and Zoe, it is my privilege and joy to be your father.

To my parents, for supporting me, praying for me, and modeling Christian love throughout my life.

To Dr. Daniel Janosik, for believing in this project and supporting me in countless ways. This book would not exist without you.

To Dr. Steve Baarendse and Dr. Charlie Starr, whose thoughtful critiques and clarifications substantially improved this work.

To Dr. Greg Welty, who generously offered helpful feedback on the ontological argument and allowed me to share his words.

To Caleb Woodbridge, you are a providential editor. This book is significantly improved because of your additions, skill, and craft. I am truly grateful.

Finally, I am thankful to the Lord. I have learned a great deal studying C. S. Lewis. As creative and contagious as Lewis is to me, it reminds me that as his maker, the Lord is the fountain of all creativity and the true satisfier of our longing hearts.

Soli Deo Gloria.

Introduction

STORIES ARE POWERFUL WAYS of building bridges and communicating ideas deeply. I've seen this for myself, particularly through C. S. Lewis's series of children's fantasy novels, *The Chronicles of Narnia*. Several years ago, I was teaching about the life of Jesus at a Christian university. The challenge was that most of my students were from non-Christian backgrounds, with little if any exposure to Christianity. In many ways these students lacked Christian categories to understand what we were discussing. Everything was new and unfamiliar. For better or worse, I chose to show some of the *Narnia* stories that had been adapted into movies. I found that because the students had experienced something like the Christian story, it was easy to communicate what the Bible was saying about Jesus and basic Christian beliefs. In an important sense, these college students were already familiar with the biblical story of Jesus when we talked about him in the Bible.

I've also seen this in my family life while listening to an audio version of *The Lion, the Witch and the Wardrobe*. My wife and I, along with our five children (ages five through seventeen at the time), were traveling back from a family vacation. As we listened to the story, there was an unseen weight felt in our vehicle when Aslan exchanged his life for Edmund's. Sensing the seriousness of the moment for my youngest daughter, Zoe, I asked why she thought Aslan had died. As we discussed the story, it was easy for her to understand how Edmund's heart had been ugly and that his consequences were real. The depth of love and Christlike quality of Aslan's grace was understandable to her in a potent way. This allowed me to share about the similar ugliness of our hearts, the true consequences of our sin from a biblical perspective, and the love and grace that Jesus shows those who trust in him.

NARRATIVE—A WAY OF SHAPING OUR BELIEFS

How do story and imagination help shape our Christian beliefs? How do they also contribute to shaping people's beliefs in other worldviews? These are questions of Christian apologetics, which defend and advocate the truth and goodness of the Christian faith. Apologetics doesn't need to be aggressive. Rather, following the example of twentieth-century pastor and apologist Francis Schaeffer, Christian apologetics should seek to lovingly remove false shelters that keep a fellow image bearer from seeing his or her need for the gospel (see 1 Pet 3:15).[1] Schaeffer explains this well: "Emotionally as well as intellectually, we must look at the man [or woman] before us as *our kind*. This man [or woman] is our counterpart; he [or she] is lost, but so once were we."[2] When effective, apologetics points to the truth of Christianity and removes obstacles that get in the way of Christian belief. *Narrative apologetics* is an approach that uses the resources of story and the imagination to help people believe.

The potential force of imagination is vividly seen in the life of systematic theologian Ellen Charry of Princeton Seminary. As a student at Temple University, Charry was studying the Augsburg Confession, trying to understand the doctrine of grace as a nonbeliever:

> Justification by grace through faith . . . justification by grace through faith—what are they talking about? So I decided to try it on. I lifted my arms up and I put over me like a dress, the doctrine. I tried it on myself. It wasn't just words. I tried it out. And I fell off the chair. It was in July, it was very hot; I was on the third floor in my study . . . I tried it on like a dress, and I just fell over.[3]

Charry's imagination helped translate an otherwise obscure Christian doctrine from a meaningless concept to a life-changing message that knocked her out of her seat. Narrative apologetics does not force a person to believe. Instead, it invites you to see, experience, savor, and, upon reflection, to understand and contemplate the truth of Christianity. It is a kind of pre-evangelism.

---

1. Schaeffer, *Complete Works*, 131–39.
2. Schaeffer, *Complete Works*, 131.
3. From an interview with Ellen Charry in Stafford, "New Theologians," 47. I first became aware of this story in Sire, *Habits of the Mind*, 73.

NARRATIVE—PART OF LEWIS'S JOURNEY OUT OF ATHEISM

C. S. Lewis also knew the power of the imagination, and literature played a significant role in him becoming a Christian. Lewis's path to Christianity was not a straight one, as he describes in several places.[4] There were many twists and turns, and Lewis entertained various beliefs along his road, including atheism, idealism, and the occult. Nevertheless, narrative played an important role, especially in evoking what he termed *Joy* or *Sehnsucht*. Lewis found throughout his life that he experienced a longing evoked by beauty and great literature that was curiously enjoyable and yet also painful because there was no obvious fulfillment. As a child Lewis's older brother made a miniature garden in a biscuit tin that stirred this longing. Lewis calls this "the first beauty" he ever knew.[5] Among his experiences, he notes that he encountered joy when reading Beatrix Potter's *Squirrel Nutkin*, in looking at a drawing with the words "Siegfried and the Twilight of the Gods," and in reading Norse mythology.[6] Then, when he was seventeen years old, an especially memorable encounter occurred when reading George MacDonald's *Phantastes*. Lewis recalls how *Phantastes* aroused his desire for joy to the highest level and brought about the recognition not only that he *desired* joy, but also that it was *right* to desire it.[7] While reading MacDonald's novel, Lewis's imagination was "baptised," as he described it, and it caused him to grasp the idea of holiness.[8] He was still miles from Christian faith, but literature was one of the ropes that was reluctantly drawing him to God.

THE ROLE OF CULTURE AND MAKING

Given the role that narrative played in Lewis's conversion, it might surprise you to know that in the close of his important work on literature, *An Experiment in Criticism*, Lewis rejected the idea that the value of literature lies in communicating truths about life.[9] Earlier in the same work,

---

4. Lewis, "Early Prose Joy"; Lewis, *Surprised by Joy*; also see Lewis, *Pilgrim's Regress*.
5. Lewis, *Surprised by Joy*, 6.
6. Lewis, "Early Prose Joy," 15, 19.
7. Lewis, "Early Prose Joy," 22.
8. Lewis, "Early Prose Joy," 23.
9. Lewis, *Experiment in Criticism*, 130.

he says that we "use" rather than "receive" fiction when we value it mainly for ideas or morals we can draw out of it.[10]

As Lewis describes in his essay "Christianity and Culture," he struggled to understand the place of culture-making early in his Christian life. His question was due in part to his vocation as a scholar of literature and his prior belief that culture is inherently valuable on its own terms and good for human beings. But following his conversion, he began to question an elevated view of culture as offering almost a secular alternative to salvation. He began to ask, If glorifying God and saving souls are what is really important, what is the place of culture? In the end, Lewis came to see that while humility about the role of culture is needed, culture-making is both good and pleasurable within the moral law and can be done to God's glory, just as *any* earthly activity can be offered up to him, even as simple as sweeping the floor.[11]

Lewis became convinced that it may even be the Christian's duty to create culture.[12] Still, he saw doing a bait and switch where you promise your readers a story and use it as a chance to preach at them as a kind of fraud or stealing. Instead, Christians need to simply have a presence among a culture's storytellers.[13]

There are two important insights that are worth hearing from Lewis before considering how narrative can play a part in apologetics. First, as we have seen, Lewis believed that the primary purpose of culture-making is enjoyment.[14] Charlie Starr summarizes this well:

> The purpose of sub-creation ["doing on a finite level what God did infinitely at the creation"] is not to make something to be used for other purposes, but to participate in pleasure and worship in acting out in ourselves the Divine impulse of creativity given us as bearers of the image of God . . . we make for the delight of making. That act alone is sufficient reason for a book's, painting's, or movie's existence—it is made out of delight, out of a God given desire to imitate Him. It is an act of worship.[15]

10. Lewis, *Experiment in Criticism*, 82–83.

11. Lewis, "Christianity and Culture," 21.

12. Lewis, "Christianity and Culture," 25. This recalls James Hunter's concept of "faithful presence." Hunter, *To Change the World*.

13. Lewis, "Christianity and Culture," 34.

14. This section was significantly improved by insights from Charlie Starr. See, for example, Starr, "Aesthetics vs. Anesthesia"; Starr, "Meaning, Meanings, and Epistemology"; Starr, "How Sho*uld We* Teach English?"

15. Starr, "Aesthetics vs. Anesthesia," 124.

Lewis maintains that artworks should be received as they are intended. Most literature was made to be read for pleasure, and if we don't engage with it "for fun," we are missing the point. As he memorably puts it, "It is no good judging a butter-knife by seeing whether it will saw logs."[16] Butter knives are not intended to saw logs, and literature is not primarily intended for analysis.

Not only are stories intended to be enjoyed, true knowledge of a story comes through *experiencing* it rather than analyzing it. Lewis explains what may be called the problem of looking along and looking at the sunbeam.[17] He uses the illustration of being in a darkened toolshed. If there's a crack, you can *look at* the beam of light from the outside. But if you move to stand in the beam, *looking along* it, you see out into the world beyond. He explains, "The more lucidly we think, the more we are cut off: the more deeply we enter into reality, the less we can think. . . . Of this tragic dilemma myth is the partial solution. In the enjoyment of a great myth we come nearest to experiencing as a concrete what can otherwise be understood only as an abstraction."[18] This observation is profound: as a rule, we cannot know experientially and in abstraction at the same time. If we are analyzing, we are not experiencing the art, which, from Lewis's perspective, is its primary purpose.

Two Years After *An Experiment in Criticism*

Reason, nevertheless, plays an important role in literature for Lewis. While valuing myths highly, Lewis also believed that myths need to be judged by reason. Adam Barkman explains why: "If the images in the imagination cannot be so judged, then there is no way to say that one myth is truer than another or one religion better than the next."[19]

---

16. Lewis, "Christianity and Culture," 34.

17. Lewis, "Meditation in a Toolshed," 230.

18. Lewis, "Myth Became Fact," 65–66. This insight was significantly helped by Starr, "Meaning, Meanings, and Epistemology," 176–78; also see Starr, "How *Should* We Teach English?" 63–81.

19. Barkman writes, "The key element of disagreement between Barfield and Lewis ['Lewis's Great War development'] was over, as Lewis argued, the inability of the imaginations to judge their own content. . . . Lewis always asserted that even myths, those concrete universals that refuse to be allegorized or whittled down by reason, must be judged by reason as being either true or false, for if the images in the imagination cannot be so judged, then there is no way to say that one myth is truer than another or one religion better than the next." Barkman, *C. S. Lewis & Philosophy*, 315.

Similarly, two years after the publication year of *An Experiment in Criticism*, Lewis wrote a letter to Nancy Warner dated October 26, 1963. In the letter, Lewis applauds a perceptive young man who recognized a narrative form of the ontological argument (an argument for the existence of God) in *The Silver Chair*, where Puddleglum puts out the Green Witch's fire with his foot. Lewis credits Anselm and Descartes for the argument, saying that he simply adapted it for children.[20]

With this said, I agree with Lewis that narrative and culture-making should chiefly be valued for enjoyment or for the enlargement of seeing through another's eyes. The *best* is to simply read literary art and enjoy it, to be enlarged by seeing from another point of view, or to simply create a story for the pleasure of making. As J. R. R. Tolkien's theologically rich reflections suggest, we make because we are made in the image of God as the Maker.[21] These are goods in themselves.

ON SECONDARY GOODS

If culture-making and enjoyment are the primary goals of storytelling, are there other secondary goods and possibilities too? I believe so. As I will make the case in this book, narrative apologetics, *The Chronicles of Narnia* in particular, can contribute to cross-cultural apologetics by helping translate relevant Christian beliefs, advocating Christianity's truth and goodness, subverting the adequacy of non-Christian beliefs, and helping respond to objections made against Christian belief.[22]

First of all, I should emphasize that I am looking at *The Chronicles of Narnia* as *one* particular example of what can be done in narrative. Other works and types of examinations are possible. I will also explore how they relate to various narrative and cross-cultural apologetic models. These different models provide insight into what can be done and how a given work could apply to cross-cultural readers in its final form. Second, my argument does not exclusively depend on Lewis's intent. A story's applicability can exceed original intent. With this said, my personal experience, Lewis's own words (e.g., his 1963 letter), and others' experiences that I

---

20. Lewis, *Collected Letters*, 3:1472.

21. Tolkien, *On Fairy-Stories*, 66.

22. *Cross-cultural* as it is used here applies to international contexts, but it is considered according to general worldview or belief system.

share later, all give good reasons for exploring the *Chronicles* as being stories first, but narrative apologetics as a significant secondary purpose.

Think back to my opening experiences. Showing some of the *Narnia* stories to non-Christian students highlights their potential for *cross-cultural communication*. The conversations I had with my children as they listened to *The Lion, the Witch and the Wardrobe* illustrate *The Chronicles of Narnia's* ability to create *bridges for theological discussion*. Here is a critical point: neither of these examples was forced or contrived. It was perfectly natural and understandable to talk about Jesus and core Christian beliefs because Narnia was already familiar and known. And yet, in both instances, I was talking with individuals who were only beginning to understand Jesus and Christian concepts like guilt, justice, grace, and forgiveness.

Finally, Lewis's own words invite analysis beyond enjoyment. He claims that, as an author, he wrote fairy tales because they seemed the right form for what he wished to communicate. However, once the form was established, "the man" in him had his turn at bringing out themes from what had arisen imaginatively, and he could see an opportunity to "steal past the watchful dragons" of not being able to see or feel the Christian story in its full power.[23]

But what could this mean? If we know that Christian-like truths and images are in some sense embodied in *The Chronicles of Narnia*, how might these serve cross-cultural apologetic purposes? Because *The Chronicles of Narnia* are now translated into some forty-seven different languages, they are especially well positioned for this. Lewis's stories and mythic images also continue to expand in other contexts, such as new series and films being developed by Netflix.[24]

PURPOSE

Very simply, I want to show some of the ways that narrative apologetics can contribute to cross-cultural apologetics. Three groups may especially benefit from what I have found. First, normal Christians looking for natural paths to discuss the truth, goodness, and beauty of Christianity in a pluralistic world. Second, Christians living in closed countries or missionaries who want to communicate Christianity or contrast Christian truths with other belief systems. Third and finally, for Christian writers,

---

23. Lewis, "Sometimes Fairy Stories," 57–59.
24. Halcombe, "Netflix to Develop Series and Films."

where artistically appropriate, I have identified themes that are both naturally relevant because of their existential significance and important dividing lines among worldviews.

I noted earlier that Lewis distinguishes between Lewis "the man" and Lewis "the artist." Lewis completely rejects the charge that he took a list of Christian truths and then crafted allegories to embody them.[25] The form of a fairy-story came first to him as the artist, and the embellishment of the story with Christian themes followed as the work of the man. Even fellow Inkling J. R. R. Tolkien, who was especially reticent about his faith in association with his art, acknowledges his *conscious* "revision" in private correspondence with Robert Murray on December 2, 1953, where he described it as a "fundamentally religious and Catholic work," though with its religious themes "absorbed into the story and the symbolism."[26] The key point for an author is this: the integrity of the story should come first, but themes should be developed where it is artistically appropriate.

AN OVERVIEW

Narrative Apologetics

In this chapter, I will explore some of the best work that has been done in narrative apologetics. First, I consider three "classic" examples: George MacDonald (1824–1905), J. R. R. Tolkien (1892–1973), and C. S. Lewis (1898–1963). They might not all have seen themselves as engaging in narrative apologetics as such, but they all reflected on the relationship between their storytelling and Christian faith in ways that implicitly offer a model for understanding narrative apologetics. Next, I explore three contemporary thinkers who offer models of narrative apologetics: Alister McGrath, Holly Ordway, and Justin Bailey. For each model, I look to consider the needs they address, their relevance, potential, and helpful insights. Each of these models contributes to a fuller understanding of what can be done to advocate Christian belief using imaginative and

---

25. It should be noted that Lewis did value John Bunyan's allegory, *The Pilgrim's Progress*, and celebrated Bunyan's self-reflection as an author. Lewis writes, "Then come the words which describe, better than any others I know, the golden moments of unimpeded composition: 'For having now my Method by the end; Still as I pull'd, it came.' It came. I doubt if we shall ever know more of the process called 'inspiration' than those two monosyllables tell us." See Lewis, "Vision of John Bunyan," 207.

26. Carpenter and Tolkien, *Letters of Tolkien*, 172.

narrative paths. They also provide a more robust appreciation of the kind of apologetic features that exist in *The Chronicles of Narnia*.

Cross-Cultural Apologetics

After identifying some of the best resources for narrative apologetics, I turn to cross-cultural apologetics. In chapter 3, I look at two cross-cultural apologetic models to identify the particular needs, barriers, and possibilities for cross-cultural engagement. This will help us identify some of the most critical pathways and targets for narrative apologetics and begin to identify ways that *The Chronicles of Narnia* naturally advocate belief to cross-cultural readers. I consider two cross-cultural apologetic projects, those of Benno van den Toren and Harold Netland. I first show how each of them understands cross-cultural apologetics and then consider some of the most essential needs, barriers, and engagement pathways identified by their models.

Six Keys for Cross-Cultural Narrative Apologetics

Drawing on the different models examined, I identify six keys, or narrative motifs, that are especially relevant for cross-cultural apologetics in *The Chronicles of Narnia*: (1) translation, (2) transformation, (3) treasure, (4) tension, (5) concern, and (6) call. These keys are informed by the strengths of narrative apologetics, insights from cross-cultural and traditional apologetics, relevant insights from conversion stories, and scholarship related to leaving a given belief system. After identifying a given challenge, I examine the challenge in relation to these motifs.

Translation is understood as how *The Chronicles of Narnia* help to communicate core doctrines, values, and practices of Christianity.[27] *Transformation* considers how Aslan and his kingdom impact people and places positively or how a rejection of Aslan and his kingdom has a detrimental effect. *Treasure* focuses on what is celebrated and what is not in *The Chronicles of Narnia*. Where is longing satisfied, and where is it not? What is true, good, and beautiful, and what is not? *Tension* is how Narnia engages with the existential tensions inherent in a given belief system. Tensions include cosmic security, questions of immortality and life after

---

27. For fuller explanation, see chapter 4: Six Keys for Cross-Cultural Narrative Apologetics.

death, meaning and purpose, fulfillment, forgiveness, truth and living against truth, and love. Tension also includes known problems in each worldview. *Concern* relates to a response to relevant objections to Christianity from a given worldview such as evil, exclusive religious claims, skepticism about the goodness of Christianity, and the like. Finally, *Call* is a lens that considers how Christian belief is advocated. This includes narrative forms of arguments or aspects of arguments such as the moral argument, ontological argument, or argument from desire, as well as any other means. My six motifs are then used as categories to identify and analyze how *The Chronicles of Narnia* engage a given worldview in part two of my project.

In part two, I analyze how *The Chronicles of Narnia* advocate Christian belief to a specific belief system through the lens of my six narrative motifs: translation, transformation, treasure, tension, concern, call. Because much of the potency is in Lewis's actual story, I have tried to avoid fragmenting his stories as much as possible. This is why I focus on a specific book of *The Chronicles of Narnia* series for a given worldview:

- *The Lion, the Witch and the Wardrobe* and Islam;
- *The Voyage of the Dawn Treader* and naturalism;
- *The Magician's Nephew* and Eastern pantheistic monism; and
- *The Last Battle* and apatheism.

I also include a chapter on *The Silver Chair* and the ontological argument for God's existence. This isn't specific to a particular worldview but is a good case-study of how Lewis weaves in a classic apologetics argument into a story.

Because the atmospheric qualities of Lewis's stories are so critical for appreciating how his story advocates or challenges a given belief, I try to convey Lewis's storylines as fully as I can. Of course, his own writing is simply irreplaceable, so they are best read with the books close at hand. I recommend reading the *Narnia* stories alongside my book for a full appreciation of what I'm discussing in my summaries and analysis.

By the end of the book, I aim to have shown you the cross-cultural potential of narrative apologetics with *The Chronicles of Narnia* as a prime example. I hope this will inspire and equip you for cross-cultural apologetic conversations and for the writing of new stories that can themselves build bridges for communicating the gospel story and significant Christian truths. Stories, like the wardrobe to Narnia, have the potential to be the doorway into a new world, into embracing Christianity and discovering the one in our world who Aslan points to.

PART ONE

Past Watchful Dragons

Exploring Narrative and Cross-Cultural Apologetics

1

Classic Narrative Apologetics

INTRODUCTION

CAN LITERATURE AND THE imagination contribute to forming Christian beliefs? If so, can they help people who currently hold other worldviews to come to accept Christian beliefs? Christian apologetics is broadly understood as an effort to defend or advocate the truth of the Christian faith. Narrative apologetics uses the resources of literature and the imagination to accomplish the same purpose.

    C. S. Lewis is a leading example of a writer who self-consciously understood his fiction as having an apologetic dimension. In this section, I will consider his approach to narrative apologetics alongside two other classic examples, each of which influenced Lewis, specifically George MacDonald, who was influential in baptizing the imagination of Lewis,[1] and J. R. R. Tolkien, who was Lewis's long-time friend and fellow Inkling. This is not to say that MacDonald and Tolkien would have seen what they were doing as "narrative apologetics"—Tolkien may well have resisted the idea as too close to "allegory," which he claimed to dislike.[2] But because each author still contributes to the general aims of narrative apologetics, such as familiarization with Christian themes and having an embedded Christian worldview, I have included them. In the next chapter, I will go on to consider some contemporary models of narrative apologetics. Together,

---

1. Lewis, *Surprised by Joy*, 222.
2. Tolkien, *Lord of the Rings*, xxiv.

they offer a broader canvas for understanding Lewis's achievement in *The Chronicles of Narnia* and the wider possibilities of narrative apologetics.

GEORGE MACDONALD: BAPTIZING THE IMAGINATION

George MacDonald (1824–1905) was a Scottish author and pastor whose work influenced many notable writers, including C. S. Lewis, J. R. R. Tolkien, G. K. Chesterton, and Owen Barfield. In the wake of numerous scientific and philosophical developments that were taken to challenge traditional Christian thought, it was a time widely seen as an "age of doubt." This growing uncertainty around the Christian faith was a *need* that MacDonald addressed with an imaginative response. Perhaps surprisingly, Lewis writes that MacDonald's literature, when defined as "art whose medium is words," was perhaps not even second rank. Yet, he also describes MacDonald's fantasy writing as "better than any man."[3]

Art for Truth's Sake

MacDonald's writing was intentional in rousing people toward truth. He believed the imagination and fairy tales are uniquely suited to convey truth in ways that could not be accomplished through propositions alone. MacDonald was not advocating a shallow didacticism. Rather, he writes, "The best thing you can do for your fellow, next to rousing his conscience, is—not to give him things to think about, but to wake things up that are in him; or say, to make him think things for himself."[4] MacDonald responded to the literary ideal of "Art for art's sake" that was current in his day, acknowledging the "half wisdom" of protesting the pursuit of art for the sake of money or fame, but contending that the right cry should be "Art for truth's sake!"[5] He continues, "But when certain writers tell us that the true aim of the author of fiction is to give the people what they want, namely, a reflection, as in a mirror, of themselves—a mirror not such as will show them to themselves as they are, but as they seem to each other, some of us feel that we stand on the verge of an abyss of

---

3. Lewis, *George MacDonald*, xxix.

4. MacDonald, "Fantastic Imagination," 18745.

5. MacDonald, preface to *For the Right*, 3; first seen in, Johnson, "Rooted in All Its Story," xvii.

falsehood."⁶ MacDonald believed that fiction is potentially transformational and, more importantly, that it *should* be.⁷ He contends, "Whoever has an ideal and is making no struggle toward it, is sinking into the outer darkness. The ideal is the end, and must be the object of life. Attained, or but truly conceived, we must think of it as the indispensable."⁸ As George MacDonald scholar Kirstin Johnson remarks, "MacDonald firmly believed that art itself arises as a response, and is an effort on the part of one person to communicate that response to another person or persons."⁹ Elsewhere she adds, "[MacDonald's] prime intent in writing is to 'wake up' his readers to the proffered revelation of the Divine Imagination."¹⁰ MacDonald's writing, in this sense, had an intentional narrative apologetic dimension.

Relevance of MacDonald to Narrative Apologetics

MacDonald's understanding of imagination and his writing offer three important underpinnings for narrative apologetics:

1. human imagination as an aspect of being image bearers;
2. the relationality of God; and
3. God as an artist.

First, MacDonald believed that the imagination has a God-given function for humans as image bearers. The imagination has a divine function and duty because of its relation to the Father. To follow and "find out the divine imagination in whose image it was made . . . he must contemplate what the Hebrew poets call the works of His hands."¹¹ Second, MacDonald believed that because God is a relational God, relationship is better conveyed through story than propositions. Johnson explains, "MacDonald believes that an understanding of the intrinsically relational God cannot be grasped outside of a relational hermeneutic; that a list of dry

---

6. MacDonald, preface to *For the Right*, 3.

7. Justin Bailey is right to caution against viewing MacDonald's mythopoetic art as "instrumental." That said, this suggests that MacDonald is also purposed; see Bailey, *Reimagining Apologetics*, 127.

8. MacDonald, preface to *For the Right*, 3.
9. Johnson, "Rooted in All Its Story," xviii.
10. Johnson, "Rooted in All Its Story," xxi.
11. MacDonald, "Imagination: Functions and Culture," 18481.

propositions would never be able to convey what the fullness of poesis could."[12] Finally, MacDonald believes that God is better understood as a personal artist, rather than mechanistically. The scientific revolution had led to an increasingly mechanistic view of the world. Even the Christian case for a creator was framed by William Paley (1743–1805) by analogy with clockwork: he likened the discovery of the natural order of the world to finding a watch, which implies that there must be a "divine watchmaker." MacDonald writes that more than a "mechanical God"—what he thought Paley proved, at best—God is "the first of artists."[13] He continues, "If man be the child of God, would he not feel to be out of his element if he lived in a world which came, not from the heart of God, but only from his hand?"[14] He also says, "To the man of God, all nature will be but changeful reflections of the face of God."[15] These convictions anticipate the method of MacDonald's art.

MacDonald and the Potential of Narrative Apologetics

There are at least four potentials that MacDonald sees for fairy tales:

1. They communicate what is difficult to define.
2. They create an atmosphere for belief.
3. They wake what is already within the reader.
4. They transform.

First, *fairy tales communicate what is difficult to define*. In his essay "The Fantastic Imagination," MacDonald offers a description of what he calls a fairy tale. Rather than define it, he recommends reading *Undine* by Friedrich de la Motte Fouqué—a fairy tale that he finds "most beautiful."[16] For MacDonald, fairy tales are more easily experienced than defined. It is like describing an abstract human face—"a face is just a face."[17] In addition to communicating what is difficult to define, MacDonald argues that a fairy tale that is a genuine work of art will mean many things. He writes,

---

12. Johnson, "Rooted in All Its Story," xxi.
13. MacDonald, "Wordsworth's Poetry," 18683.
14. MacDonald, "Wordsworth's Poetry," 18683.
15. MacDonald, "Wordsworth's Poetry," 18693.
16. MacDonald, "Fantastic Imagination," 18740.
17. MacDonald, "Fantastic Imagination," 18740.

"The truer its art, the more things it will mean. . . . It is there not so much to convey a meaning as to wake a meaning."[18] MacDonald likens the true fairy tale to a sonata:

> We all know that a sonata means something. . . . But if two or three men sat down to write each what the sonata meant to him, what approximation to definite idea would be the result? Little enough—and that little more than needful. We should find it had roused related, if not identical, feelings, but probably not one common thought. Has the sonata therefore failed?[19]

Good fairy tales will mean more than what is written. Like music, MacDonald believes that a fairy tale can "impress" or convey what is at times "undefinable." He writes, "A fairytale, a sonata, a gathering storm, a limitless night, seizes you and sweeps you away: do you begin at once to wrestle with it and ask whence its power over you, whither it is carrying you?" He continues, "To one the sonata is a world of odour and beauty, to another of soothing only and sweetness. To one, the cloudy rendezvous is a wild dance, with a terror at its heart; to another, a majestic march of heavenly hosts, with Truth in their centre pointing their course, but as yet restraining her voice." Most notably, MacDonald contends that the greatest forces exist "in the region of the uncomprehended."[20] Fairy tales communicate experience in a way that goes beyond simple description.

Second, *good fairy tales create an atmosphere for belief*, in much the same way as nature. MacDonald asks,

> Does any aspect of Nature wake but one thought? Does she ever suggest only one definite thing? Does she make any two men in the same place at the same moment think the same thing? Is she therefore a failure, because she is not definite? Is it nothing that she rouses the something deeper than the understanding—the power that underlies thoughts? Does she not set feeling, and so thinking at work? Would it be better that she did this after one fashion and not after many fashions? Nature is mood-engendering, thought-provoking: such ought the sonata, such ought the fairytale to be.[21]

---

18. MacDonald, "Fantastic Imagination," 18743.
19. MacDonald, "Fantastic Imagination," 18743–44.
20. MacDonald, "Fantastic Imagination," 18745.
21. MacDonald, "Fantastic Imagination," 18745.

MacDonald explains that nature works "moods" into us, and in this atmosphere, "thoughts of high import arise."[22] This is why these created worlds must operate by laws. "Law," he writes, "is the soil in which alone beauty will grow; beauty is the only stuff in which Truth can be clothed; and you may, if you will, call Imagination the tailor that cuts her garments to fit her, and Fancy his journeyman that puts the pieces of them together." The moral laws of the invented world are not flexible, even if clothed in new forms. MacDonald explains, "The laws of the spirit of man must hold, alike in this world and in any world he may invent . . . it would be wicked to write a tale representing a man it called good as always doing bad things, or a man it called bad as always doing good things."[23] Once the fairy-tale world is created, it must operate with harmonious laws that cannot be violated; otherwise, the world will be "incredible."[24] Good fairy tales create an atmosphere, one of moral order and meaning, that set a context where belief can grow.

Third, *fairy tales attempt to wake up what is already within the reader.* As discussed earlier, MacDonald argues that the best thing he can do for a reader, other than "rousing his conscience," is to wake the unseen music within his reader if it is there to be awakened.[25] Waking what is already in a reader connects with a final potential that MacDonald sees in fairy tales—transformation.

Fourth, *fairy-stories attempt to transform the reader.* C. S. Lewis, who was both a literary scholar and one who knew firsthand about the waking and transforming force of MacDonald's work, writes this of MacDonald's mythopoetic art:

> It may even be one of the greatest arts; for it produces works which give us (at the first meeting) as much delight and (on prolonged acquaintance) as much wisdom and strength as the works of the greatest poets. It is in some ways more akin to music than to poetry—or at least to most poetry. It goes beyond the expression of things we have already felt. It arouses in us sensations we have never had before, never anticipated having, as though we had broken out of our normal mode of consciousness and "possessed joys not promised to our birth." It gets under our skin, hits us at a level deeper than our thoughts

---

22. MacDonald, "Fantastic Imagination," 1874 5.
23. MacDonald, "Fantastic Imagination," 1874 2.
24. MacDonald, "Fantastic Imagination," 1874 1.
25. MacDonald, "Fantastic Imagination," 1874 5.

or even our passions, troubles oldest certainties till all questions are reopened, and in general shocks us more fully awake than we are for most of our lives.[26]

As Lewis recounts in *Surprised by Joy*, he began his move from atheism to theism while reading MacDonald's book *Phantastes, a Faerie Romance*.[27] Fairy-stories can transform a reader, and MacDonald wrote stories capable of working powerful transformation.

The Apologetic Potential of Fairy Tales

MacDonald uses several pathways to advocate Christian belief. Two are especially important: (1) encountered beauty and (2) argumentation.

One way that MacDonald also advocates belief is through *encounters with beauty*. In his piece "Wordsworth's Poetry," delivered extempore at Manchester, MacDonald posits that the created world is "an expression of the thought, the feeling, the heart of God himself." The poets of the Old and New Testament, he remarks, viewed the world as the "work of his hand," and even more intimately, that "we are his offspring"—the children that came "forth from his heart." MacDonald argues that the world comes "from the heart of God," not only from his hand.[28] Again, MacDonald believed that God was "the first of artists." He continues,

> Let us go further; and, looking at beauty, believe that God is the first of artists; that he has put beauty into nature, knowing how it will affect us, and intending that it should so affect us; that he has embodied his own grand thoughts thus that we might see them and be glad. Then, let us go further still, and believe that whatever we feel in the highest moments of truth shining through beauty, whatever comes to our souls as a power of life, is meant to be seen and felt by us, and to be regarded not as the work of his hand, but as the flowing forth of his heart, the flowing forth of his love of us, making us blessed in the union of his heart and ours.[29]

This beauty is what MacDonald believed Wordsworth saw when beheld in "the awful mountain-peak, sky-encompassed with loveliness, or upon the

---

26. Lewis, *George MacDonald*, xxxi.
27. Lewis, *Surprised by Joy*, 220–23.
28. MacDonald, "Wordsworth's Poetry," 18683.
29. MacDonald, "Wordsworth's Poetry," 18683.

face of a little child."³⁰ MacDonald explains this further: "When we understand the Word of God, then we understand the works of God; when we know the nature of an artist, we know his pictures; when we have known and talked with the poet, we understand his poetry far better. To the man of God, all nature will be but changeful reflections of the face of God."³¹ Dean Hardy observes that, for MacDonald, "the signaling of aesthetic experience, and the ability of human nature to indicate and enjoy beauty was a sign of God's existence and his creative handiwork."³² Moreover, Hardy continues, "the ability to find new meaning in a work of art, and a meaning that was not intended by the artist, also signals a divine cause."³³ Notice MacDonald's words: "The fact that there is always more in a work of art—which is the highest human result of the embodying imagination—than the producer himself perceived while he produced it, seems to us a strong reason for attributing to it a larger origin than the man alone—for saying at the last, that the inspiration of the Almighty shaped its ends."³⁴

Building on MacDonald's conviction that beauty points to God, Hardy argues that MacDonald uses the "reflection of aesthetic experience" to point to God's existence. Hardy explains, "MacDonald often used a reflection of the aesthetic experience to draw the reader toward the beautiful, then redirects them to the existence of the grand and ultimate artist."³⁵ One example is seen in MacDonald's autobiographical novel *Wilfrid Cumbermede*:

> It was the loveliest evening that brooded round us as we walked. The moon had emerged from a rippled sea of grey cloud, over which she cast her dull opaline halo. Great masses and banks of cloud lay about the rest of the heavens, and, in the dark rifts between, a star or two were visible, gazing from the awful distance.
> "I wish I could let it into me, Wilfrid," said Charley, after we had been walking in silence for some time along the grass.
> "Let what into you, Charley?"
> "The night and the blue and the stars."
> "Why don't you, then?"³⁶

---

30. MacDonald, "Wordsworth's Poetry," 18683. MacDonald uses the somewhat confusing words "Christian pantheism" to mean that God is "overwhelmingly immanent." See Hardy, *Waking the Dead*, 45.

31. MacDonald, "Wordsworth's Poetry," 18693.

32. Hardy, *Waking the Dead*, 146.

33. Hardy, *Waking the Dead*, 146.

34. MacDonald, "Imagination: Function and Culture," 18495.

35. Hardy, *Waking the Dead*, 143.

36. MacDonald, *Wilfrid Cumbermede*, 5854–55.

Charley is moved by the atmosphere and drawn to the beauty of creation, yet hesitant to follow the beauty in the way it seems to point him. Wilfrid asks him why. Charley replies, "I hate being taken in. The more pleasant a self-deception, the less I choose to submit to it."[37]

As they talk, Wilfrid presses Charley on the nature of beauty from his perspective. Wilfrid asks, "Suppose I asked you wherein its beauty consisted: would you be satisfied if I said—In the arrangement of the blue and the white, with the sparkles of yellow, and the colours about the scarce visible moon?" But Charley is dissatisfied with the emptiness of that thought. He responds, "Certainly not. I should reply that it lay in the gracious peace of the whole—troubled only with the sense of some lovely secret behind, of which itself was but the half-modelled representation, and therefore the reluctant outcome."[38]

Wilfrid offers another perspective, consistent with a world that wasn't created: suppose this perceived beauty is merely the "fortuitous result of the half-necessary, half-fortuitous concurrences of nature." He continues,

> "Suppose I said:—The air which is necessary to our life, happens to be blue; the stars can't help shining through it and making it look deep; and the clouds are just there because they must be somewhere till they fall again; all which is more agreeable to us than fog because we feel more comfortable in weather of the sort, whence, through complacency and habit, we have got to call it beautiful:—suppose I said this, would you accept it?"

Charley's response is striking: "Such a theory would destroy my delight in nature altogether."[39]

This is part of a longer passage that is saturated with beauty and desire that feels like the real world. In this imaginative brush with reality, MacDonald invites the reader to reflect on beauty. MacDonald's reflection trades on satisfaction, desire, pleasure, and delight, as well as reason. The dialogue repeatedly, but gently, asks this question about beauty: "Would this explanation satisfy you?" The answer is considered through two views of the world: purposeful or accidental. One world is an accidental, purposeless world, in which peace, grandeur, and beauty are only a mirage. The other world is created with purpose by a God with preexistent beauty, who has fashioned us to stand in awe and wonder at beauty.

37. MacDonald, *Wilfrid Cumbermede*, 5854.
38. MacDonald, *Wilfrid Cumbermede*, 5854–55.
39. MacDonald, *Wilfrid Cumbermede*, 5855.

A second way that MacDonald advocates Christian belief is through *argumentation*. Although MacDonald did not think argumentation itself results in faith, he does use arguments in his imaginative work. Hardy explains MacDonald's general posture toward reason and argumentation: "While rationality did not produce faith, it could prompt someone to search for God, and that could lead the way for an inspired searcher to look further." Hardy continues, "Rationality could never twist arms, but it could direct the mind, and by steps of varying degrees, eventually help change the heart."[40]

One such example occurs in MacDonald's *There and Back* (another of his realist novels, also published as *The Baron's Apprenticeship*). In the context, Richard (who does not believe) experiences the wonder and desire of music as he had not before:

> The first throbbing flash of the violins cleft his soul as lightning cleaves a dark cloud, and set his body shivering as with its thunder—and lo, a door was opened in heaven! and, like the writhings of a cloud in the grasp of a heavenly wind, all the discords of spirit-pain were breaking up, changing, and solving themselves into the song of the violins! After that, he went every Monday night to the same concert-room. It was his church, the mount of his ascension, the place whence he soared—no, but was lifted up to what was as yet his highest consciousness of being. All that was best and simplest in him came wide awake as he sat and listened.

MacDonald conveys the worship-like experience evoked by music for Richard. He is drawn with wonder like a churchgoer, but his affections don't move beyond himself. From a Christian perspective, he was made for worship, but he doesn't know it. The narrative reflects on Richard's situation further as it continues:

> What fact did the music prove? None whatever. Yet would not the logic of all science have persuaded Richard that the sea of mood and mystic response, tossing his soul hither and thither on its radiant waters, as, deep unto deep, it answered the marching array of live waves, fashioned one by one out of the still air, marshalled and ranked and driven on in symmetric relation and order by those strange creative powers with their curious symbols, throned at their godlike labour—that the answer of his soul, I say, was but an illusion, the babble of a sleeping child in

---

40. Hardy, *Waking the Dead*, 140.

reply to a question never put. If it was an illusion, how came it that such illusion was possible?[41]

Here MacDonald appeals to reason and wonder. He highlights the existential barrenness of logical explanations for what Richard (and the captivated reader) is experiencing. The music seems to point beyond itself to another dimension; and it is good and hopeful: "All that was best and simplest in him came awake as he sat and listened." Much more transpires in the scene, but MacDonald closes the chapter with an informal argument:[42]

> Who invented music? Some one must have made the delight of it possible! With his own share in its joy he had had nothing to do! Was Chance its grand inventor, its great ingenieur? Why or how should Chance love loveliness that was not, and make it be, that others might love it? Could it be a deaf God, or a being that did not care and would not listen, that invented music? No; music did not come of itself, neither could the source of it be devoid of music![43]

Notice several features. First, music is captivating to many people. Richard's experience is likely to be familiar to the reader. Second, MacDonald's appeal is to a cosmological argument—*ex nihilo nihil fit*—out of nothing, nothing comes. The music does not plausibly originate from nothing, and it is not self-created. Third, the cause of this beauty delights in aesthetic goodness, and it must be good and orderly. Finally, as hearers we are fit to receive his grace—could it be a deaf God, or a being that did not care and would not listen? MacDonald argues that God is a much better fit for the beauty of music than a world without him.

Helpful Insights from MacDonald

There are several important points to take from studying George MacDonald. First, history testifies to MacDonald's effectiveness. His project was not just theory. C. S. Lewis, for example, describes a significant debt he felt to MacDonald in the preface of the collection he assembled.[44]

---

41. MacDonald, *There and Back*, 15288.

42. Justin Bailey, for example, importantly notes the "Dantean moment" of the scene as MacDonald writes, "Hell became purgatory, for there was hope in it." See Bailey, *Reimagining Apologetics*, 145.

43. MacDonald, *There and Back*, 15291.

44. Lewis, *George MacDonald*, xxxvii.

Lewis regarded MacDonald as his mentor and regularly featured MacDonald's writing in his own. Lewis even includes a character named George MacDonald in *The Great Divorce*, who guides the narrator in a way that recalls Virgil guiding Dante in *The Divine Comedy*.

MacDonald's fantasy writing also impacted G. K. Chesterton. In the introduction to *George MacDonald and His Wife*, Chesterton remarks that, as a rule, our minds function like "a vast uncatalogued library."[45] For Chesterton, the thought of ranking the best or most influential books like contemporary top-ten lists felt contrived. But this is what he writes about MacDonald's fantasy novel *The Princess and the Goblin*:

> But in a certain rather special sense I for one can really testify to a book that has made a difference to my whole existence, which helped me to see things in a certain way from the start; a vision of things which even so real a revolution as a change of religious allegiance has substantially only crowned and confirmed. Of all the stories I have read . . . it remains the most real, the most realistic, in the exact sense of the phrase the most life-like.[46]

Standing out as the best or most memorable writer in any category by both of these men is a strong argument that you are doing something right. The fact that they both point to his fantasy writing suggests that we should pay attention to what MacDonald did.

Second, MacDonald helpfully recognized that there are desires within us as image bearers that can be engaged in ways that reason might not accomplish. MacDonald did this very effectively, as demonstrated earlier and corroborated by Lewis and Chesterton. Lewis and Chesterton both reference the atmospheric qualities of MacDonald's fantasy writing. Beyond the lifelike feeling of the worlds that MacDonald created, Chesterton recalls the recurring image of a great white horse. Chesterton vividly reminisces, "To this day, I can never see a big white horse in the street without a sudden sense of indescribable things."[47] The key point is that Chesterton's encounter with MacDonald's fantasy writing transformed the ordinary world for Chesterton, and it was not merely rational.

Finally, MacDonald's writing demonstrates that narrative can be rationally compelling without sacrificing excellence. He uses reason within his narrative work. This insight can apply to fantasy writers in general or to

---

45. Chesterton, introduction to *MacDonald*, 9.
46. Chesterton, introduction to *MacDonald*, 9.
47. Chesterton, introduction to *MacDonald*, 10.

narrative apologetics, whether it is writers or those who use stories to engage in apologetics. MacDonald is generally more explicit about Christian themes and claims than Lewis is in *The Chronicles of Narnia*. Nevertheless, MacDonald shows that writers can be more overt than some may assume. At a minimum, MacDonald shows one way to advocate for Christian truth using stories that influenced some of the greatest British writers.

J. R. R. TOLKIEN: THE POWER OF SUB-CREATION

J. R. R. Tolkien (1892–1973) is the well-known author of *The Hobbit* and *The Lord of the Rings*, as well as a medieval scholar and philologist. He was a close friend of C. S. Lewis, and they mutually encouraged one another in several important ways in their lifetime. Tolkien's view of Christianity as "true myth" was influential in Lewis's conversion to Christianity. Conversely, Tolkien credited Lewis with convincing him to move his writing beyond a hobby and later was instrumental in motivating Tolkien to complete *Lord of the Rings*. Tolkien was a fellow "Inkling" with C. S. Lewis and several others, which was a circle of friends and literary community that met in Oxford in the 1930s and 1940s. Tolkien's Christianity is expressed in his fiction in a more subdued way than Lewis's approach. But his writing is nonetheless underpinned by a strong Christian worldview and theology of art. It can help us understand the range of approaches that narrative apologetics can take.

Relevance of Tolkien to Narrative Apologetics

Whereas Lewis saw himself as a Christian apologist, both explicitly in his works like *Mere Christianity* and *The Problem of Pain*, and weaving in apologetic elements into his narratives, there is good reason to believe that Tolkien would dislike associating his work with narrative apologetics. He prefers the language of "art" or "sub-creation," as explained in his well-known essay *On Fairy-Stories*. He believed that we are hardwired for world-making, which arises from being hardwired for language and for stories.[48] Similar to MacDonald, who rooted his understanding of human imagination in his view of God as artist, Tolkien saw human beings as "sub-creators," making like God as the great Maker. In a foreword to the second edition of *Lord of the Rings*, Tolkien denies any inner message,

---

48. Flieger and Anderson, introduction to *On Fairy-Stories*, 23.

intention, or allegory, saying that its theme arose from choosing the Ring as the basis of a sequel to *The Hobbit*.[49] Later he adds to this:

> I cordially dislike allegory in all its manifestations, and always have done so since I grew old and wary enough to detect its presence. I much prefer history, true or feigned, with its varied applicability to the thought and experience of readers. I think that many confuse "applicability" with "allegory"; but the one resides in the freedom of the reader, and the other in the purposed domination of the author.[50]

Tolkien had a "cordial dislike" for allegory in "all its manifestations," such that he grew "old and wary enough to detect its presence." This sentiment is repeated in a letter to Michael di Capua of Pantheon books in response to a request to write a preface to George MacDonald's *The Golden Key*. As Tolkien explains, he is not the admirer of MacDonald that Lewis was, and he adds, "I am not at all confident that I can produce anything worthy of the honorarium that you offer. I am not naturally attracted (in fact much the reverse) by allegory, mystical or moral."[51]

The Potential of Sub-Creation

With Tolkien's dislike of allegory noted, we should also pay attention to his comments that his fantasy epic is religious in nature. In reply to Robert Murray on December 2, 1953, Tolkien wrote,

> *The Lord of the Rings* is of course a fundamentally religious and Catholic work; unconsciously so at first, but consciously in the revision. That is why I have not put in, or have cut out, practically all references to anything like "religion," to cults or practices, in the imaginary world. For the religious element is absorbed into the story and the symbolism.[52]

This comes in reply to Murray's perception that *Lord of the Rings* had "a strong sense of a 'positive compatibility of the order of Grace'" and compared the image of Galadriel to that of the Virgin Mary.[53]

---

49. Tolkien, *Lord of the Rings*, xxiii.
50. Tolkien, *Lord of the Rings*, xxiv.
51. Carpenter and Tolkien, *Letters of Tolkien*, 351.
52. Carpenter and Tolkien, *Letters of Tolkien*, 172.
53. Carpenter and Tolkien, *Letters of Tolkien*, 172.

Lord of the Rings is interrelated with Tolkien's celebrated essay *On Fairy-Stories*. As Flieger and Anderson explain, for Tolkien, *Lord of the Rings* was a "practical demonstration" of what he wrote in his essay.[54] Let's look at how *On Fairy-Stories* helps us understand narrative apologetics and then look at specific examples in *Lord of the Rings*.

Narrative Apologetic Elements in *On Fairy-Stories*

In *On Fairy-Stories*, Tolkien explores two key questions: What are fairy-stories? And what is their use? His answers point to their usefulness to narrative apologetics. First, similar to MacDonald, Tolkien does not believe fairy-story can be defined, but he does not consider this a weakness. Fairy-stories are not necessarily stories about fairies: Flieger and Anderson explain that they are "stories about humans in Faerie," understood as "the realm or state in which fairies have their being." Provisionally, a fairy-story is one that "touches on or uses Faerie."[55]

This may lead some to believe that fairy-stories are just for children. Tolkien is adamant that this is false. He maintains that fairy-story is a legitimate branch of art and literature. For Tolkien, if a fairy-story is worth reading at all, it also deserves to be enjoyed by adults.[56] The successful creator of a fairy-story is a "sub-creator."[57] Furthermore, when done with fitting skill by the artist, a secondary world is created; one that may be inhabited by the reader. Tolkien explains,

> [The writer] makes a Secondary World which your mind can enter. Inside it, what he relates is "true": it accords with the laws of that world. You therefore believe it, while you are, as it were, inside. The moment disbelief arises, the spell is broken; the magic, or rather art, has failed. You are then out in the Primary World again, looking at the little abortive Secondary World from outside.[58]

Tolkien's concepts of sub-creation and secondary world are very important to the narrative apologetic task. A skilled writer who creates a world

---

54. Flieger and Anderson, introduction to *On Fairy-Stories*, 16; See also, Carpenter and Tolkien, *Letters of Tolkien*, 310.

55. Flieger and Anderson, introduction to *On Fairy-Stories*, 10.

56. Tolkien, *On Fairy-Stories*, 58.

57. Tolkien, *On Fairy-Stories*, 52.

58. Tolkien, *On Fairy-Stories*, 52.

that feels real to the reader helps the reader to invest it with secondary belief, being "true" inside that world (contrasting with Coleridge's idea of the willing suspension of disbelief[59]). In the context of cross-cultural narrative apologetics, readers from non-Christian worldviews who imaginatively enter the secondary world have experiences as "believers" in the land. If the sub-creation has core elements that are consistent with the Christian worldview, they will have a glimpse of what it is like to believe. Furthermore, if the core elements are desirable and good, readers will cultivate a taste for them as well. This is why excellence is needed. Great literature has the feeling of the primary world.

Fairy-stories, Tolkien maintains, trade on desirability, not just possibility. As a boy, Tolkien found the land of Merlin and Arthur desirable. Even more, he found the nameless North of Sigurd of the Völsungs and the prince of all dragons more so, carrying the appeal of Faërie or an "Other-world." He writes, "Fantasy, the making or glimpsing of Other-worlds, was the heart of the desire of Faërie. I desired dragons with a profound desire."[60] Fairy-story can awaken desire. Notice in this instance, it comes through glimpsing secondary worlds.

Three Uses of Fairy-Stories

In addition to desirability, Tolkien highlights three other uses for fairy-stories: recovery, escape, and consolation. While recognizing that these aren't unique to fairy-stories, he maintains that this genre offers these to a particularly high degree.[61] He also notes that children tend to need these uses less than older people, so if anything, fairy-stories are *more* relevant for adults.[62]

Recovery is the first application. Tolkien maintains that fairy-stories are well-suited to recover wonder in the primary world. For Tolkien, recovery is the idea of removing familiarity.[63] According to Tolkien, the "windows" of our lives have become clouded with the "blur of triteness or familiarity," of "possessiveness," and he suggests that this is the "penalty

---

59. Coleridge, *Biographia Literaria*, 208.
60. Tolkien, *On Fairy-Stories*, 55.
61. Tolkien, *On Fairy-Stories*, 58–59.
62. Tolkien, *On Fairy-Stories*, 58–59.
63. Tolkien, *On Fairy-Stories*, 67.

of 'appropriation.'"[64] We are so familiar with the world that we can't see it. We think we know it, so we quit looking.

I once asked a local girl who worked at a tourist shop at the edge of the clear turquoise water of the Caribbean if she ever got used to the stunning view. She replied, "I barely notice the ocean anymore." Visitors to her island could see the beauty of her home more clearly than she did. She needed to recover her view of the ocean because it was too familiar. In Tolkien's language, she had come to view the ocean panorama as "known," and lamentably, "ceased to look" at it.[65]

Tolkien believed that fantasy can help displace familiarity. The best ones from his perspective primarily dealt with basic things like wood, stone, trees, and bread, but the setting re-enchanted the familiar. Tolkien also knew the recovery power of fairy-stories firsthand. He writes, "It was in fairy-stories that I first divined the potency of the words, and the wonder of the things, such as stone, and wood, and iron; tree and grass; house and fire; bread and wine."[66] By encountering ordinary things dipped in fantasy, they sometimes lose their familiarity and cultivate wonder. This was the effect of the great white horse of MacDonald's fantasy on G. K. Chesterton. Chesterton could not simply see a big white horse in the street when it passed; the white horse of the primary world now evoked a sense of "indescribable things."[67] Concerning narrative apologetics, Christianity, and even Jesus himself are sometimes perceived as known or "known enough" by those inside and outside the faith. For some, fantasy could help displace familiarity.

Escape is the second use of fairy-stories. For Tolkien, to escape into fairy-story is not a weakness, and it doesn't have to be mercenary. He compares it to the escape of a prisoner who enjoys imagining life beyond prison walls rather than the "flight of a deserter."[68] Escape includes social pressures of the day, such as the utilitarian march of progress in his day, as something to escape. Perhaps unexpectedly, Tolkien contrasts the "permanent things" in fairy-story like lightning and trees, with the transient nature of science. He writes, "[Fairy-stories] have many more permanent and fundamental things to talk about. . . . The escapist is not

---

64. Tolkien, *On Fairy-Stories*, 67.
65. Tolkien, *On Fairy-Stories*, 67.
66. Tolkien, *On Fairy-Stories*, 69.
67. Chesterton, introduction to *MacDonald*, 10.
68. Tolkien, *On Fairy-Stories*, 69.

so subservient to the whims of evanescent fashion as these opponents."[69] Tolkien recounts a meeting with an Oxford academic who celebrated the arrival of "mass-production robot factories" because it brought the university in contact with "real life."[70] Tolkien protests, "The maddest castle that ever came out of a giant's bag in a wild Gaelic story is not only much less ugly than a robot-factory, it is also (to use a very modern phrase) 'in a very real sense' a great deal more real."[71]

For Tolkien, fairy-stories escape and temporarily satisfy the limitations of lesser longings like the desire to communicate with animals, reflected in talking animals, similar to what Lewis does in *The Chronicles of Narnia*, or the desire to fly like a bird or explore the depths of the sea as seen in Hans Christian Andersen's "The Little Mermaid."

Fairy-stories also escape more weighty concerns like suffering, hunger, ugliness in the world, and even death. Tolkien remarks, "Few lessons are taught more clearly in them than the burden of that kind of immortality, or rather endless serial living, to which the 'fugitive' would fly."[72] Some contemporary examples include Voldemort's pursuit of immortality in J. K. Rowling's *Harry Potter* series or Emperor Palpatine in *Star Wars* by George Lucas.

Consolation is a final use for fairy-stories. For Tolkien, consolation is a necessary ingredient of fairy-stories. So crucial, Tolkien created the word *eucatastrophe* to describe the joy of an unexpected happy ending against impossible odds and almost certain failure. This unexpected grace strikes the reader with joy in the face of overwhelming despair. When the Ring of Power was shockingly destroyed in *Lord of the Rings* or when the Death Star was destroyed in *Star Wars*, a joy is conferred to the captivated imagination. Tolkien explains eucatastrophe "denies (in the face of much evidence) . . . universal final defeat and in so far is *evangelium*, giving a fleeting glimpse of Joy, Joy beyond the walls of the world, poignant as grief."[73] Tolkien believed this joy was a glimpse or echo of the

---

69. Tolkien, *On Fairy-Stories*, 70.

70. Tolkien, *On Fairy-Stories*, 70. Earlier drafts say "the head of an Oxford college," see Flieger and Anderson, editors commentary in *On Fairy-Stories*, 117.

71. Tolkien, *On Fairy-Stories*, 72.

72. Tolkien, *On Fairy-Stories*, 75. Elsewhere Tolkien states that this is the real theme in *Lord of the Rings*, even more important than power: death and immortality. See Flieger and Anderson, editors commentary in *On Fairy-Stories*, 119.

73. Tolkien, *On Fairy-Stories*, 75.

gospel, the true and greater eucatastrophe. This momentary joy answers the question about whether or not there is hope for the world's sorrows.

For Tolkien, the most complete conceivable eucatastrophe that occurred in the primary world was the birth of Christ, which is "the eucatastrophe of Man's history. The Resurrection is the eucatastrophe of the story of the Incarnation."[74] This true story, he maintains, begins and ends in joy. Fairy-stories, then, have a particular ability to tap into our longings for "something more," and through eucatastrophe, point us toward the Christian gospel as the fulfilment of that longing.

Narrative Apologetic Elements in *The Lord of The Rings*

Building on this understanding, there are at least two ways that Tolkien advocates Christian belief that are consistent with narrative apologetics: (1) art as witness and (2) sub-creation through Christian eyes.

The Christian Witness of Art

One thing that Tolkien accomplished with few peers is to create an entire world for his readers to inhabit. Tolkien's sub-creation in *Lord of the Rings* is remarkable. Few works in English rival the excellence of what Tolkien achieved. As a philologist who was passionate about the aesthetics of language, languages were foundational to the world and the story he created. In a letter to the Houghton Mifflin Company, Tolkien explained that his narrative was designed to give expression to languages he invented rather than the other way around.[75] As a linguistic craftsman, Tolkien invented multiple languages for Middle-earth. Two were exceptionally comprehensive and included a history and a shared linguistic origin. The languages were also used to create the majority of the names in the collective work. Tolkien explains, "This gives a certain character (a cohesion, a consistency of linguistic style, and an illusion of historicity)."[76]

I remember where I was when I first heard that Tolkien created a language for *Lord of the Rings*. I remember wondering, "Why would someone spend so much time making a language for a fictional book?" Awe and curiosity naturally entered my mind. Who is this guy? What

---

74. Tolkien, *On Fairy-Stories*, 75.
75. Carpenter and Tolkien, *Letters of Tolkien*, 219.
76. Carpenter and Tolkien, *Letters of Tolkien*, 143.

is going on here? A more refined appreciation of my sentiment was expressed by C. S. Lewis in a scholarly review of Tolkien's *The Fellowship of the Ring*, where he praised how intricate and exhaustive Tolkien's world was, recognizing Tolkien's concept of sub-creation at work.[77]

Sub-creation is essential to understanding why Tolkien went to such lengths. In Tolkien's words, "Fantasy remains a human right: we make in our measure and in our derivative mode, because we are made: and not only made, but made in the image and likeness of a Maker."[78] This making is a kind of witness. For those looking at Christianity from the outside, there is a depth of excellence and beauty that glorifies God and points beyond the art. Ralph Wood remarks, "Tolkien's work is all the more deeply Christian for not being overtly Christian. He would have violated the integrity of his art—and thus the faithfulness of his witness—if he had written a 1,200-page novel to illustrate a set of ideas that he could have expressed apart from the story itself. This is a principle not only of good art but also of good theology."[79] This is consistent with Donald Williams's encounter with *Lord of the Rings*. Williams writes, "[Tolkien] shows us what it looks like when an intelligent and creative person has [a Christian worldview] and applies it with confidence in his efforts to see, understand, and appreciate the world."[80] He continues, "*The Lord of the Rings* . . . showed me the difference a Christian worldview could make before I even knew that such a thing existed or what to call it. Tolkien's doctrine of sub-creation flows from the very heart of who God is and who we are: creative because we are made in the image of the Creator."[81] The quality of Tolkien's creative masterpiece honors his maker but also points beyond him to the author of all language and creation.

Sub-Creation Through Christian Eyes

A second significant way that *Lord of the Rings* advocates Christian belief is through a Christian view of the world embodied in fantasy.[82] Peter Kreeft insightfully observes that "all literature incarnates some philosophy. Thus

---

77. Lewis, *Image and Imagination*, 99–100.
78. Tolkien, *On Fairy-Stories*, 66.
79. Wood, *Gospel According to Tolkien*, 4.
80. Williams, *Encouraging Thought*, 52.
81. Williams, *Encouraging Thought*, 52.
82. Tolkien specifically affirms that *Lord of the Rings* is monotheistic and embodies natural theology. See Carpenter and Tolkien, *Letters of Tolkien*, 220.

all literature teaches."[83] He explains this further, "The philosophy is in the point of view, and the point of view lies not in the picture but in the frame. For example, a theistic frame, or point of view, is present in Shakespeare's *Macbeth* and is deliberately removed in Faulkner's *The Sound and the Fury*. . . . When we read Shakespeare we judge Macbeth to be insane from an implicitly higher point of view, which 'frames' the portrait of Macbeth."[84] It is in this sense that one can see the Christian worldview as depicted in *Lord of the Rings*.

There are several representative examples. One is the *sense of paradise lost* (see Gen 3). Clyde Kilby is correct when he writes that the story of *Lord of the Rings* suggests "the sadness of a paradise lost and the glory of one that can be regained."[85] This is seen in Frodo's desire to return to his home of the Shire as he faces the perils of Middle-earth, though even after he returns, he must leave with the elves in going into the West to find relief from his sorrows. Frodo *longs for home*, to flee the brokenness of the world, and to feel the goodness of home again. This longing is likely amplified by the reader's felt *sense of exile* in the primary world. In a letter to his son, Tolkien writes, "We all long for [Eden], and we are constantly glimpsing it: our whole nature at its best and least corrupted, its gentlest and most humane, is still soaked with the sense of 'exile.'"[86] Another glimpse of the world through Christian sight is the *fallen nature of humanity* and the *consequences of sin* in Middle-earth. The character of Gollum displays this with acute force: he is a "ruined," hollowed-out version of himself. Sméagol (his real name) is who he should be. Gollum is something of a possessed version of himself, now corrupted by his Ring lust. Gollum is willing to exchange everything for the Ring of Power. His lust corrupts him to the point that he despises the light and all that is good. Sin has deformed him, and it invites reflection from the primary world of the reader.

Christian mercy or grace is another feature of Tolkien's work. When Bilbo had the opportunity to kill Gollum in *The Hobbit*, after winning the Ring in the riddling contest, he was moved by pity to spare him. Bilbo escapes, while Gollum vows hatred against him as a thief. There is a repeated reflection on sparing Gollum's life. Frodo remarks, "What a pity that Bilbo did not stab that vile creature, when he had a chance!"[87]

83. Kreeft, *Philosophy of Tolkien*, 23.
84. Kreeft, *Philosophy of Tolkien*, 24.
85. Kilby, *Well of Wonder*, 174.
86. Carpenter and Tolkien, *Letters of Tolkien*, 110.
87. Tolkien, *Lord of the Rings*, 59.

However, Gandalf responds, "It was Pity that stayed his hand. Pity, and Mercy: not to strike without need."[88] Pity stayed him. Kilby's words are instructive. It is the "quality of mercy" that reflects the mercy of God.[89]

A final point is the *sense of paradise regained* on the heels of impossible deliverance. Following the destruction of the Ring, Sam wakes up in bed to glimmers of sunlight, the gentle green of trees, and the smell of sweetness in the air. Sam says in surprise, "'Gandalf! I thought you were dead! But then I thought I was dead myself. Is everything sad going to come untrue? What's happened to the world?' 'A great Shadow has departed,' said Gandalf, and then he laughed, and the sound was like music, or like water in a parched land."[90] Much more can be said, but in this short space, Tolkien presents resurrection, longing, shalom, paradise regained, and deliverance at great sacrifice.

Helpful Insights from Tolkien

Tolkien makes several significant contributions to narrative apologetics. Excellence is one of the most important. Christian writers and artists are sometimes rightly accused of creating subpar work. It is important that authors create stories to the glory of God. Excellence is part of the Christian witness, and Tolkien does this well. Similarly, Tolkien's commitment to quality, instruction, and understanding regarding sub-creation is standard-setting and informative for Christian writers in public spaces. Finally, the natural strengths that he identifies in fairy-stories (e.g., recovery, escape, and consolation) as well as less overt Christian themes such as the sense of paradise lost, monotheistic worlds, the fallen nature of humanity, the quality of mercy, and the feeling of paradise regained are natural paths for narrative apologetic exploration and other relevant fields. Austin Freeman's recent work, for example, uses Tolkien's writing to see theology better. Freeman explains, "We should look for Christian theology not in the explicit elements of the tales (after all, they are set in a pre-Christian world) but in the deep structure of the story, in its metaphysics, ethics, and in the shape of its plot."[91]

---

88. Tolkien, *Lord of the Rings*, 59.
89. Kilby, *Well of Wonder*, 168.
90. Tolkien, *Lord of the Rings*, 951–52.
91. Freeman, *Tolkien Dogmatics*, 3.

Tolkien is clearly different than MacDonald in his style and methodology. MacDonald is much more forthright about Christian themes and ideas, while Tolkien's Christian ideas are latent. Both authors, however, draw on theological understandings and assumptions about human beings. MacDonald attempts to wake things within a reader that are asleep. This assumes humans have something to wake. Tolkien believed fairy-stories can help the reader escape or find glimpses of consolation and joy—these trade on the belief that reality is ordered in a specific way and humans can relate to it in a right or wrong way. Moreover, both writers believed that humans have a certain kind of blindness that narrative can help overcome. As we will see, Lewis shared some of these convictions and contributes other insights as well. Lewis's works tend to be less overt than MacDonald but not as subtle as Tolkien.

C. S. LEWIS: PAST WATCHFUL DRAGONS

Now we come to C. S. Lewis (1898–1963) himself, who as well as writing *The Chronicles of Narnia* reflected in his nonfiction, essays, and letters on the relationships between myth and history, imagination and reason, his storytelling and his apologetics—rich territory for understanding narrative apologetics. Because I discuss Lewis's life and work in various aspects throughout the book, in this section, I have focused on a few core examples of the themes of narrative apologetics.

Needs Addressed by Lewis

Lewis sees the need for *familiarization* of readers with certain ideas that will make them more spiritually receptive. One example of this conviction is found in Lewis's *Space Trilogy*. At the close of *Out of the Silent Planet*, the main character, Ransom, comments on how fiction might get a hearing where "fact" would not; where the "true" story would appear more plausible if its ideas were clothed in fiction.[92] The events of the book, in which Ransom is kidnapped and taken to Malacandra (Mars) and encounters the creatures of that world and the ruling spirit Oyarsa, coming to realize the nature of the "Heavens" as full of spiritual life, are portrayed as a fictionalized account of real events. Ransom says, "What we need for the moment is not so much a body of belief as a body of

92. Lewis, *Out of the Silent Planet*, 152.

people familiarized with certain ideas. If we could even effect in one per cent of our readers a changeover from the conception of Space to the conception of Heaven, we should have made a beginning."[93] Notice that Ransom's goal (and that of Lewis) is very modest: *familiarized* with certain ideas. Further, success is obtained if effective with even "one percent."

Another potential that Lewis sees for narrative is to cultivate *favorable conditions* for belief in a time of religious decline.[94] This relates to the need for what lifelong friend and biographer George Sayer says about Lewis's hope for *The Chronicles of Narnia*: "His idea, as he once explained it to me, was to make it easier for children to accept Christianity when they met it later in life. He hoped that they would be vaguely reminded of the somewhat similar stories that they had read and enjoyed years before. 'I am aiming at a sort of pre-baptism of the child's imagination.'"[95]

Defamiliarization as well as familiarization has a role to play. Lewis believes that myth can help with the *removal of the veil of familiarity* to restore the significance of things no longer fittingly appreciated. Lewis explained in his review of Tolkien's *Lord of the Rings* that the putting of ordinary things into myth does not take us away from reality but helps us rediscover it, echoing Tolkien's theme of fairy-stories providing "recovery" of sight.[96]

Relevance of Lewis's Narrative Apologetics

The power of story was not just a theory for Lewis; he knew the potential of literature from experience. As a seventeen-year-old, Lewis expressed his view of Christianity in personal correspondence to a close friend dated October 12, 1916, saying that he thought Christianity was lacking in proof and was just one invented myth among many.[97] This was the year that he first read George MacDonald's *Phantastes*. Later, in retrospect, Lewis vividly recalled the impact that MacDonald's fantasy had on him:

> *Unde hoc mihi?* In the depth of my disgraces, in the then invincible ignorance of my intellect, all this was given me without asking, even without consent. That night my imagination was,

---

93. Lewis, *Out of the Silent Planet*, 152.
94. Lewis, "Decline of Religion," 221.
95. Sayer, *Jack*, 192.
96. Lewis, "Tolkien's *Lord of the Rings*," 138.
97. Lewis, *Letters of C. S. Lewis*, 59.

in a certain sense, baptised; the rest of me, not unnaturally took longer. I had not the faintest notion what I had let myself in for buying *Phantastes*. . . . I saw the bright shadow coming out of the book into the real world and resting there, transforming all common things and yet itself unchanged.[98]

As I noted in the section on MacDonald, Lewis experienced a powerful encounter with holiness through reading imaginative fantasy literature.

Lewis believed in the potential goodness of culture and culture-making when rightly enjoyed under the moral law, as discussed in the introduction. Moreover, Lewis wondered if it is even the Christian's duty to create culture and to cultivate right responses. He recognizes that culture can be harmful, but he also believed it is important for Christians to be involved in creating good culture as an "antidote."[99] In addition to this, Lewis also believes that the enjoyment of culture often opens doors into an otherwise closed view of thinking. Culture can shake people out of a sense of complacency, of believing everything is already explained, already understood—culture can awaken a sense of mystery, and the realization that ultimate truth is likely to seem strange and fantastic at first.[100]

Lewis also believed that narrative is needed to cultivate what he termed "just sentiments." In his work *The Abolition of Man*, Lewis argues that until modern times, people believed that objective truths and values were real features of the world, and not just projected onto it by human reaction or preferences, and so our emotional reactions could be fitting or not.[101] Lewis perceived a threat in an English book that challenged the objective status of values and corresponding sentiments. Responding to this Lewis maintains that a right defense of these objective values is to teach people to respond fittingly to the truly good and beautiful by creating a taste for them. He writes, "The task of the modern educator is not to cut down jungles but to irrigate deserts. The right defence against false sentiments is to inculcate just sentiments."[102]

Elsewhere he used the language of "stock responses" to describe rightly ordered affections. This was a significant priority for him. In *A Preface to Paradise Lost*, Lewis responds to a critique against Milton that,

98. Lewis, *Surprised by Joy*, 222.
99. Lewis, "Christianity and Culture," 20–21.
100. Lewis, "Christianity and Culture," 23.
101. Lewis, *Abolition of Man*, 16.
102. Lewis, *Abolition of Man*, 14.

because he overused stock responses, it cheapened the quality of *Paradise Lost*. Lewis replies that efforts to cultivate stock responses or rightly ordered affections is "one of the first necessities of human life, and one of the main functions of art is to assist it."[103] Notice the relevance to narrative apologetics: one of the main functions of art is to help cultivate these responses and affections. Consequently, art, like *The Chronicles of Narnia*, can and should assist in inculcating these rightly ordered affections. This also neatly fits into the purposes of narrative apologetics, which seeks to cultivate affections for the Lord and his kingdom purposes.

Lewis furthermore believes that stories enlarge our being in a good way. In *An Experiment in Criticism*, Lewis considers why we should give our time and attention to things that never happened and concludes that the best answer he can find is that stories make us more than ourselves.[104] He says, "In reading great literature I become a thousand men and yet remain myself."[105] There is a goodness in seeing through others' perspectives, and narrative does this. This also applies to narrative apologetics, especially for those from other worldviews. Stories allow a person to safely explore a different belief system embedded in the narrative. Consider Tolkien's monotheistic world for someone who is an atheist or is a polytheist. This is a significant part of what I explore later in the book.

Lewis and the Potential of Narrative Apologetics

There are many ways that Lewis advocates the Christian faith in his literary work, which shows the potential that narrative apologetics has. Here I focus on six general categories: (1) familiarization, (2) supposal, (3) atmosphere, (4) the creation of favorable conditions, (5) past watchful dragons, and (6) Christian experiences.

Familiarization

As we saw in relation to Lewis's *Space Trilogy*, stories can help provide familiarization "with certain ideas." In a letter written to Sister Penelope, a close friend and long-running correspondent of Lewis, wrongly dated July (rather than August) of 1939, Lewis describes his surprise that so few

---

103. Lewis, *Preface to Paradise Lost*, 69.
104. Lewis, *Experiment in Criticism*, 137.
105. Lewis, *Experiment in Criticism*, 141.

people recognized the theological underpinnings of his work and observed that "any amount of theology can now be smuggled into people's minds under the cover of romance without their knowing it."[106] This is an opportunity that Lewis would make the most of in writing the *Narnia* books.

Supposal

Lewis is clear that he did not create Narnia as an allegory of Christian truths. The stories began with vivid images, and he wrote fairy tales because the fairy tale, as a genre, allowed him to express his ideas best. In his words, it "seemed the ideal Form for the stuff I had to say."[107] The inclusion of Christian truths came later in the process, and Lewis did not consider Narnia an allegory, but a "supposal," a way of exploring the question: "'What might Christ become like, if there really were a world like Narnia and He chose to be incarnate and die and rise again in that world as He actually has done in ours?' This is not allegory at all."[108] Lewis believes that fairy tales can "steal past watchful dragons"—inhibitions or dispositions that block thoughtful consideration—so that the ideas can, for the first time, be experienced in their full power.[109] This happened to Lewis while reading *Phantastes*, and it is something that he evokes in his readers—skeptical or receptive.

Quality of Atmosphere

Much of Lewis's writing evokes what he terms *Sehnsucht* or longing. Lewis often creates an atmosphere that depicts the experience of *Sehnsucht* in his actual characters. This otherworldly vision luridly prompts *Sehnsucht* in some readers. This effort is unsurprising when one considers Lewis's conviction about what he calls "The Kappa element in Romance." Michael Ward explains that Kappa is taken from the Greek word *krypton*, which is translated "hidden" or "cryptic."[110] In that paper, Lewis defends romantic literature, but he was especially concerned about the atmospheric quality of stories. According to Ward, "Again and again, in defending works of

---

106. Lewis, *Collected Letters*, 2:262.
107. Lewis, "Sometimes Fairy Stories," 58.
108. Lewis, *Collected Letters*, 3:1004.
109. Lewis, "Sometimes Fairy Stories," 58.
110. Ward, *Planet Narnia*, 15.

romance, Lewis argues that it is the quality or tone of the whole story that is its attraction."[111] Later Ward comments that Lewis was "continually preoccupied with God's unperceived ubiquity and propinquity."[112] Similarly, Timothy Willard stresses Lewis's use of atmosphere. Willard writes, "It is helpful to think of *Numinous* and Northernness as the atmosphere created by paint on a canvass. It is the unsafeness of Aslan, the apocalyptic feel in *That Hideous Strength*, it is Orual's breath leading her into terror, joy, and overpowering sweetness as the god approached."[113] Willard elsewhere points to what he calls a "progression of beauty." Lewis uses this progression as a literary device to "quicken his stories and to incite the wonder and curiosity of his readers."[114] Willard explains,

> The subject experiences an object, person, or place that strikes the subject with its beauty (form and/or splendor). Mingled in this encounter is the *numinous tremendum*. The *numinous* is the experience of dread or even terror that often accompanies the encounter of the beautiful, or the sublime.... Next, the encounter of that object, person, or place, possibly through *numinous* means, produces an aesthetic gasp in the subject, what Lewis describes as "Joy."... Joy remains through the aesthetic progression and, when the subject obtains the object, in a purely physical and perhaps spiritual manner, the subject then experiences the perpetuity of Joy. The Joy experienced, however, connects to the divine, to the God of Christianity.[115]

Atmosphere is vital to Lewis's advocacy of Christian belief. It is also instructive to narrative apologetics in its focus on experience and aesthetics.

Creation of Favorable Conditions

Lewis also believed that the imagination can contribute to favorable conditions for belief. Lewis saw literature as a sort of pre-evangelism. His firsthand experience with MacDonald's work gave him an awareness of the fertile soil of the imagination. MacDonald's literature prepared the soil of Lewis's faith. Lewis wrote in his essay "The Decline of Religion" about the value of creating a favorable intellectual climate for Christian

---

111. Ward, *Planet Narnia*, 15.
112. Ward, *Planet Narnia*, 227.
113. Willard, "C. S. Lewis's Language of Beauty," para. 11.
114. Willard, "Endless Twilight," 70.
115. Willard, "Endless Twilight," 69–70.

CLASSIC NARRATIVE APOLOGETICS 43

belief, so that when someone reaches the point of whether or not to accept Christ, their reason and imagination might be inclined toward faith. Lewis is not overly optimistic here, emphasizing the modest role that those who prepare the ground in this way play. The imagination is only one facet of a favorable intellectual climate, but it plays a significant role in human thought about reality.[116]

Past Watchful Dragons

Lewis also believed that fantasy literature can slip past what he calls "watchful dragons." Lewis noted how the obligation to feel a certain way, or the reverence attached to religion, can get in the way of a real emotional response to the Christian story, but imaginative storytelling has potential to bypass these barriers: "But supposing that by casting all these things into an imaginary world, stripping them of their stained-glass and Sunday school associations, one could make them for the first time appear in their real potency? Could one not thus steal past those watchful dragons? I thought one could."[117] Lewis remembered his own response to being told to believe this or that—what would reach him? What would entice him? How could Lewis get some of his adult, Christian understanding and wonder at the world through to his own childhood resistance? Story was at least part of the solution.

Christian Experience

A final potential for narrative is enabling readers to enter into Christian experience. As a literary scholar, Lewis's conviction about his role as a reader is that he should enter a story and avail himself of the total experience of that created world. He writes:

> In reading imaginative work, I suggest, we should be much less concerned with altering our own opinions—though this of course is sometimes their effect—than with entering fully into the opinions, and therefore also the attitudes, feelings and total experience, of other men. Who in his ordinary senses would try to decide between the claims of materialism and theism by reading Lucretius and Dante? But who in his literary senses would

---

116. Lewis, "Decline of Religion," 221.
117. Lewis, "Sometimes Fairy Stories," 58.

not delightedly learn from them a great deal about what it is like to be a materialist or a theist? In good reading there ought to be no "problem of belief."[118]

Lewis distinguishes between ordinary and literary senses. It is the literary sense, or the nature of good reading, that offers a natural path for seriously experiencing otherwise implausible beliefs. In his well-known essay "Meditations in a Toolshed," Lewis describes the difference between looking at a beam of light that breaks into a dark toolshed versus looking along the beam of light: "Looking along the beam, and looking at the beam are very different experiences."[119] Imaginative literature invites the reader to look along and to experience. This is what one author calls a "lived-in experience of theology." By seeing through the eyes of and along with the characters, both the reader and the characters see how the ideas play out.[120] When Lewis entered *Phantastes*, his life was forever changed. These otherworldly experiences contributed to that end.

Helpful Insights from Lewis

Lewis makes a number of additions to classic narrative apologetics. His unique take on familiarization, supposal, atmosphere, favorable conditions, moving past inhibitions, and creating narrative experiences with Christianity are helpful tools for writers and natural places for talking points for those who want to use written works for Christian conversations and apologetics. Lewis is similar to Tolkien in recognizing the need to displace familiarity but also acknowledges a need for familiarization. Whether it was his aim or not, the need for familiarization is especially true for those who lack the fundamental categories of Christianity across worldviews.

The importance of cultivating favorable conditions and of atmosphere are other points that are worthy of note. Like MacDonald and Tolkien, Lewis believed that atmosphere played a vital role in the power of literary art. Similarly, he was convinced that narrative helps cultivate affections and sentiments. Lewis was very conscious of the role of a person's inhibitions about belief, but he felt that narrative was especially suited to get around this obstacle.

---

118. Lewis, *Experiment in Criticism*, 85–86.
119. Lewis, "Meditation in a Toolshed," 230.
120. McCarty, "*Narnia* and the Philosophy of Religion," 119.

Finally, Lewis provides us with another model that is intentional but more indirect than MacDonald. Supposal is one of Lewis's most significant contributions to narrative apologetics. Using supposal skillfully as a writing tool, an author can explore Christian truths without forcing a contrived, inauthentic world. In Tolkien's essay *On Fairy-Stories*, Tolkien observes that a fairy-story's building material, like a craftsman's clay or stone, is fantasy even though it draws on the primary world.[121] Similarly, for a writer, supposal offers distinctly Christian world-building material that can be organically included among a writer's options. Even Tolkien used theistic concepts like providence. Although not every stone or clay can or should be used, some can.[122]

THE VALUE OF CLASSIC NARRATIVE APOLOGETICS

I have termed these three models *classic* because of their impact as pioneer fantasy writers and their influence. MacDonald's fantasy is not as mainstream in the contemporary world as Lewis and Tolkien, but his effect is still felt in those he influenced, if nothing else. These three authors show some of the most important elements and strengths of narrative apologetics. Before moving to some of the work done in contemporary narrative apologetics, notice several aspects shared among these models.

First, all three writers emphasize the significance of narrative atmosphere. MacDonald believed specific atmospheric contexts lend themselves to thinking about matters of importance. Tolkien believed the best fairy stories stir feelings of wonder about things in the primary world. Lewis also emphasized atmosphere as supremely important and actively used it to cultivate longing.

Narrative influence is another shared theme. While avoiding a sense of instrumentality, all three authors believed stories should impact the reader. MacDonald believed that fiction should be transformational and push the reader toward some ideal. Lewis believed that one of the jobs of art is to cultivate a fitting response to what is true and good, as he discusses in *The Abolition of Man* and *A Preface to Paradise Lost*. Even Tolkien believed fairy stories should remove familiarity and facilitate "escape." In a related sense, all three authors believed that people are blind to things

---

121. Tolkien, *On Fairy-Stories*, 68.

122. With this said, it is essential to reemphasize that Lewis did not set out to teach specific things about Christianity; he began his writing with images that inspired him and also imagined what it would be like for Jesus to enter a world like Narnia.

that matter. MacDonald believed inner needs needed to be awakened and sought to do that with his writing. Lewis, like Tolkien, believed familiarity hinders seeing reality with full potency, and both believed narrative was a path to remedying this.

A final similarity is the role of existential need or desire in narrative. All three classic writers recognized that narrative can engage and direct a reader's existential desire using stories. MacDonald regularly featured beauty and reflections about encountering beauty in his work, often noting how God fits the desire for beauty better than alternatives. Tolkien maintained that consolation that evokes joy is indispensable for fairy-stories and points us to the Christian gospel as the true fulfillment of this longing. Lewis regularly features existential needs in his work, as I develop more fully in later chapters. Among these existential needs is a longing for joy that he believed was uniquely satisfied in God. Lewis regularly features this longing and often hints at the source and solution.

These are just some of the features identified in these classic writers. For writers, these themes help identify some of the most important elements in writing, as noted by some of the best writers in English literature. They also prepare us to consider how the power of stories might intersect with cross-cultural apologetic needs. It begins to answer the question, How could narrative apologetics serve cross-cultural apologetics? Moreover, these models prepare nonwriters to understand narrative apologetics better and recognize potential bridges for cross-cultural apologetics and dialogue.

Beyond the classic models, there has been considerable contemporary reflection on narrative apologetics since the works of MacDonald, Tolkien, and Lewis. In the next chapter, I explore some of the best works in contemporary narrative apologetics, before considering cross-cultural apologetics in chapter 3.

2

Contemporary Narrative Apologetics

INTRODUCTION

WHAT ABOUT CONTEMPORARY NARRATIVE apologetics? What recent thinking is there on how literature and imagination can contribute to Christian belief formation? How can literature create favorable conditions for belief or overcome barriers to belief in our current cultural moment, as well as cross-culturally?

While the example and insights of George MacDonald, J. R. R. Tolkien, and C. S. Lewis are extremely valuable, some things have changed since they were writing, and many Christian writers and apologists have built on their work since. In what follows, I explore three recent models: Alister McGrath, Holly Ordway, and Justin Ariel Bailey. The classic narrative apologists in the previous chapter are all celebrated story makers, while the contemporary models focus on analysis and application. Nevertheless, each project provides essential insights into narrative apologetics and will help us understand the cross-cultural potential of narrative apologetics in general.

ALISTER MCGRATH: NARRATIVE APOLOGETICS AND USING STORIES TO COMMUNICATE TRUTH

Alister McGrath's 2019 book *Narrative Apologetics: Sharing the Relevance, Joy, and Wonder of the Christian Faith* helped popularize and formalize "narrative apologetics" as a branch of apologetics, though as we have seen, the concept goes back much further.[1] McGrath defines narrative apologetics as an approach to affirming, defending, and explaining the Christian faith by telling stories.[2] McGrath says that narrative apologetics explores how stories can "open up important ways of communicating and commending the gospel, enabling it to be understood, connecting it with the realities of human experience, and challenging other stories that are told about the world and ourselves."[3] He regards the narrative approach as working alongside reasoned argumentation. Rational arguments are important, but by themselves can fall short in accounting for ultimate things.[4] Facts, he contends, are not enough. We need stories to more fully communicate the depths and reality of God and the Christian faith in meaningful ways.

Moreover, empirical studies show that human beings try to understand the world and our role within it through stories—that is, by positioning ourselves within a narrative framework.[5] Using sociologist Christian Smith's classifications, McGrath identifies several relevant categories of meaning that operate in people living in the twenty-first century, including the "Christian metanarrative," the "Scientific Enlightenment narrative," and the "Chance and Purposelessness narrative."[6] Although recognizing that we rely on multiple narratives to make sense of reality and our place in it, McGrath argues that this question remains: "Which story do we allow to serve as our main narrative, and which do we treat as ancillary?"[7]

The Seed of Story

McGrath makes the case for narrative apologetics both from Scripture and from human nature. From Scripture, he notes Nathan's criticism of David's adulterous relationship with Bathsheba and the parable of the good Samaritan as two examples of a kind of narrative apologetics within

---

1. For completeness, it is worth noting McGrath did author a children's fantasy series called *The Aedyn Chronicles*.
2. McGrath, *Narrative Apologetics*, 7.
3. McGrath, *Narrative Apologetics*, 7.
4. McGrath, *Narrative Apologetics*, 8.
5. McGrath, *Narrative Apologetics*, 9.
6. McGrath, *Narrative Apologetics*, 13.
7. McGrath, *Narrative Apologetics*, 13.

Scripture. In the first case, Nathan chose to criticize David's adulterous relationship with Bathsheba by first telling a moving story of deceit and corruption, stirring David's sense of injustice. Nathan then identified David within the story: "You are the man!" (2 Sam 12:1–25).[8] Similarly, when Jesus addresses the theological question, "Who is my neighbor?" (Luke 10:29) he tells a story rather than offering a theological analysis.[9] Of the good Samaritan, McGrath writes, "The story itself is a vehicle for disclosure, which draws its readers into that story and invites them to correlate it with their own personal stories."[10]

As well as Scripture, McGrath draws on a concept termed *mythos spermatikos*. Patristic apologist Justin Martyr used the term *logos spermatikos* to mean "'seed-bearing reason,' . . . God's implanting, through the act of creation, rational tendencies, and intuitions that were capable of leading individuals to discover God."[11] In kind, *mythos spermatikos* is a way of making sense of the human use of stories to convey meaning and identity.[12] The idea of *mythos spermatikos*, McGrath writes, "helps us grasp that this created capacity to intuit the divine is to be seen in terms of creating and telling stories, not simply in terms of developing arguments or rational concepts."[13] He continues, "[Stories] express something profound about who we are—which in turn expresses something of the God who created us in this manner."[14] This idea suggests that we are primed to receive truth via "seed-bearing myth," through an affinity for story implanted in us by God.

This is similar to Tolkien and Lewis's understanding of myth. For Lewis, myth is "a story that evokes awe, enchantment, and inspiration and conveys or embodies an imaginative expression of the deepest meanings of life."[15] As McGrath observes, one of the central themes of Lewis's apologetics is that Christianity offers a narrative that can generate a "big picture" of reality that makes sense of our subjective experiences and our observations of the world.[16] The Christian narrative, as the big picture of reality,

---

8. McGrath, *Narrative Apologetics*, 11–12.
9. McGrath, *Narrative Apologetics*, 12.
10. McGrath, *Narrative Apologetics*, 12.
11. McGrath, *Narrative Apologetics*, 12.
12. McGrath, *Narrative Apologetics*, 47.
13. McGrath, *Narrative Apologetics*. 47.
14. McGrath, *Narrative Apologetics*, 48.
15. McGrath, *Narrative Apologetics*, 31.
16. McGrath, *Narrative Apologetics*, 25.

"brings to fulfillment and completion imperfect and partial insights about reality, scattered abroad in human culture."[17] On this view, similarities in pagan myths are expected; they are "'dim dreams or premonitions' of the greater and fuller truth of the Christian gospel," and Christianity is the "true myth."[18] Christianity, McGrath explains, possesses the literary form of a myth, with the critical difference that it is true.[19]

McGrath is helpful in identifying precedents for narrative apologetics in Scripture, and in recognizing features of human nature such as *mythos spermatikos*, and these revalidate the importance of the narrative apologetic task. Moreover, they give reason to expect stories to play an important role in understanding and commending the Christian faith. In McGrath's words, "[They] give us reason to believe that stories are a God-given means of telling people about God, making sense of their worlds, and ultimately allowing them to grasp something of the relevance of God for life and thought."[20]

McGrath on the Potential of Narrative Apologetics

McGrath identifies at least six important applications for narrative apologetics. These include meeting objections, explaining significance, translation and transposition, non-spectator evidence, best explanation deliberation, and relevance.

First, narrative apologetics can *meet objections* to religious belief. A common claim is that God is a projection (e.g., Freud). McGrath briefly points to C. S. Lewis's "ontological proof" in *The Silver Chair* as an example of a response to this in narrative form.[21]

Second, a narrative apologetic story can *explain significance* by showing the ways that Christianity can connect with people's lives and concerns. One example is the significance of the incarnation of Christ. McGrath features Lewis's depiction of the incarnation in *The Lion, the Witch and the Wardrobe*.

Third, a narrative apologetic story can *translate and transpose*. It can present Christian beliefs in a way that contemporary culture can appreciate

---

17. McGrath, *Narrative Apologetics*, 46.
18. McGrath, *Narrative Apologetics*, 46.
19. McGrath, *Narrative Apologetics*, 31.
20. McGrath, *Narrative Apologetics*, 48.
21. McGrath, *Narrative Apologetics*, 58. I discuss this argument in more detail in chapter 7.

and understand. One relevant example is visualizing sin, such as the "un-dragoning" of Eustace in *The Voyage of the Dawn Treader*. McGrath discusses how Lewis's narrative transposes Christian themes of sin and salvation by portraying sin as an "enslaving force" that requires outside intervention. Thus, "God's grace alone can break the power of sin and liberate us from its spell."[22] Moreover, McGrath notes that the un-dragoning of Eustace instructs apologists on transposal. McGrath explains, "It invites apologists to reflect on what stories they might tell to make those same points in an imaginatively engaging and compelling manner."[23]

Fourth, a narrative apologetic story can create a form of *non-spectator evidence*. McGrath observes, "Lewis's apologetic strategy is to invite his readers to step into the Christian way of seeing things, imagine how things look and feel from this perspective, and assess the quality of the Christian narrative. Does this story seem to ring true to life and experience?"[24]

Fifth, a narrative apologetic story can seek *the best explanation of the world*. McGrath identifies a scene in *The Lion, the Witch and the Wardrobe* as an example of this kind of application. He writes, "At an early stage . . . the four Pevensie children begin to hear stories about the true origins and destiny of Narnia. Puzzled, they find they have to make decisions about which persons and which stories are to be trusted."[25] The reader must wonder with the Pevensie children: "Is Narnia really the realm of the White Witch? Or is she a usurper? . . . Gradually, one narrative emerges as supremely plausible: [noble Aslan]."[26] This application is also consistent with Lewis's belief that Christianity offers the "big picture" of reality, and that makes sense of subjective experiences of our observed world.[27]

McGrath helpfully notes that crime fiction trades on this feature and its potential for narrative apologetics, based on the essay "The Slaughterhouse of Literature" by Franco Moretti. Moretti ponders why Sir Arthur Conan Doyle remains so widely read when other Victorian crime authors are overlooked or neglected. His conclusion is that "Conan Doyle makes systematic use of clues: entities or observations that demand an explanation that can only be provided by a coherent narrative that binds them

22. McGrath, *Narrative Apologetics*, 70.
23. McGrath, *Narrative Apologetics*, 70.
24. McGrath, *Narrative Apologetics*, 55.
25. McGrath, *Narrative Apologetics*, 107.
26. McGrath, *Narrative Apologetics*, 107.
27. McGrath, *Narrative Apologetics*, 25.

together."²⁸ Clues, McGrath writes, "are pointers to a larger picture."²⁹ This also invites best explanation deliberation.

Relevance is the final feature of narrative apologetics that he emphasizes: story helps connect ideas to our deepest questions. According to McGrath, metanarratives must engage humanity's deepest cares and concerns if they are to gather attention. Drawing on social psychologist Roy Baumeister, McGrath maintains that religions must offer a credible explanation for the meaning of life by answering core questions: (1) Identity: Who am I? (2) Value: Do I matter? (3) Purpose: Why am I here? (4) Agency: Can I make a difference?

Considered in turn, McGrath maintains that the Christian story does answer these: *Who am I?* As Christians, we are given a new identity as a person of significance by the God who has created and redeemed us and called us by name.³⁰ *Do I matter?* The core ideas of incarnation and atonement affirm that we matter to God and that we are sufficiently important to God to motivate this great drama of solidarity, restoration, and redemption.³¹ *Why am I here?* Christianity satisfies the ancient human quest for wisdom and fulfills our deepest longings, as historically recognized by Augustine and others.³² *Can I make a difference?* Through faith, Christian believers become part of God's unfolding story. McGrath remarks that we must think of ourselves as graciously invited to become part of God's cast and so are made capable of undertaking roles of real importance.³³

Helpful Insights from McGrath

McGrath makes several important observations. His insights from sociology, related to the way humans gain meaning from multiple stories simultaneously, are helpful. Theologically, the concept of *mythos spermatikos*, builds on Lewis's understanding of myth and helps form an important background of possibility for the task of narrative apologetics. Finally, he identifies a range of applications important for narrative apologetics. McGrath's book helps consolidate and establish narrative apologetics as

---

28. McGrath, *Narrative Apologetics*, 114.
29. McGrath, *Narrative Apologetics*, 114.
30. McGrath, *Narrative Apologetics*, 126.
31. McGrath, *Narrative Apologetics*, 131.
32. McGrath, *Narrative Apologetics*, 132.
33. McGrath, *Narrative Apologetics*, 135.

an approach within the broader field of apologetics, emphasizing the importance of appealing to both reason and imagination.

HOLLY ORDWAY: APOLOGETICS AND THE CENTRALITY OF IMAGINATION

Holly Ordway's *Apologetics and the Christian Imagination* focuses on imagination as central to an integrated approach to apologetics. It draws on her experience of coming to faith as an adult, including the role that *The Chronicles of Narnia* played in engaging her imagination. For Holly Ordway, apologetics is for everyone who wants to develop a stronger faith, understand why we believe what we believe, and know and love the Lord more fully.[34] Rooted in the Greek word *apologia*, apologetics is an effort to explain why we believe Christianity is true.[35] Apologetics functions negatively and positively. It works negatively to "address challenges to the faith, resolve doubts, remove obstacles to belief, and dismantle false ideas; and positively, to show the truth, coherence, power, and beauty of Christianity."[36] But Christians are also called to evangelize, "to share the good news," and to help people understand that the gospel really is good news and that it is *true*."[37] A problem exists, however, in what Ordway calls an "essentially post-Christian age."[38] According to Ordway, access to Christianity is not the primary issue. People think they know what they are rejecting. She writes, "All too often, people think they already know what Christianity is—and they don't particularly want to hear any more about it. . . . Christianity is just one more option on the spiritual menu, and an outdated one at that."[39] Ordway argues that there is a need for a new and likewise ancient approach: people need to come and see Christianity for themselves. This is the same basic appeal recorded in Scripture, what Andrew told the apostle Peter, and the Samaritan woman told her peers: "Come and see for yourself."[40] This is an invitation into the Christian story.

34. Ordway, *Apologetics*, 1–2.
35. Ordway, *Apologetics*, 1.
36. Ordway, *Apologetics*, 2.
37. Ordway, *Apologetics*, 2.
38. Ordway, *Apologetics*, 2.
39. Ordway, *Apologetics*, 4.
40. Ordway, *Apologetics*, 5.

Imagination and Incarnation

Ordway's project is informed by her own experience as a once-convinced atheist. She writes, "I was so firmly an atheist, I found the very idea of faith to be so repellent that I would not have listened to the arguments that ultimately convinced me."[41] As a college professor, Ordway was revisiting classic poetry to prepare for a class when she found that she was "deeply moved" by distinctly Christian poets.[42] Ordway recalls, "I had to admit that whatever it was that these authors believed, it was not simplistic or silly. Eventually, I realized that this question of 'faith' was more complex, and more interesting, than I had thought . . . and I decided to learn more."[43] Imagination opened the door to an otherwise hostile outlook on Christianity. *The Chronicles of Narnia*, in particular, played a significant role in her conversion. Although Ordway understood the concept of an incarnation, she felt that she could not grasp it. As she reread *The Chronicles of Narnia*, she went "looking for Aslan." In reading these works, she recalls, "my imagination was able to connect with what my reason already knew, and I was able to grasp, as a whole person, that it could be true: that God could become Incarnate."[44] This removed her last stumbling block to accepting Christ.[45] As well as narrative helping Ordway understand Christ's incarnation, she sees literature as offering a mode for bringing to life concepts that we might struggle to grasp in a solely rational way.

Reason, Imagination, and Meaning

Similarly to C. S. Lewis, Owen Barfield, and J. R. R. Tolkien, Ordway broadly understands the imagination as the mental power that allows us to conceive in our minds the image of something that is not present.[46] The faculty of the imagination "assimilates sensory data into images, upon which the intellect can then act."[47] Ordway explains this relationship by considering how one normally identifies a friend in a crowd:

41. Ordway, *Apologetics*, 9.
42. Ordway, *Apologetics*, 9–10.
43. Ordway, *Apologetics*, 10.
44. Ordway, *Apologetics*, 10.
45. Ordway, *Apologetics*, 10.
46. Ordway, *Apologetics*, 15.
47. Ordway, *Apologetics*, 16.

"You see someone coming toward you—is this your friend? There is a moment when you have the sensory data available to your eyes, but you are unsure of the identification—is this really the person you're looking for, or a stranger?"[48] As the data is processed, she writes, "there is a moment when the data resolves into meaning, and you are able to identify the person."[49] Ordway continues, "The senses bring the data; the reason makes the identification; the imagination mediates between the two."[50]

This sort of process occurs in reading as well. "Until sensory data has been assimilated," she writes, "reason cannot judge whether the meaning of the words is true or false."[51] For something to be judged true or false by reason, it must first have meaning. Ordway explains, "Only when something has meaning, which is generated by the imagination, can we begin to use our reason to judge whether it is true, or false."[52] This is one reason why the imagination has an important role to play in apologetics, evangelism, and even catechesis; Christian truths must first have meaning before they can take root.[53] "If someone can find the idea of the supernatural to be meaningful—an idea that can be grasped, that is worth grasping—then, and only then, is the question 'Is it true?' significant."[54] Understanding meaning comes before deciding whether something is true or not.

Similarly, to believers and unbelievers, Christian language often "rings empty." Ordway explains that although words like grace, sin, heaven, hell, and even "Jesus loves you" point to reality, for many, they are received like empty slogans: they are "words that are received without attention, and without a grasp of their meaning."[55] They are functionally meaningless. Ordway says that it is a "lack of meaning" rather than a specific dispute with Christian doctrine that is the strongest barrier to a serious consideration of the Christian faith.[56]

---

48. Ordway, *Apologetics*, 17.
49. Ordway, *Apologetics*, 17.
50. Ordway, *Apologetics*, 17.
51. Ordway, *Apologetics*, 18.
52. Ordway, *Apologetics*, 29.
53. Ordway, *Apologetics*, 10–11.
54. Ordway, *Apologetics*, 29.
55. Ordway, *Apologetics*, 21–22.
56. Ordway, *Apologetics*, 21–22.

Ordway on the Potential of Imaginative Apologetics

Ordway offers at least four ways that imaginative apologetics engages these challenges: (1) communicating meaning through metaphors, (2) recovering our sight of the world, (3) reordering our emotions, and (4) engaging with our experiences of life. Ordway suggests that imaginative literature is especially helpful for making ideas meaningful and for communicating ideas to those who may resist rational argumentation.[57]

Metaphor is one tool available to the apologist for conveying Christian meaning. Ordway explains that a metaphor is a comparison of one thing to a second thing that is outwardly dissimilar but that has some inner likeness to it, in order to convey something true about the first thing.[58] She identifies biblical examples, such as "the Lord is my shepherd" and the word of God as "a lamp to my feet," as examples of metaphors that bridge the known and the unknown.[59] Ordway elaborates, "If we do not know Christ, but have seen a lion at a zoo or at least seen television documentaries of lions, the phrase 'the Lion of Judah' can convey meaning that the phrase 'the Lord God' does not."[60] Metaphor allows the apologist to create a bridge for meaning.

Ordway believes that C. S. Lewis was especially effective in communicating Christian truth through metaphor. She cites Michael Ward's essay "Escape to Wallaby Wood: C. S. Lewis's Depictions of Conversion" as an example of this. In Ward's essay, he finds some thirty conversion metaphors in Lewis's *Mere Christianity*:

> Becoming a Christian (passing over from life to death) is like joining a campaign of sabotage, like falling at someone's feet or putting yourself in someone's hands, like taking on board fuel or food, like laying down your rebel arms and surrendering, saying sorry, laying yourself open, turning full speed astern; it is like killing part of yourself, like learning to walk or to write, like buying God a present with his own money; it is like a drowning man clutching at a rescuer's hand, like a tin soldier or a statue coming alive, like waking after a long sleep, like getting close to someone or becoming infected, like dressing up or pretending

---

57. Ordway, *Apologetics*, 39.
58. Ordway, *Apologetics*, 47.
59. Ordway, *Apologetics*, 47, 52.
60. Ordway, *Apologetics*, 52. As a side, Ordway importantly notes that Aslan is neither a symbol nor a metaphor for Christ since in Narnia Aslan is the Christ of the world of Narnia. Ordway, *Apologetics*, 50.

or playing; it is like emerging from the womb or hatching from an egg; it is like a compass needle swinging to north, or a cottage being made into a palace, or a field being plowed and resown, or a horse turning into a Pegasus, or a greenhouse roof becoming bright in the sunlight; it is like coming around from anesthetic, like coming in out of the wind, like going home.[61]

Ordway reflects, "Is it any wonder that *Mere Christianity* has had such a powerful effect on so many readers?"[62] Metaphors create a bridge for understanding meaning.

Ordway does make the important qualification that metaphors are contextually received. While some metaphors effectively communicate in some places, times, and people, they may not fit all contexts.[63] For example, while images of the ocean may evoke relaxation and holiday for some hearers, it may evoke ideas of danger or solitude in others.[64] Similarly, the language of God the Father may require contextualization. Biblical stories, such as the prodigal son, may not convey as well in certain contexts. Ordway remarks, "There may be no father in the picture at all for many of the people we want to reach. The Parable of the Prodigal Son will be more difficult to understand by someone for whom 'father' means 'one of my mother's ex-boyfriends.'"[65]

A second application of imaginative apologetics is the *recovery of sight* in relation to truth and meaning. Ordway believes the explanatory power of the Christian worldview is the most convincing argument for the faith: "everything coheres."[66] The Christian worldview, she explains, "encompasses all of reality—spiritual, mental, material, emotional."[67] The problem is that there are several obstacles to meaningful sight. Christians and skeptics have different understandings about "what they see."[68] A person's worldview impacts how they interpret the world and events within it. For example, those who believe in karma and reincarnation may view a leper as paying the price for past sins, so they may lack empathy; while a person operating within a Christian worldview may view

61. Ward, "Escape to Wallaby Wood," 151, quoted in Ordway, *Apologetics*, 56–57.
62. Ordway, *Apologetics*, 57.
63. Ordway, *Apologetics*, 53–54.
64. Ordway, *Apologetics*, 54.
65. Ordway, *Apologetics*, 56.
66. Ordway, *Apologetics*, 85.
67. Ordway, *Apologetics*, 85.
68. Ordway, *Apologetics*, 79.

the leper as one who needs help.[69] Another issue is a sense of "familiarity" and indifference. Ordway writes, "We live in a culture that is paradoxically both jaded by and ignorant about Christianity. People think they know who Jesus is, what the Church is, what it means to have faith . . . and they think it's boring, or stupid, or irrelevant."[70] She continues, "We need to help people recover a fresh view of the truth—to see Jesus for the first time, and really see him; to actually see the reality of sin, and the beauty and brokenness of the world, not to just gloss over it."[71]

The imagination is one pathway for recovering sight. The imagination affords the opportunity to *step into another perspective*, and through the faculty of reason, we can "assess the truth or falsity of what we discover."[72] Although people see through particular perspectives, Ordway notes, "our context is our home, not our prison."[73] Following Tolkien's *On Fairy-Stories*, Ordway sees fantasy literature and stories as a fruitful path for meaningful sight. It can recover the familiar or help readers to see things as a whole. Moreover, stories open the door to *seeing the world afresh*. She cites Tolkien's Middle-earth as an example of how:

> After reading about the Ents, Tree-beard and the other shepherds of the trees, we can look at an ordinary tree, a pine or oak, and think: how extraordinary, really, is a tree! . . . We can be moved by the self-sacrifice of Frodo and the kingliness of Aragorn and thus respond more immediately, more intuitively, to these ideas when we hear them in the Gospel.[74]

Ordway maintains that "good stories and poetry help us to see more clearly when we close the book and re-enter ordinary life."[75] This is very relevant for the apologist.

A third application of imaginative literature is the *reordering of emotion*. Ordway maintains that literature offers "a mode of apologetics in which we can guide the natural human emotional response toward its right end."[76] Literature presents truth such that the reader is emotionally

---

69. Ordway, *Apologetics*, 81.
70. Ordway, *Apologetics*, 88.
71. Ordway, *Apologetics*, 89.
72. Ordway, *Apologetics*, 89.
73. Ordway, *Apologetics*, 85.
74. Ordway, *Apologetics*, 89.
75. Ordway, *Apologetics*, 89.
76. Ordway, *Apologetics*, 102.

moved as well as intellectually convinced.[77] She maintains that "when emotion and intellect are in line, rather than at odds, with each other and both are oriented toward the good, then it becomes easier for the will to direct action toward the good."[78] Ordering the emotion prepares the reader to respond to the Christian truth.

A final application of imaginative apologetics is that it can engage or provide biblical solidarity with *our experiences of human life*, such as pain and doubt, struggle and longing. Ordway notes, "If we tell the truth about the experience of pain, our witness is more credible when we speak about joy. When there are Christians who can speak honestly about suffering in their art, it provides the necessary context for other Christians to speak about hope and love."[79] Ordway suggests that authenticity about pain, doubt, and struggle is an important facet of imaginative apologetics. She concludes, "Here, imaginative apologetics can shine, as literature and the arts provide ways to illuminate questions of suffering and joy in ways that argument cannot."[80]

Longing is another point of contact with our lived experience. Ordway asks, "Why do people so often feel a desire for something more—something they can't even articulate, perhaps—even when they are fed, clothed, sheltered, and entertained?"[81] Why, she asks, do we desire meaning in our lives from a materialist worldview?[82] C. S. Lewis's answer, writes Ordway, is that we are not merely material.[83] If this holy longing points beyond the material world, it is a natural path for apologetics. Ordway asks, "How, then, do we help to cultivate this 'holy longing' in ways that will bear fruit? One way is through stories that evoke joy and make our Christian joy credible.... What we need are convincing portraits of Christian hope and joy."[84] Ordway says that part of the work of imaginative apologetics is to stir up a longing for meaning, truth, beauty, and goodness: "We must, in a sense, be gadflies for beauty: rousing people from their contentment with the status quo."[85] Ordway sees literature, the

---

77. Ordway, *Apologetics*, 102.
78. Ordway, *Apologetics*, 124.
79. Ordway, *Apologetics*, 124.
80. Ordway, *Apologetics*, 124.
81. Ordway, *Apologetics*, 135.
82. Ordway, *Apologetics*, 135.
83. Ordway, *Apologetics*, 131.
84. Ordway, *Apologetics*, 139–40.
85. Ordway, *Apologetics*, 129.

arts, and architecture as tools that help stir, attract, and show "the beauty of Christ."[86] They provide a kind of glimpse into the kingdom of Christ.

In the end, Ordway says we need both reason and imagination. "Our fullest understanding of any truth," she writes, "comes when we both look at (Contemplate) it and look along (Enjoy) it, bearing in mind that both reason and imagination are involved in the operation of these two modes of seeing."[87] Following Lewis, Ordway notes that some things, such as love, cannot be enjoyed and contemplated at the same time. The apologetic task requires "both propositional argument and imaginative engagement, continually shaped and re-shaped to show the truth in fresh ways."[88] In this sense, apologists must become "gadflies" for truth and beauty.[89]

Helpful Insights from Ordway

Ordway offers a first-person account of the potential for imaginative apologetics, including the impact of *The Chronicles of Narnia* on her path to faith. As a convinced atheist, she would not listen to rational argumentation, so her interest needed to be piqued first. She highlights the potential for imagination to overcome the very important obstacle of indifference, one that continues to grow as a recognized obstacle in the field of apologetics.[90] Further, she recognizes the need for a both/and approach to apologetics. Rational argumentation may ring hollow, while narrative alone does not automatically point us to truth in the real world. Ordway also offers a helpful explanation about the way metaphors can serve apologetically to convey meaning, as well as the needed insight that metaphors must be contextualized. She identifies the importance of emotion in the apologetic task, as well as what I have termed points of contact. By exploring the nature of the imagination in relation to reason, she focuses on the aspects of human beings that respond to stories, adding a helpful dimension to our understanding of narrative apologetics.

86. Ordway, *Apologetics*, 129.
87. Ordway, *Apologetics*, 164.
88. Ordway, *Apologetics*, 176.
89. Ordway, *Apologetics*, 129.
90. See chapter 9 on apatheism.

JUSTIN ARIEL BAILEY: IMAGINATION AND THE SECULAR AGE

If McGrath shows the breadth of narrative's potential for apologetics and Ordway the power of language and imagination, Justin Ariel Bailey shows the urgency of narrative apologetics in the contemporary Western context. Bailey's project in his book *Reimagining Apologetics* is a call to reconsider our approach to apologetics to accommodate what Charles Taylor has termed the "social imaginary" of our secular age.[91] As Bailey explains, a social imaginary is "an unarticulated and often unexamined sense of the world and our place in it. It consists of habitual ways of experiencing the world, worked in, and worked out by the rhythms of our common life. It is carried around and carried on through practices, stories, and cultural artifacts, which are often profoundly dissonant with what we say we believe."[92] The Christian faith is no longer taken for granted in the contemporary Western world. Bailey finds that traditional apologetic arguments often fall flat or go unheard, and he believes an adjustment is needed for today.

Thick Authenticity and the Theater of God's Glory

Traditional apologetics typically appeals to authority and external proof, what Bailey calls "Uppercase Apologetics." But he argues that people within our present context are more likely to connect with authenticity. Authenticity, as Bailey defines it, is the "internal call to compose an original life, a life that makes sense."[93] Unlike "thin versions" of authenticity that drift toward narcissism and sociopathy, Bailey maintains that "thick" authenticity invites a more "examined, creative, and self-responsible life."[94] In keeping with Charles Taylor, Bailey argues that authenticity is one of the most important factors for making belief believable in a secular context. To engage authentically, Bailey maintains, one must account for a person's "embodied, aesthetic experience of the world, their felt sense of their place in the world, and the possibilities that are available."[95] This

---

91. Bailey, *Reimagining Apologetics*, 54; see Taylor, *Secular Age*, 224.
92. Bailey, *Reimagining Apologetics*, 54.
93. Bailey, *Reimagining Apologetics*, 8.
94. Bailey, *Reimagining Apologetics*, 8.
95. Bailey, *Reimagining Apologetics*, 8.

human quest in the world is "fundamentally" imaginative.[96] He writes, "In an age of authenticity, faith and doubt are first navigated imaginatively and affectively, and the felt dimension of faith is most decisive in belief."[97] This is why the imagination very naturally plays such an important role.[98]

Related to the age of authenticity is Bailey's theological conviction that the world is "the theater of God's glory."[99] Bailey says that God is at work in the human quest for authenticity in ways that are often underappreciated.[100] An apologetic that fittingly calls for "thick authenticity," he writes, will "join our neighbors in the quest for authenticity, offering a larger horizon in which God's active presence can be named as it is felt."[101] This stands in contrast to our culture's "thin authenticity," which focuses on the idea of being "true to yourself" in an individualistic and often relativistic way. Bailey continues, "It is in moments of imaginative excess, when Reality breaks through—perhaps summoning unlooked-for tears to our eyes—that we are especially open to the provocations of belief."[102] As such, theologically informed authenticity is an important pathway for advocating Christian belief.

The Apologetics of Hope

Blaise Pascal is sometimes associated with the "apologetics of despair."[103] Pascal drew attention to an existential void created by humanity's alienation from God as a kind of apologetic engagement. In contrast, Bailey

---

96. Bailey, *Reimagining Apologetics*, 8.

97. Bailey, *Reimagining Apologetics*, 14.

98. Bailey defines the imagination as a faculty concerned with *possibility* (what could be), that is responsive to real presence (God is at work in creation and creativity). He also believes it can be directed to participate in the "theodrama" of Scripture. By this he means the world of meaning has been gifted to our perception, ultimate reality is personal, and it is most fully revealed in Jesus Christ. See Bailey, *Reimagining Apologetics*, 5, 85.

99. This is John Calvin's language. See Bailey, *Reimagining Apologetics*, 33, 163, 187, 206, 240.

100. Bailey, *Reimagining Apologetics*, 8–9, 206–7.

101. Bailey, *Reimagining Apologetics*, 9.

102. Bailey, *Reimagining Apologetics*, 9.

103. Bailey, *Reimagining Apologetics*, 11. Following William de Wit, Bailey identifies three features of the apologetics of despair: (1) Address the worldview that excludes God. (2) Use a reductio ad absurdum argument that shows the absurdity of unbelief. (3) Use this sensitivity to the existential implications of belief, especially whether the worldview is satisfying on its own terms. De Wit, *On the Way*, 62–63.

argues for "the apologetics of hope" as a more fruitful path.[104] He suggests that an apologetic of despair may unnecessarily level in order to build, rather than to address ways that God is already at work.[105] As Bailey explains, the apologetics of hope tries to help non-Christians to attend to God's work in and through creation and creativity.[106] This version of apologetics "seeks to explore the experience of presence in creation and creativity, inviting seekers to consider whether the presence might have a transcendent source and a personal name."[107] Bailey continues, "It seeks the source of our imaginative longings as well as a larger context in which these musings can be explored, deepened, negotiated, and fulfilled."[108] Bailey says that while rationality and truth remain essential, in the present Western context the apologist first needs to convey the beauty and fruitfulness of the Christian faith.[109] The apologist needs to show how Christianity blesses and enlarges the created order.

Bailey argues that we need to pay attention to a person's hopes and imaginings—that is, to the realm of desire ("the aesthetic realm"), and this realm is where the "felt experience of meaning is most important."[110] Our desires are not delusions; rather, they are "responsive to the provocations of God's active presence" and "evidence of God's continued engagement."[111]

Bailey makes the case that the apologetics of hope provides compelling reasons for taking the Christian message seriously. First, the very idea of hope invites us to consider what could establish grounds for a person to hope and never despair. Second, it seeks to show that Christianity is consistent with this type of hope.[112] Rather than attempting to prove that Christianity is undoubtedly true, this approach seeks "epistemic permission"—that is, showing how faith is plausible and rational, so people

104. Bailey, *Reimagining Apologetics*, 11.
105. Bailey, *Reimagining Apologetics*, 12.
106. Bailey, *Reimagining Apologetics*, 13, 207.
107. Bailey, *Reimagining Apologetics*, 13.
108. Bailey, *Reimagining Apologetics*, 13.
109. Bailey, *Reimagining Apologetics*, 10. Bailey extends his desire for generativity in a call to the apologetic posture of culture care rather against culture war. If the world is the arena of God's glory, it has implications for all areas of life. Bailey writes, "If the world is saturated with God's presence and address, despite our attempts to deny or shut it out, Christian engagement with culture becomes more a matter of discernment than defense." Bailey, *Reimagining Apologetics*, 226–27.
110. Bailey, *Reimagining Apologetics*, 12.
111. Bailey, *Reimagining Apologetics*, 12, 262.
112. Bailey, *Reimagining Apologetics*, 12.

have good reason to choose to believe, even if they don't have an absolute proof or an irrefutable argument. Bailey believes this is consistent with many apologists of church history. He explains, "The wider tradition begins in faith, seeks understanding in hope, and commends the gospel in love. It does not secure epistemic obligation."[113]

Three Elements for Reimagining Apologetics.

In addition to bringing attention to the roles of authenticity and apologetics of hope, Bailey advances three essential elements for reimagining apologetics: (1) the aesthetic sense, (2) an orienting vision, and (3) poetic participation.[114] He also features prominent writers George MacDonald and Marilynne Robinson as examples of nontraditional apologists who demonstrate his reimagined apologetic in action.

Element One: Aesthetic Sense

Bailey's reimagined apologetics prioritizes the aesthetic dimension, understood as our "felt sense" or the "embodied experience" of what is meaningful.[115] The apologist asks questions such as, "What would make belief beautiful and believable for this person?" or "What makes belief ugly and unbelievable?"[116] These questions are informed, Bailey says, by the social, cultural, and relational contexts of your life that make up your "lived, felt sense of the world," especially as it relates to possibilities. Bailey illustrates this with Esqueleto, a character in the movie *Nacho Libre*, who "only believes in science."[117] Bailey asks, "What is it about science that feels more capacious than Christianity?"[118] Or, how does Christianity or scientism limit our view of the world?

The first question of our "post-romantic situation" is not "Is it true? But rather "How does it move Esqueleto?"[119] If the solution resonates, connects with his desires, or generates new possibilities for exploring the

---

113. Bailey, *Reimagining Apologetics*, 7.
114. Bailey, *Reimagining Apologetics*, 229–35.
115. Bailey, *Reimagining Apologetics*, 229, 262.
116. Bailey, *Reimagining Apologetics*, 229.
117. Hess, *Nacho Libre*.
118. Bailey, *Reimagining Apologetics*, 230.
119. Bailey, *Reimagining Apologetics*, 230.

world, it has the "ring of authenticity," so he may now seek its truth.[120] This approach draws out desire through the imagination by identifying the desires and imaginative intrigue that animate Esqueleto's life (e.g., what in science gives him security, is beautiful, or desirable?).[121] In kind, the imaginative apologist contextualizes the beauty and desirability of the Christian faith, and seeks to cultivate a humble hope by translating how the gospel offers something more satisfying in the heart language of the individual.[122] Bailey maintains that the apologist can act with confidence because the Holy Spirit is already at work in the person's human longings. Imaginative apologetics starts with human meaning-making but directs the desire toward God, "who moves toward creation in love."[123] Even if openness is not apparent, Bailey maintains, addressing the imagination through story or supposition offers an immersive experience of the logic of faith.[124]

Bailey identifies this pattern in George MacDonald's work in several ways. First, he describes MacDonald's basic strategy as follows: "[MacDonald] begins with the assumption that things we love have a source beyond themselves, that our deepest longings are not lies. Next, he wakes the imagination to consider what kind of God would be worth having, worth believing in. Next, he aims to fill the heart with hope that such a God actually exists."[125]

As Bailey explains, "The first movement of MacDonald's imaginative apologetic is to find a God worthy of belief, one whose presence accounts not just for truth and goodness but also for beauty."[126] One example from MacDonald's imaginative work is *Thomas Wingfold, Curate*. Bailey writes, "When Wingfold tells Faber that he is searching for 'an idea of a God large enough, grand enough, pure enough, lovely enough to be fit to believe in,' Faber asks him if he has found one. Wingfold replies, 'I think I am finding such.' 'Where?' 'In the man of the New Testament.'"[127] Bailey explains, "Throughout the Wingfold series, the hunger for beauty, goodness, and truth finds its most concrete ground in the incarnate Christ."[128]

120. Bailey, *Reimagining Apologetics*, 230.
121. Bailey, *Reimagining Apologetics*, 230.
122. Bailey, *Reimagining Apologetics*, 231.
123. Bailey, *Reimagining Apologetics*, 231.
124. Bailey, *Reimagining Apologetics*, 232.
125. Bailey, *Reimagining Apologetics*, 150.
126. Bailey, *Reimagining Apologetics*, 143.
127. Bailey, *Reimagining Apologetics*, 148.
128. Bailey, *Reimagining Apologetics*, 149.

Element Two: An Orienting Vision

Reimagining apologetics invites exploration of a larger vision of the world by asking questions such as, "What would it be like to see the world through eyes of faith?"[129] Bailey writes, "We inhabit vision, asking, "What would faith feel like?"[130] This element seeks to invite people to see the world in a Christian perspective via imaginative rather than intellectual grounds. This can be done through stories or through personal testimony about how faith opens the world to a greater vision.[131] The invitation to an "empathetic gaze" requires space for mutual understanding and includes showing hospitality toward doubt and unbelief.[132] It also requires that human desire be situated in the "theodrama" in which all humans participate.[133] The imagination plays an important role in cultivating empathy and translation. The goal, Bailey says, is "an experience of seeing the world in all its particularities through the lens of the Christian story: creation, fall, and redemption."[134]

Bailey believes that Marilynne Robinson accomplishes this by giving her readers a "vicarious vision." He explains, "She ravishes with revelatory perception. Her writing invites outsiders to see the world through the shocked eyes of wonder, even as it invites insiders to a posture of generous love.[135] Her readers get a sense of what it "feels like to live within the Christian imaginary."[136] Bailey observes, "[Robinson] celebrates epiphanies of the ordinary. If the world is truly the theater of God's glory, then everyday life holds revelatory potential."[137] He continues, "Robinson depicts John Ames [a chief character and Congregationalist pastor in *Gilead*] in awe of the prairie at dawn, astonished at being 'allowed to

---

129. Bailey, *Reimagining Apologetics*, 232.
130. Bailey, *Reimagining Apologetics*, 236.
131. Bailey, *Reimagining Apologetics*, 232.
132. Bailey, *Reimagining Apologetics*, 233.
133. Bailey, *Reimagining Apologetics*, 233; "Theodrama" depends on Kevin J. Vanhoozer. It means that a world of meaning has been gifted to our perception, and ultimate reality is personal, revealed most fully in Jesus Christ. Bailey, *Reimagining Apologetics*, 5.
134. Bailey, *Reimagining Apologetics*, 235.
135. Bailey, *Reimagining Apologetics*, 155–56.
136. Bailey, *Reimagining Apologetics*, 155.
137. Bailey, *Reimagining Apologetics*, 163.

witness such a thing."[138] This vision leads to what Bailey describes as a kind of epiphany in the final pages of Robinson's *Gilead*:

> It has seemed to me sometimes as though the Lord breathes on this poor gray ember of Creation and it turns to radiance—for a moment or a year or the span of a life. And then it sinks back into itself again, and to look at it no one would know it had anything to do with fire, or light. . . . But the Lord is more constant and far more extravagant than it seems to imply. Wherever you turn your eyes the world can shine like transfiguration. You don't have to bring a thing to it except a little willingness to see. Only, who could have the courage to see it?[139]

Bailey continues, "Epiphanic vision is not abolished by fallenness, though it does require 'a little willingness to see,' itself a gift of grace."[140] Bailey concludes that Robinson's primary apologetic contribution is that she "blesses and baptizes the imagination of her reader by providing a visionary experience of the world."[141]

Element Three: Poetic Participation

Reimaging apologetics, Bailey writes, "situates human projects within the redemptive project of God."[142] The pathway for exploration is participation. It asks, "What new possibility would faith facilitate?"[143] A search for meaning based around the created order is especially fruitful. Bailey writes, "Instead of saying, 'Here is why you should believe,' imaginative apologetics says, 'Here is how faith could reframe your quest.'"[144] Similar to what Augustine did in the *City of God*, the apologist helps situate human projects within the larger plan of God.[145] For example, in the quest for authenticity, imaginative apologetics helps a person to see how the search for a "beautiful, resonate life" fits with the active presence of God

---

138. Bailey, *Reimagining Apologetics*, 163.
139. Quoted in Bailey, *Reimagining Apologetics*, 163.
140. Bailey, *Reimagining Apologetics*, 163.
141. Bailey, *Reimagining Apologetics*, 189.
142. Bailey, *Reimagining Apologetics*, 235.
143. Bailey, *Reimagining Apologetics*, 236.
144. Bailey, *Reimagining Apologetics*, 237.
145. Bailey, *Reimagining Apologetics*, 238.

in the world.¹⁴⁶ Added to this is the unexpected beauty of the cross, as well as the promise that death will ultimately be swallowed up, which discloses "the most capacious possible life."¹⁴⁷

Everyday and Extended Imaginative Apologetics

Bailey offers two additional models for imaginative apologetics: (1) everyday imaginative apologetics and (2) extended imaginative apologetics. He illustrates the first model with a story about his wife, Melissa. A coworker once asked Melissa why she would indoctrinate her children into Christianity rather than allow them to choose. Bailey writes, "Melissa understood that a frame had been placed on faith; for this coworker, faith is opposed to freedom and thus should always be consciously chosen. Underneath the objection is the ethic of authenticity: people should believe what feels right to them rather than being told what to believe."¹⁴⁸ Melissa's response was to offer an alternative picture: "For us, faith is the most liberating thing we have ever experienced. We feel like it is this amazing gift that we get to pass on to our children."¹⁴⁹ The coworker was stunned and admitted that she had not thought of faith in that way. Melissa articulated the "generative" picture of faith that her friend had not imagined—"a glimpse of what faith feels like from the inside."¹⁵⁰

The final model presented is what Bailey terms "extended imaginative apologetics." For this, Bailey turns to an episode of the PBS series *Closer to Truth*, in which Robert Kuhn interviewed Anglican scholar Sarah Coakley.¹⁵¹ This interview forcefully corroborates the potency of Bailey's general project. In the series, the host travels and interviews some of the world's most brilliant minds, exploring humanity's deepest questions.¹⁵² In this conversation, instead of offering classical arguments for God, though Coakley does find some value in them, she addresses Kuhn's existential longing with the question: "*Quid petis?*" "What do you seek?"¹⁵³

---

146. Bailey, *Reimagining Apologetics*, 237.
147. Bailey, *Reimagining Apologetics*, 238–39.
148. Bailey, *Reimagining Apologetics*, 241–42.
149. Bailey, *Reimagining Apologetics*, 242.
150. Bailey, *Reimagining Apologetics*, 242.
151. Kuhn, "Why Believe in God?"
152. Bailey, *Reimagining Apologetics*, 242.
153. Bailey, *Reimagining Apologetics*, 243.

Bailey finds that Coakley's interview aligns well with his project of reimagining apologetics. She uses a suggestive, inviting tone rather than directly challenging Kuhn. She uses amicable language like "Let's say" or "I would ask you" to invite Kuhn's imaginative consideration. She also uses Bailey's "first essential element" by beginning with the aesthetic dimension—"that it is in the spaces of longings and losses that God may be reaching out to him."[154] Curiously, Kuhn feels that he has numerous reasons to want to believe, and even claims that he would love to believe in God. Still, he doesn't want to "fool himself."[155]

Coakley also uses Bailey's second essential element. She invites Kuhn to see the world with her through her eyes as a believer.[156] Coakley says, "As a believer, I find that it is in silent waiting on God that ultimate, transcendent reality impinges on me. And every time I do that I think of it as a sort of rehearsal for the moment when I have to give over control, which will be the moment I die . . . because when we're no longer afraid of death, we're no longer afraid of life."[157] Bailey explains, "She allows him to vicariously experience the presence and solace that she feels in surrendering to God."[158] He continues, "Coakley offers an example of what imaginative apologetics looks like, even with an interlocutor who is resistant to the provocations of desire. She begins and ends with the aesthetic dimension that situates his unbelief, reframes his creative projects in terms of a spiritual quest, and offers a vision of life through the eyes of faith."[159] It is also one of the most impactful interviews that I have seen with Kuhn. He was unusually moved.[160]

Helpful Insights from Bailey

Bailey's approach is both thoughtful and attentive to the distinctives of the contemporary Western context. Context matters a great deal for apologetics. He identifies the cultural shift toward authenticity and a general distaste for authority. He also shows us some advantages of adopting

---

154. Bailey, *Reimagining Apologetics*, 243.
155. Bailey, *Reimagining Apologetics*, 243.
156. Bailey, *Reimagining Apologetics*, 243.
157. Bailey, *Reimagining Apologetics*, 243.
158. Bailey, *Reimagining Apologetics*, 242.
159. Bailey, *Reimagining Apologetics*, 243.
160. See Kuhn, "Why Believe in God?" 2:19–11:33.

a posture of "epistemic permission," inviting people to see and believe, rather than "epistemic obligation," which involves trying to persuade them that they must believe.

Bailey also identifies a theologically informed basis for narrative apologetics as a discipline, and for expecting it to connect with people. If the whole world is "the theater of God's glory," everyday life, as well as literature and art, has the potential to point people to God.

Further, Bailey's concept of "thick authenticity" when considering how God may be at work in and through imaginative pathways is excellent. The Christian faith offers a true and deeper authenticity that fulfils the longing for authenticity in our culture, but that is met only superficially by individual self-expression. He also highlights how narrative apologists can address doubt with empathy in a way that connects with the desire for authenticity. Bailey furthermore shows how reimagined apologetics has generative potential, the ability to produce meaning and beauty, in kind with artist Makoto Fujimura's view of culture care.[161] Moreover, he shows the strengths of an apologetic centered on hope, beauty, and desire rather than despair.

THE INSIGHTS OF CONTEMPORARY NARRATIVE APOLOGETICS

All three contemporary models identify the relevance of narrative apologetics, particularly in a post-Christian world. They identify the generative capability of stories to enlarge our view of Christianity. They recognize the power of narrative to convey significance in ways that reason alone does not accomplish. All three also recognize the potential to see better or freshly through the eyes of characters or through the story.

One place that none of the contemporary models seriously develop is the "negative" side of narrative apologetics. They recognize authenticity concerning brokenness, but not the potential presented by despair and fear while living in a broken world. Lewis, however, thought one of the essential roles of fairy stories for children was to prepare them to be courageous and to cultivate courage. By encountering fearful experiences and brave characters in fairy stories, he believed it prepared children for the fallen world.

---

161. Fujimura, *Culture Care*.

To be fair, Bailey does reference the apologetics of despair, but his point is to contrast his model with it. While the apologetics of hope is an excellent focus, the apologetics of despair is also vital. Consider Bailey's discussion of Sarah Coakley's engagement with Robert Kuhn. Coakley fruitfully began with the aesthetic dimension but did not end there. Bailey does not discuss that Coakley includes something closer to an apologetic of despair even more forcefully. Coakley graciously but forcefully helps Kuhn to imagine and concede that there will come a point when he will no longer be able to maintain his false sense of control—the day that he takes his last breath. Kuhn's filmed reflection on the interview suggests that the strongest impact was the apologetics of despair, not the apologetics of hope. In fact, when transitioning to Kuhn's following interview, he reflects, "I do fear death. I shudder at the finality of utter nonexistence. I'd wish to be no longer afraid." Then he continues, "But before I give in to *easy answers*, I seek out the other side."[162] Narrative apologetics can engage hope and despair, pointing people to the only sure foundation. Although it may be closer to seed planting, it still has a role to play.

---

162. Kuhn, "Why Believe in God?" 11:33–11:46; emphasis added.

3

Cross-Cultural Apologetics

INTRODUCTION

GIVEN NARRATIVE APOLOGETICS' UNIQUE strengths and abilities to communicate Christian truths, how could these strengths be applied across cultures and worldviews? My contention is that narrative apologetics can contribute to cross-cultural apologetics by helping translate relevant Christian beliefs, advocating Christianity's truth and goodness, subverting the adequacy of non-Christian beliefs, and helping respond to objections. In this chapter, I consider two models of cross-cultural apologetics to identify important needs, barriers, and possibilities for engagement, and how these overlap with narrative apologetic approaches. What are the specific challenges of cross-cultural apologetics, and how can story and imagination help us address them? Considering these models will prepare us for part two, where we will explore how *The Chronicles of Narnia* connects with a range of worldviews and cultures.

BENNO VAN DEN TOREN AND CROSS-CULTURAL PERSUASION

The first model we will turn to is that of Benno van den Toren, professor of intercultural theology at the Protestant Theological University (Groningen). Van den Toren taught in French-speaking Africa for eight years, as well as at Wycliffe Hall at the University of Oxford, before his present position. His time in non-Western contexts significantly shapes his theological understanding and methodology, and his work explores how the Christian faith can be faithfully communicated in different cultural contexts, both the post-Christian West and other cultures globally.[1] I will focus on his book *Christian Apologetics as Cross-Cultural Dialogue* to explore the possibilities and overlap with narrative apologetics.

What Is Cross-Cultural Apologetics?

Van den Toren prefers the language of persuasion rather than argument in his approach to cross-cultural apologetics.[2] All arguments are culturally embedded, he says, so they will encounter significant barriers. Instead of "knock-down arguments," we should seek to persuade our conversation partners of the liberating truth and goodness of Jesus Christ.[3] This echoes Bailey's emphasis on the apologetics of hope and creating "epistemic permission" rather than compulsion. Van den Toren argues that we need culture-sensitive apologetics in part because of globalization and cultural diversity. Because diverse cultural outlooks regularly intersect, it tends to diminish the plausibility of each of them.[4] This need is compounded by the difficulty of cross-cultural communication in general, as well as of communicating the gospel.[5]

Van den Toren's cross-cultural persuasion model can be considered in two main parts: (1) identifying barriers to cross-cultural persuasion and (2) exploring mutually reinforcing possibilities for cross-cultural persuasion.

Barriers to Cross-Cultural Persuasion

Van den Toren identifies three types of barriers to cross-cultural persuasion, relating to

---

1. Van den Toren, "Prof. Dr. B. van den Toren."

2. Van den Toren, *Christian Apologetics*, 178; Van den Toren, "Challenges and Possibilities"; Van den Toren, "Inter-Religious Dialogue."

3. Van den Toren, *Christian Apologetics*, 178.

4. Van den Toren, *Christian Apologetics*, 155.

5. Van den Toren, *Christian Apologetics*, 170–77.

1. the nature of the human being itself;
2. the nature and impact of worldviews on our lives; and
3. the way individuals and communities deal with objections to their basic outlook.[6]

First, Van den Toren identifies the nature of the human being as one barrier to cross-cultural persuasion. As human beings, we are profoundly bound to the community where we are socialized, and which provides our identity. He explains that Christians from Western, individualistic communities sometimes do not appreciate the level of support experienced by other communities. So they do not acknowledge this additional cost of following Jesus, which would put them at odds with their community. Van de Toren explains that a Muslim in the West considering conversion is not only considering a new religious allegiance and a new outlook on the world. She is also considering converting to the community of the church, which often seems rather shallow compared to the close-knit Muslim communities in the diaspora on which she depends.[7] This is one of her barriers to coming to the Christian faith.

A second barrier to persuasion relates to the nature of worldviews. Van den Toren says, "Worldviews do not represent a loose collection of ideas that can be exchanged for others in a piecemeal manner. The different basic elements of a worldview do reinforce each other . . . [it also] coheres with an *ethos*—a way of life."[8] Worldview also involves what we consider a worthy pursuit. He explains, "A worldview also coheres with a certain allegiance to what we consider most worthwhile to pursue, be it individual happiness, the continuation and flourishing of our clan, entry in the Koranic Paradise, absorption in the *Nirvana*, loving communion with God, or whatever."[9] Furthermore, he writes, "threads of allegiance, worldview, ethos, and spiritual power weave together to an almost unbreakable bond(age) in which our mind, will and emotions are all pulled in one direction."[10] Persuasion is challenging due to the tightly woven nature of worldviews, which bind beliefs with values and desires.

---

6. Van den Toren, *Christian Apologetics*, 179–81.
7. Van den Toren, *Christian Apologetics*, 179.
8. Van den Toren, *Christian Apologetics*, 180.
9. Van den Toren, *Christian Apologetics*, 180.
10. Van den Toren, *Christian Apologetics*, 180.

A final barrier that Van den Toren identifies is the way individuals and communities deal with objections that do not fit their outlook. Unexpected anomalies are often set aside, similar to how scientific anomalies do not immediately overturn a paradigm. This means that a real objection that does not fit the current belief system is simply set aside without serious consideration. The anomaly does not displace current belief unless there is a sufficient build-up of pressure. A similar factor is what Michael Polanyi terms the "principle of suppressed nucleation." This is when "counter-instances do not seem important enough to give them real attention."[11] People tend to ignore or explain away things that don't fit their worldview, and it takes a lot for people to seriously consider changing their whole worldview.

Another factor that Van den Toren observes is social pressures, such as those described by Peter Berger and Thomas Luckman's *The Social Construction of Reality: A Treatise on the Sociology of Knowledge* and Thomas Kuhn's *The Structure of Scientific Revolutions*. Taken together, all these factors might make the prospects for persuasion seem bleak. But Van den Toren maintains that a range of possibilities for apologetic dialogue opens up if we move away from efforts at "watertight arguments to checkmate our dialogue partners."[12] Dialogue is key.

Possibilities for Cross-Cultural Persuasion

Van den Toren finds formal argumentation somewhat unhelpful, but he identifies three mutually reinforcing possibilities for cross-cultural apologetic persuasion:

1. the power of the whole;
2. points of contact that show that the Christian faith is coherent and the fulfillment of what is best and true in one's present worldview; and
3. exposing tensions and antinomies in cultures, worldviews, and lifestyles that reveal the need to explore alternatives.[13]

Van den Toren emphasizes the illuminating power of the whole—and of Jesus. He sees Christ as the clue to an alternative way of life. He

---

11. Van den Toren, *Christian Apologetics*, 182.
12. Van den Toren, *Christian Apologetics*, 182.
13. Van den Toren, "Challenges and Possibilities," 64.

explains, "Because of the inner coherence of the Christian worldview and of alternatives, we will *in the final analysis* only be able to persuade our dialogue partner because of the persuasive power of the person and message of Jesus Christ and the window He opens on our world and condition as a whole."[14] He continues, "Because the new perspective we gain in Christ illuminates our world and lives and the whole of our experience," this allows us to confidently point to clues for understanding life.[15] Further, because the Christian story gives a "better reading of all aspects of life as we encounter it, we consider it better than its alternatives."[16]

Van den Toren believes "the power of the whole" should be introduced from the beginning.[17] He offers two reasons for this; one is its invitation to dialogue. The second is a more fitting expectation of what to anticipate with Christianity. He explains,

> They need to understand that our initial explanations of the Gospel can only be considered *initial* introductions into a whole new world, which they will not be able to understand adequately at first glance. They especially have not understood the Christian faith, if they dismiss it from the outset for not making sense *from their own perspective*.[18]

Instead of magic bullets to the gospel, Van den Toren invites more modest expectations about what should be anticipated from someone's first encounter with Christianity.

Van den Toren also notes that we as human beings desire existential security. Similar to Thomas Kuhn's understanding of paradigm shifts in science, Van den Toren says that "people will never seriously reconsider their own outlook and way of life, when they see no alternative."[19] He continues, "If we have no other place to go, we will defend the only place we have, whatever its limitations."[20] We need a plausible alternative before we can seriously reconsider our present belief system. Van den Toren illustrates this by inviting us to imagine two circles on a floor, which represent worldviews. He writes, "Let us imagine our dialogue-partner

---

14. Van den Toren, "Challenges and Possibilities," 49.
15. Van den Toren, *Christian Apologetics*, 183.
16. Van den Toren, *Christian Apologetics*, 183.
17. Van den Toren, *Christian Apologetics*, 183.
18. Van den Toren, *Christian Apologetics*, 183.
19. Van den Toren, *Christian Apologetics*, 183.
20. Van den Toren, *Christian Apologetics*, 183.

standing in a circle which represents her own world."[21] He continues, "The best way to bring her so far that she leaves this circle is to invite her to explore the Christian way of life in a non-committal way with one foot already within the Christian circle, the Christian world, to see if it is tenable."[22] It is only when a person feels that another circle is viable that he or she feels comfortable putting both feet in the Christian circle.

Van den Toren furthermore sees the value of the apologetic use of narrative. This shows the intersection of cross-cultural and narrative apologetics. He sees narrative as especially apt for introducing our dialogue partner to the Christian world, due to its existential appeal and ability to fully immerse the reader in another world.[23] Van den Toren writes, "[Narrative in apologetics] appeals to other and more comprehensive sides of our humanity than the classical types of argument—particularly the imagination and the emotions."[24] He continues, "Narrative does not lead us step by step into another world, but *plunges us right in the middle*. The world from the very beginning *retains its strangeness* in comparison to what the reader or hearer is used to. It becomes *bit by bit more familiar* but not by accommodating it to the world we know but by expanding our experience of its foreignness."[25]

Van den Toren identifies Tolkien's *The Hobbit*, Lewis's "Narnia-cycle," and nineteenth-century Russian novels as examples of when the reader gradually becomes accustomed to the logic of the created world. Van den Toren suggests that one likely reason for the neglect of narrative in modern apologetics is that moderns may view narrative and argumentation as mutually exclusive. "Narrative," he remarks, "embodies different types of argumentation.... It evokes a valid experience from a wholly different domain."[26] The ability of narrative to immediately immerse us into the whole and retain strangeness, while progressively increasing familiarity, is apologetically helpful.

Cross-cultural apologetics builds bridges. Van den Toren identifies several accessible bridges for dialogue, including Jesus, the human condition, and other worldview-specific questions. The story of Jesus is central to a Christ-centered apologetic witness and dialogue. He writes Jesus is

21. Van den Toren, *Christian Apologetics*, 184.
22. Van den Toren, *Christian Apologetics*, 184.
23. Van den Toren, "Challenges and Possibilities," 51.
24. Van den Toren, "Challenges and Possibilities," 51.
25. Van den Toren, "Challenges and Possibilities," 51; emphasis added.
26. Van den Toren, *Christian Apologetics*, 52.

"the clue to reality, to our lives, to history, and to God."[27] Furthermore, it is in Jesus that we find that God is not "irrelevant or far-off."[28] As he explains, apologetic dialogue in relation to Jesus is essentially "witness to this person and an invitation to further personal discovery of what life with this Jesus entails and what the world with Him at the centre looks like."[29] Jesus is central to apologetic dialogue.

A second bridge is the human condition, understood as the gap between the high calling of a being human and "the way he actually lives."[30] Van den Toren explains, "All religions and worldviews that I know of provide some explanation of the human condition that is partly adequate and partly inadequate. These explanations need to prove their soundness precisely in the face of the enigma."[31] Van den Toren suggests that the question for most humans about who they are and what they want to be touches a central tension in their lives, and this creates openness to dialogue.[32] By building bridges to relevant culture and worldview-specific points of contact, the Christian faith is shown to be "coherent with and the fulfillment of what is best and most true in the former worldview."[33]

A third bridge that Van den Toren identifies is worldview-specific interests. He explains that dialogues with traditional Africans often deal with questions concerning "illness, healing, curses, and protection" in ways that are typically less urgent in Western contexts.[34] Similarly, dialogues with Hindus must address reincarnation and the afterlife; with Muslims, the relationship between prophets and scriptures; with moderns, the success of modern science.[35] Van den Toren insightfully points out that worldviews are structured in terms of relevance.[36] For example, while many believe in the possibility of extraterrestrial intelligence, it functions as a peripheral belief. However, some beliefs are central and are key bridges for dialogue: for example, our indignation at the reality of evil is in tension with certain worldviews, in a way that points to the existence

27. Van den Toren, *Christian Apologetics*, 52.
28. Van den Toren, *Christian Apologetics*, 53.
29. Van den Toren, *Christian Apologetics*, 52.
30. Van den Toren, "Challenges and Possibilities," 53.
31. Van den Toren, "Challenges and Possibilities," 53.
32. Van den Toren, *Christian Apologetics*, 64.
33. Van den Toren, *Christian Apologetics*, 210.
34. Van den Toren, *Christian Apologetics*, 187.
35. Van den Toren, *Christian Apologetics*, 187.
36. Van den Toren, *Christian Apologetics*, 191.

of a personal and good God.[37] Van den Toren says that anger toward evil in a naturalistic evolutionary, pantheist, or monist universe should be dismissed as deceptive, because these worldviews do not ultimately allow for real moral distinctions. You can only have a problem with evil in a worldview where there is a genuine basis for good and evil, something that human beings usually recognize intuitively. The difficulty in rejecting such a strong and basic awareness, he writes, "opens up the possibility for an argument for the existence of God based on the experience of evil."[38]

Cross-cultural apologetics can expose tensions and antinomies. Van den Toren suggests that tensions, anomalies, and antinomies can push people to change their beliefs. Studies in cultural linguistic frameworks, he writes, have found that changes in worldview are most likely to occur when "tensions arise within a given understanding of reality."[39] He explains, "Many people experience moments of sudden or slowly mounting crisis in their (a-)religious perspective on life, which opens them up to a serious consideration of the Christian faith," such as when confronted with death or a new life phase (e.g., parenthood).[40]

Van den Toren identifies several examples of tension within a given belief system. In Zen Buddhism, "the relationship between the high moral awareness with the understanding of ultimate reality that surpasses the distinction between good and evil" creates such a tension. For example, while the Holocaust should be condemned as an unpardonable, absolute evil, the distinction between good and evil is actually relative and not absolute.[41]

This worldview tension is also revealed in the Japanese poet Issa when he was shaken by the death of his five children and wife. A Zen master explained to Issa: "All our grief is only a sign that we are unable to overcome our egotistic bondage to this reality."[42] Issa's poem betrays his tension at the thought of such a conclusion—"and yet, and yet," Issa writes. He cannot dismiss the reality of his profound loss. His worldview came into tension with his existential experience. Van den Toren concludes, "One is never entirely imprisoned by the symbolic universe one

---

37. Van den Toren, *Christian Apologetics*, 190.
38. Van den Toren, *Christian Apologetics*, 190.
39. Van den Toren, *Christian Apologetics*, 195.
40. Van den Toren, *Christian Apologetics*, 196–97.
41. Van den Toren, *Christian Apologetics*, 197.
42. Van den Toren, *Christian Apologetics*, 197.

inhabits."[43] Such tensions are bridges for the gospel, and a potential trigger to start exploring the new world inaugurated by Jesus.[44]

Van den Toren is not, however, content with an impasse. He argues that we must point out that "the most crucial antinomies can be solved, when Christ is brought into the centre of our life and worldview."[45] Van den Toren concludes,

> It is the anomalies that show the need to look elsewhere. It is by building bridges that we show that the Christian faith is coherent with and the fulfilment of what is best and what is most true in the former worldview. It is the rearrangement of all these elements around Christ that reveals first and foremost the illuminating power of the whole picture.[46]

These tensions and antinomies are natural paths for sharing the gospel.

Helpful Insights for Cross-Cultural Apologetics

Van den Toren's model helps understand Christianity through the eyes of other cultures. The portrait he paints recalls Tolkien's readers of fairy stories, who stand outside the story and to whom Christianity feels foreign. To consider the Christian story from the inside, the cross-cultural apologist needs to communicate the Christian worldview in a way that feels safe to explore. It needs to interest them or relate to things that matter to them, and in some cases, it will need to displace caricatures or false ideas that are hindrances. Van den Toren also shows that there are some unavoidable conflicts. The cross-cultural apologist will need to displace relativism, account for past beliefs, and, for those deeply committed to the non-Christian worldview, more direct apologetics will be required. This is especially true of those deeply connected with their community because their conversion might, for some people, risk the loss of family relationships.

Van den Toren's model also provides several helpful pathways for cross-cultural apologetics that naturally fit the strengths of narrative

43. Van den Toren, *Christian Apologetics*, 198.

44. Van den Toren, *Christian Apologetics*, 60. Other points of tension include "legalism and mysticism in Islam"; rival pictures of Muhammad—"a mere man" versus the "persistent tendency to sacralise him." Another is the tension between concerns about human rights and "evolutionism." Van den Toren, *Christian Apologetics*, 199.

45. Van den Toren, *Christian Apologetics*, 199.

46. Van den Toren, *Christian Apologetics*, 210.

apologetics. Some of these include exposing tensions of a given belief system, communicating ways that Christ satisfies core antinomies of the belief system, engaging points of interest, communicating an appropriate sense of mystery, and, for apologists discussing a shared narrative with a non-Christian, it allows for meaningful dialogue.

HAROLD NETLAND AND CONTEXTUALIZED APOLOGETICS

Now retired, Harold A. Netland was professor of philosophy of religion and intercultural studies at Trinity Evangelical Divinity School. Before his time at Trinity, he was a missionary educator in Japan. Netland received his PhD in philosophy from Claremont Graduate School. He is another Christian academic whose work on cross-cultural apologetics can help us see the overlap with narrative apologetics.

What Is Contextualized Apologetics?

We can think about apologetics either in a general sense, or in a culture-specific sense. Netland describes the distinction as being between transcultural and culture-specific (contextualized) apologetics.[47] Elsewhere he uses the language of theoretical versus applied apologetics.[48] According to Netland, both transcultural and culture-specific (contextualized) apologetics are concerned with the intelligibility and credibility of Christianity, and the evidence for it.[49] The distinction mainly relates to their purposes and the kinds of questions that are being addressed.[50] Transcultural apologetics is concerned with an objective justification for the Christian faith, regardless of the human response to the answers.[51] Contextualized apologetics, however, focuses on the human response to the proclamation and

---

47. Netland, "Toward Contextualized Apologetics."
48. Netland, *Encountering Pluralism*, 250. Theoretical apologetics is concerned with the objective justification of the Christian faith, regardless of how an audience responds to it, while applied (context-specific) apologetics occurs in a specific sociocultural context and is concerned with human response.
49. Netland, "Toward Contextualized Apologetics," 293.
50. Netland, "Toward Contextualized Apologetics," 293.
51. Netland, "Toward Contextualized Apologetics," 293–94.

defense of the gospel and is concerned with effectively persuading the target audience.[52] Elsewhere he explains further:

> [Contextualized apologetics] receives its agenda largely from its target audience and cultural context, the questions dealt with and the appropriate answers, as well as the proper methods of communication and persuasion, will vary greatly—not only from culture to culture but even from person to person within the same culture. Thus the person engaging in [contextualized apologetics] must be flexible, sensitive, and creative. Not only must he or she understand well the prevailing presuppositions of the target audience, but he or she must also be sensitive to the felt needs of the moment.[53]

Netland maintains that more is required than simply showing why people's prior assumptions do not hold up; it is also necessary to persuade people to change their views, rejecting old assumptions and embracing a biblical viewpoint.[54] This is why apologetics is needed.

Six Needs for Cross-Cultural Apologetics

Netland presents six needs for cross-cultural apologetics that a contextualized approach addresses. The first need is to *clarify basic Christianity*. Netland maintains that because there are distortions of the gospel, the cross-cultural apologist must explain what Christianity actually is. A second need is to *respond to key criticisms* of the Christian faith. A third need is a *positive presentation of the gospel*. This means that the gospel must be presented in such a way as to seek a favorable response from the hearer who is "initially uncommitted."[55] The need to *answer key questions* about Christianity's intelligibility, credibility, and evidential basis is a fourth need.[56] *Contextual relevance* is a fifth need. Netland explains that the values, presuppositions, and interests of the target audience often dictate questions. For example, the question of the existence of God is relevant in Mexico City; in Cairo, the identity of Jesus of Nazareth is a relevant concern; while in Andhra Pradesh, a relevant question could be "Why

---

52. Netland, "Toward Contextualized Apologetics," 294.
53. Netland, "Toward Contextualized Apologetics," 295.
54. Netland, "Toward Contextualized Apologetics," 298.
55. Netland, "Toward Contextualized Apologetics," 290.
56. Netland, "Toward Contextualized Apologetics," 293.

did God not heal my child's smallpox?"[57] A final need is a *contextualized form of communication*. Netland explains that how we communicate requires contextual sensitivity. For example, although exceptions exist, in Japanese culture, direct confrontation is highly unwelcome, and an overly aggressive approach is very likely to be counterproductive.[58]

Four Barriers to Cross-Cultural Apologetics

Netland identifies at least four significant obstacles to cross-cultural apologetics. These include (1) assumptions about ultimate reality, (2) objections to exclusivism, (3) relativism (religious and ethical), and (4) common Western objections to Christianity—science and the problem of evil. As a former missionary to Japan, Netland gives special attention to the Japanese context, but his insights are relevant to other contexts.

A first obstacle for cross-cultural apologetics is an individual's view of *ultimate reality*. Netland explains that some fundamental assumptions about ultimate reality must be altered before Christian belief is possible.[59] For example, in the Hindu worldview ultimate reality is not empirically accessible. He writes, "Before the Hindu is able to respond favorably to the gospel—which is inextricably grounded in the historical events surrounding Jesus' life, death, and resurrection—certain fundamental assumptions about religious truth and history must be altered."[60] In Japan, Netland maintains, the universe is considered divine, blurring distinctions between natural and supernatural, human and divine.[61] This is clearly at odds with creation *ex nihilo*. In kind, the highest form of religion is *felt*, not analyzed. Netland explains, "The highest form of religious apprehension or 'truth' transcends all conceptual distinctions and dichotomies, defies logical categorization, and is not subject to rational analysis, but can only be intuited or 'felt.'"[62]

Exclusivism is a second obstacle for cross-cultural apologetics, in that people from many worldviews find Christianity's claim to

---

57. Netland, "Toward Contextualized Apologetics," 294.
58. Netland, "Toward Contextualized Apologetics," 300.
59. Netland, "Toward Contextualized Apologetics," 297.
60. Netland, "Toward Contextualized Apologetics," 297.
61. Netland, "Toward Contextualized Apologetics," 299.
62. Netland, "Toward Contextualized Apologetics," 299.

exclusive truth in Christ to be offensive, prioritizing tolerance as a virtue.[63] When engaging with people from Eastern worldviews in particular, offering simplistic, definite explanations about ultimate reality is likely to be counterproductive, seeming arrogant and naïve.[64] Further, certainty is not considered possible. In Japan, sincerity and virtue are valued more highly.[65]

The barrier of exclusivism is compounded in our day by a world filled with religious suspicion and strife. Netland says, "We live in a postcolonialist world that is acutely aware of the injustices of four centuries of Western imperialism and that believes—rightly or wrongly—that Christianity bears much of the blame for such injustice."[66] He continues, "Religious conversion is increasingly seen as an obstacle to peaceful coexistence."[67] As a result, Netland argues, "New models of evangelism and disciple making must be developed that are appropriate for a world increasingly hostile to evangelism."[68]

A third obstacle is *relativism*, cultural and ethical relativism. In Japan, religion is viewed as culturally relative.[69] From this perspective, Christianity is viewed as the predominant religion of the West, while the East has equally valid religious traditions. Ethical standards are understood in similar ways. Netland explains, "Moral wrong is not sin in the sense of falling short of the moral standard of a holy, righteous, and limitlessly perfect God, but is simply failure to observe socially sanctioned standards of acceptable behavior."[70]

Some final obstacles include more traditional objections to Christianity, such as *science and the problem of evil*. Netland notes that Japan is a highly industrialized and affluent nation. The Japanese people, while strongly shaped by traditional religious values, are also increasingly materialistic in their outlook. Like the West, technology and education are seen optimistically as being able to solve most problems.[71] Also similar to the West, the Japanese privilege science as providing the only or best

---

63. Netland, "Toward Contextualized Apologetics," 299.
64. Netland, "Toward Contextualized Apologetics," 301.
65. Netland, "Toward Contextualized Apologetics," 299.
66. Netland, "Christian Theology of Religions," 26.
67. Netland, "Christian Theology of Religions," 26.
68. Netland, "Christian Theology of Religions," 26.
69. Netland, "Toward Contextualized Apologetics," 298.
70. Netland, "Toward Contextualized Apologetics," 299.
71. Netland, "Toward Contextualized Apologetics," 298.

access to truth.[72] The problem of evil is another obstacle to faith identified by Netland.

Six Topics for Cross-Cultural Engagement

Netland highlights six significant topics that are pathways for cross-cultural engagement: (1) topical relevance, (2) relationships, (3) mystery, (4) appropriate methodology, (5) core beliefs, and (6) reasons to choose Christianity over alternatives. First, we must engage in contextually *relevant topics* such as the nature of reality. If you prove the existence of God to a Muslim, little is won. However, for the Hindu, some foundational issues need to be engaged to be able to introduce the reality of the life, death, and resurrection of Jesus Christ.

We have good theological reasons to expect common themes among religions, Netland says, based on biblical creation, general revelation, and common grace. He explains,

> Scripture teaches that all human beings are created in God's image (Gen 1:26–27; 5:1–3), that God has revealed something of himself and our obligation to him to all humankind through the created order (Acts 14:15–17; 17:22–28; Rom 1:18–32; 2:14–15), and that there is a sense in which God's gracious provision extends to all humankind (Matt 5:45).[73]

These are reasons to expect that we can find shared themes as bridges for engaging cross-culturally.

Relationships are a second pathway for cross-cultural engagement. In Japan, Netland writes, "truth is always transmitted through personal relationships."[74] Though in the West, it is not unusual for people to come to faith through reading privately and becoming convinced of the truthfulness of Christianity, Netland maintains that it is far more common in Japan to come to faith through interaction with someone he or she knows well and has come to respect.[75]

A third theme for cross-cultural engagement is a fitting regard for *theological mystery*. Netland observes that Western thinkers sometimes give the impression that the most profound questions of human existence

---

72. Netland, "Toward Contextualized Apologetics," 298.
73. Netland, "Christian Theology of Religions," 23.
74. Netland, "Toward Contextualized Apologetics," 300.
75. Netland, "Toward Contextualized Apologetics," 300–301.

can be neatly packaged. He writes, "This can communicate arrogance and naïveté to those in the East, who are influenced by centuries of rich religious traditions which revel in the profound mystery of the cosmos and which disdain clear-cut answers to ultimate questions."[76] We need to be careful about giving overly simplistic answers in any context, but apologists engaging with Eastern cultural contexts need to be especially careful to properly acknowledge the mystery of God.

Contextual *methodology* is a fourth topic, where we consider *how* we engage. Netland, for example, cautions against aggressive approaches within a Japanese context, which may alienate audiences.[77] Similarly, he notes that persons are not easily separated from ideas in Japanese culture. He explains, "Many Japanese tend not to distinguish clearly between ideas and the persons holding the ideas. In the West, it is often possible to launch a vigorous attack upon a particular idea while still remaining perfectly amiable toward the individual advocating that idea. . . . [In the East] an attack upon a particular idea can easily be interpreted as a personal affront to the dignity of the one maintaining the idea."[78] Because of challenges like these, varying from culture to culture, Netland contends that "considerable creativity and variety of approach are essential in applied apologetics."[79]

Because many people associate Christianity with the abuses of Western imperialism, Netland believes new models are needed today. Netland points to Terry Muck and Francis Adeney's "giftive mission" as a possible model.[80] Rather than thinking about missions as harvesting souls or conquering peoples, the twenty-first century missionary understands themself as a bearer of gifts to a world in need—the gift of the gospel that they have received themselves. The missionary gives and receives according to cultural rules.[81] Muck and Adeney explain, "If one reason Hindus, Buddhists, Muslims, and other people of well-articulated and successful civilization religions have resisted the gospel message is that they feel disrespected, then establishing a religious gift exchange might go some distance in remedying that problem. We come offering the greatest gift

---

76. Netland, "Toward Contextualized Apologetics," 301.
77. Netland, "Toward Contextualized Apologetics," 300.
78. Netland, "Toward Contextualized Apologetics," 300.
79. Netland, *Encountering Pluralism*, 250.
80. Netland, "Christian Theology of Religions," 26.
81. Muck and Adeney, *Practice of Mission*, 354.

we can imagine."[82] Missionaries bear the gift of the gospel. They explain, "Giftive mission can redirect the positive values of each culture's use of the metaphor of gift."[83] For example, in indigenous cultures "gift giving creates community," in Western cultures the "free gift of God's grace amazes us," while in eastern cultures "the best gift is one given without expectation of a return."[84] Muck and Adeney observe the value of gift in all cultures: "In their own way, [all cultures] see gift giving as important, if not central, to their ways of looking at the world."[85]

Fifth, Netland argues that the *core beliefs* of a given worldview must be true. This has important implications for religious pluralism and challenging relativism. Netland suggests that we should speak of a religion as true "if and only if its defining beliefs are true. For Christianity to be true, then, the defining beliefs of Christianity must be true. If they are true, then Christianity is true; if they are false, then Christianity is false."[86] Thus, Netland concludes,

> 'God created the universe' is true if and only if God created the universe. 'The Buddha attained enlightenment under the Bodhi tree' is true if and only if the Buddha attained enlightenment under the Bodhi tree. 'Muhammad is the final prophet' is true if and only if Muhammad is the final prophet. . . . Truth or falsity applies to particular religious claims or teachings.[87]

This key point makes the core beliefs of a given religion a truth claim. Moreover, it allows a thoughtful person to recognize that certain truth claims are mutually exclusive. For example, Netland explains, "if the notion of anattta [sic] (no self) in classical Buddhism is indeed incoherent, as many argue, then this provides positive reason for rejecting a central tenet of many Buddhist traditions."[88]

Finally, Netland argues that in many contexts of religious disagreement, it is important for Christians to provide fitting *reasons* for accepting their claims over other religious traditions.[89] Netland affirms the

---

82. Muck and Adeney, *Practice of Mission*, 354.
83. Muck and Adeney, *Practice of Mission*, 361.
84. Muck and Adeney, *Practice of Mission*, 361.
85. Muck and Adeney, *Practice of Mission*, 362.
86. Netland, *Christianity and Religious Diversity*, 186.
87. Netland, *Christianity and Religious Diversity*, 182–83.
88. Netland, *Christianity and Religious Diversity*, 225.
89. Netland, *Christianity and Religious Diversity*, 220.

value of probabilistic arguments, such as those of philosopher of religion Richard Swinburne, which make the case that "on total evidence theism is more probable than not."[90] Drawing on C. Stephen Evans, another Christian philosopher, Netland believes that a cumulative case argument can be made for the Christian God from our intuitive experience or direct knowledge of natural signs such as wonder, moral obligation, and the good order of the world, which are a kind of "direct, non-inferential evidence for God's reality."[91] Netland quotes C. Stephen Evans as saying,

> Cosmic wonder suggests that whatever lies behind the natural universe exists in some deeper, more secure way than the contingent things that cry out for explanation. It has a firmer grip on reality than the transient realities we encounter in our world. Beneficial order suggests that what lies behind the universe is intelligent because purposive. Moral obligation suggests that whatever lies behind the universe is personal and cares about moral goodness; the reality must be a being capable of creating an obligation.[92]

These natural signs can be used to build a case where the different clues together add up to a strong reason for embracing Christian theism over other alternative beliefs.[93]

HIGHLIGHTS FROM DIFFERENT MODELS OF CROSS-CULTURAL APOLOGETICS

Each of these models offers significant insights for cross-cultural apologetics. Van den Toren helpfully identifies the importance of the "power of the whole," the need for space for safe exploration by non-Christians, the need to identify and graciously engage crucial antinomies within non-Christian worldviews, as well as the relevance of narrative. Netland helpfully identifies the need to examine core beliefs, maintain a posture of apologetic humility, a biblical expectation for shared themes across worldviews, and the need for arguments and natural signs to provide a reason for embracing Christian theism over alternatives.

---

90. Netland, *Christianity and Religious Diversity*, 221.
91. Netland, *Christianity and Religious Diversity*, 226.
92. Evans, *Natural Signs*, 185, quoted in Netland, *Christianity and Religious Diversity*, 228; also see Evans, *Natural Signs*, 126, 132.
93. Evans, *Natural Signs*, 228.

There are several recurring themes among these models. For one, *apologetics is needed on both models*. This is especially true for people who are deeply committed to other faith traditions. Van den Toren's model emphasizes dialogue and how Christ, in particular, satisfies antinomies and fulfills what is best within other worldviews. Netland points to Richard Swinburne's apologetic project as a strong case for the probable truth of Christianity. He is also sympathetic with C. Stephen Evans's argument that natural signs point to the truthfulness of Christianity. Second, both models consider *topical relevance* to be important for cross-cultural apologetics. Van den Toren sees worldviews as being structured in terms of relevance and having worldview-specific interests. However, there are some broadly shared convictions about the nature of reality that can serve as a bridge between worldviews. Netland likewise observes that the target audience's values, presuppositions, and interests often dictate questions.

The challenge of *religious relativism* is the third point of agreement. Van den Toren says that the claim that Christianity is different is not enough. We must argue that critical issues of truth are at stake in the religion and worldview we embrace.[94] Netland also identifies religious relativism as a key issue for cross-cultural apologetics. Netland notes that our postcolonial world associates many historical injustices with Christianity and views religious conversion as a threat to peaceful coexistence.[95] This sentiment is exacerbated in the East by a general disdain for exclusivism, and a deep conviction that exclusive claims about religious truth are "naïve, arrogant, and false."[96]

The need for *contextually informed* communication is a fourth feature that these models share. Although Van den Toren believes there are significant challenges to cross-cultural communication, he does believe that meaningful communication and mutual understanding are possible. He attributes this partly to the fact that cultures are not, as he says, "watertight compartments" and that all cultures share a common basis in the same human nature and the same world.[97] Van den Toren maintains that the thought forms of a given culture and how the Christian message will be understood must be addressed by cross-cultural apologetics.[98] Netland

---

94. Van den Toren, "Why Inter-Religious Dialogue," 23; Van den Toren, *Christian Apologetics*, 224.

95. Netland, "Christian Theology of Religions," 26.

96. Netland, "Toward Contextualized Apologetics," 301.

97. Van den Toren, *Christian Apologetics*, 171–73.

98. Van den Toren, *Christian Apologetics*, 177.

also identifies the need for a contextualized form of communication, requiring contextual sensitivity. This includes avoiding aggressive approaches in contexts where confrontation is culturally unacceptable.

A fifth need that both models identify is the importance of communicating an accurate understanding of *who Jesus is*. Van den Toren places Jesus at the center of his model, asserting that Jesus fulfills what is good and resolves the antinomies present in non-Christian worldviews and religions. Similarly, Netland emphasizes that the cross-cultural apologist must clarify what Christianity truly is, as there are many distortions of the gospel.

Finally, the sixth point of agreement is the exhortation to recognize *theological mystery* appropriately. Van den Toren and Netland agree that cross-cultural apologists must be sensitive to mystery, especially when working with Eastern religions.

Intersections and Possibilities of Cross-Cultural and Narrative Apologetics

Several overlaps with narrative apologetics are apparent, as will be developed in more detail in the following chapters. First, consider the overlaps with Van den Toren's model. *Safe exploration*, which Van den Toren recommends, is precisely what narrative apologetics offers. *The Chronicles of Narnia* grants non-Christian readers the chance to explore an embodiment of the Christian worldview that can be safely considered while continuing to hold to one's own worldview. The *strangeness* of the Christian worldview, especially from a non-Christian perspective, is retained while imaginatively experienced. The reader is *immediately plunged* into something like the Christian world, along with imaginative emotions that recall and mirror the real world, to include: a Creator, mystery, the reality of good and evil, along with moral guilt and its remedy. The narrative world *gradually accustoms* the reader to the logic of another worldview. *Mystery* is organically maintained, and core antinomies are mirrored in forms that are more conducive to Eastern worldviews. *The Chronicles of Narnia*, in particular, centers its attention on Aslan's nearness, ubiquity, benevolence, and allure. Following C. S. Lewis, stories can get past such watchful dragons and help the reader see Jesus for the first time.

Several overlaps with narrative apologetics can be seen in Netland's model too. Mystery is an underappreciated aspect of narrative apologetics. Could it be that Rudolf Otto's *mysterium tremendum* is an integral pathway into the mystery and quest sentiment that Japan and other like-minded belief systems possess?[99] The goodness and unsafeness of Aslan are significant features of *The Chronicles of Narnia*. According to Netland, in Japan the highest form of religion is *felt*. Given this, Lewis's experience with *Sehnsucht* and the use of longing in *The Chronicles of Narnia* may also be relevant to cross-cultural apologetics in these contexts. *Desirability* is intertwined with this deep-seated feeling. *Exclusivism* may be addressed more effectively through storytelling than through argumentation in some contexts. Avoiding the topic of exclusivism is problematic. Netland notes that in some situations, believers have an epistemic and ethical duty to challenge improper beliefs, particularly in the light of Christianity's claim that salvation is found only in Jesus.[100] *Scientism* is broadly addressed in Narnia, particularly in Eustace's pre-transformation life. *The Chronicles of Narnia* does address evil and goodness, and they are distinct and objective. Natural law, moral obligation, and moral accountability are prominently featured in Narnia. This is a significant target, as Netland observes, because Buddhism is unable to address moral obligation adequately, and its view of reality is unable to account for the widespread human awareness of a fundamental distinction between good and evil, right and wrong.[101]

CONCLUSION

We have looked at examples of classic narrative apologetics in theory and practice, learned from the insights of contemporary narrative apologists, and in this chapter, we have discovered some of the ways that these overlap with cross-cultural apologetics. In the next chapter, I combine the strengths of the six models into what I call the six keys. These six keys are narrative motifs that help identify how a given story communicates Christianity, and they can also be used for effective dialogue. Additionally, the keys identify helpful pathways to communicate Christianity through story. In future chapters, we will look at how *The Chronicles of Narnia* engages specific worldviews with these six keys in mind.

99. Otto, *Idea of the Holy*.
100. Netland, *Encountering Pluralism*, 281.
101. Netland, *Encountering Pluralism*, 307.

4

Six Keys for Cross-Cultural Narrative Apologetics

INTRODUCTION

In the opening scene of *Alice in Wonderland*,[1] Alice follows a strange yet hurried white rabbit down a rabbit hole. To her surprise, she free falls for what feels like miles before safely landing in a strange world. It is dark and hopeless, but she can see the rabbit ahead. She follows him but loses him, only to find herself in a hallway of locked doors that she tries one by one in despair. Her despondency is interrupted when she finds herself in front of a small glass table with a golden key sitting on top. The key is too small for the hallway doors, but she discovers a tiny door behind a curtain she had not seen before, and the key fits. In the dark of the hallway, she kneels to look through the tiny door and sees a beautiful garden with flowers and cool streams. From the darkness, she longs for the garden. The little golden key opened a door to another world.

    I want to use the image of a key to highlight six well-suited narrative motifs that can equip us to see how stories can communicate Christianity cross-culturally. The six keys are based on what we've seen in narrative and cross-cultural apologetics, and include patterns identified in studies from those who have become Christians from other worldviews.

1. Carroll, *Alice's Adventures in Wonderland*.

The six keys are:

1. Translation
2. Transformation
3. Treasure
4. Tension
5. Concern
6. Call

The six keys are a tool that will allow us to identify and explore some of the ways that narrative, and those speaking with others about a given narrative, such as *The Chronicles of Narnia*, might contribute to cross-cultural apologetics.

KEY ONE: TRANSLATION

The *Translation* key is the communication of Christian beliefs, concepts, terms, or practices in a way that is understandable to a reader (or a conversation partner if discussing the stories). *The Chronicles of Narnia* presents the reader with a world that embodies images that recall various Christian doctrines and beliefs, such as the resurrection, the existence of true moral guilt and accountability, forgiveness, the incarnation, the reality of God, creation, and the virtue of faith in a way that is concrete and conceivable.

Translation can be intentional or unintentional on the part of the author. We can know that translation is purposeful in *The Chronicles of Narnia* because Lewis confirmed his intent. For example, in his letter to Anne Jenkins on March 5, 1961, Lewis explained what he meant by "supposing." Lewis wrote to her to encourage her to see the "deeper meaning" behind Aslan's death and resurrection, which he believes is perceptible and understandable with some reflection. Lewis went on to detail how the *Narnia* series is "about Christ": "I asked myself 'Supposing there really were a world like Narnia, and supposing it had (like our world) gone wrong, and supposing Christ wanted to go into that world and save it (as He did ours) what might have happened?' The stories are my answer."[2] Lewis goes on to explain the choice of Aslan as a lion in terms of Narnia

---

2. Lewis, *Collected Letters*, 3:1244–45.

as a world of talking beasts and because of the biblical image of the "Lion of Judah." He details the theme of each book, from Jesus's death and resurrection in *The Lion, the Witch and the Wardrobe* through to the coming of antichrist at the end of the world in *The Last Battle*. Because Lewis is explicit here, we can know exactly what Lewis intends to translate and in the coming chapters we will investigate how. Other explicit examples exist (e.g., the ontological argument, as discussed in chapter 7). Furthermore, Lewis suggests that some "deeper meanings" are perceptible without being stated.

A reader can also learn *indirectly* about Christian beliefs, concepts, terms, or practices because Lewis is using a supposal. Here's how: because we know that Aslan is a supposal of Christ, we are able to infer that Lewis is communicating something of what Christ is like, or at least what Lewis believes Christ is like. This is a kind of translation.

Alister McGrath's explanation is helpful in relation to the role of narrative apologetics for translation:

> The apologist has to translate the language of the Christian faith into the cultural vernacular. The Christian faith is traditionally expressed using a wide range of abstract conceptual terms that are becoming increasingly disconnected from contemporary Western culture. Central New Testament terms—such as "justification," "salvation," and "sin"—are now likely to be simply dismissed as antiquated and irrelevant, or at best misunderstood, generally by being inappropriately assimilated to the nearest cultural equivalent. *These terms need to be translated or transposed—that is to say, reformulated in terms of narratives or images capable of connecting with a wider audience, while retaining maximum continuity with the Christian tradition.*[3]

KEY TWO: TRANSFORMATION

Transformation is another key storytelling element in narrative apologetics, especially how a story positively depicts the change of a given character or environment because of the Christian faith (or some analogy of it in the world of the story). In *The Chronicles of Narnia*, we see the transformation motif in how Aslan or his kingdom impacts people and

---

3. McGrath, *Narrative Apologetics*, 19; emphasis added.

environments positively and in how a rejection of Aslan or his kingdom has a detrimental effect.

We can see transformation through the changes in individual characters in a given story, such as Edmund's transformation from traitor to a king of Narnia, or Eustace's un-dragoning. Emily McCarty helpfully terms this narrative device a "lived-in experience of theology": by seeing through the eyes of and along with the characters, the reader along with the characters see how the ideas play out.[4]

In *The Chronicles of Narnia*, we also see a marked difference between people and kingdoms where Aslan benevolently reigns and where he does not. There are significant differences between kingdoms where Aslan's kingdom principles govern and those that reject these principles. For example, kingdoms and people marked by Aslan's ways live by faith, know forgiveness, lead with humility, and uphold justice. Conversely, anti-type kingdoms reign with tyranny, fear, slavery, bondage, oppression, and progress disconnected from virtue. For example, George Sayer aptly notes, "the Narnia stories show a complete acceptance of the Tao, of the conventional and traditional moral code. Humanity, courage, loyalty, honesty, kindness and unselfishness are virtues."[5] Because of this, in *The Chronicles of Narnia* the tension (see Tension below) and consequences of living against the moral law are easier to see.

This transformation from one kingdom to another is particularly seen where Narnia is delivered from evil rule, such as that of the White Witch in *The Lion, the Witch and the Wardrobe* or King Miraz in *Prince Caspian*, and brought instead into Aslan's rule. The White Witch's rule is "always winter and never Christmas,"[6] with spies and secret police to oppress the Narnians. Miraz's rule is one of high taxes and cruel laws. Aslan's arrival brings spring to Narnia when he breaks the witch's spell and brings celebration and freedom to Miraz's Narnia.

This is an important motif because Christianity is often negatively associated with power, abuse, and deceit. As Harold Netland writes, "We live in a postcolonialist world that is acutely aware of the injustices of four centuries of Western imperialism and that believes—rightly or wrongly—that Christianity bears much of the blame for such injustice."[7]

---

4. McCarty, "*Narnia* and the Philosophy of Religion," 119.
5. Sayer, *Jack*, 192.
6. Lewis, *Lion*, 175.
7. Netland, "Christian Theology of Religions," 26.

Lewis's images of the transformative power of Aslan's kingdom for the good are a needed corrective for our world.

KEY THREE: TREASURE

Another narrative key is *Treasure*, what is valuable, desirable, or celebrated in a given story. This motif focuses on what is loved and celebrated and what is not. Where is longing satisfied, and where is it not? Where is hope found? What is true, good, and beautiful, and what is not? Reepicheep, as I discuss later, lives under an otherworldly promise, spoken over his life by a dryad when he was still young, that he will one day find his heart's desire in the utter East.[8] In various ways, *The Chronicles of Narnia* ultimately shows where this longing is finally satisfied and provides something of a mirror for the reader who feels similar longings.

Treasure connects with the other keys in various ways. For example, by treasuring Aslan's grace in Edmund, Lewis *translates* something of Aslan's goodness, grace, and worth. For Edmund, this alleviates the *concern* that Aslan is not good in Narnia, which suggests to the reflective reader that Jesus is likewise good and gracious. This suppoal of grace also results in *transformation* in Edmund's life and also gently *calls* one who lives under the weight of moral guilt to long for the one who gives grace to the guilty while honoring the moral law (*tension*).

KEY FOUR: TENSION

Tension is how a story engages the existential tensions that we experience as human beings. Some tensions include questions of immortality, life after death, and cosmic security; our search for meaning and purpose, fulfillment; justice and forgiveness; truth and living against truth; and love. Moreover, it also includes known tensions in a given worldview (e.g., the existence of unspeakable moral evil in tension with a belief that evil and good are illusory).[9] Francis Schaeffer said it well: "Every man is in tension until he finds a satisfactory answer to the problem of who

---

8. Lewis, *Voyage*, 623.

9. These kinds of tensions are found in numerous apologetic and theological works. Clifford Williams, for example, identifies numerous human needs: self-directed needs—cosmic security, life beyond the grave, heaven, goodness, a larger life; others-directed needs—to be loved, meaning, to be forgiven, to love, awe, delighting in goodness, being present, justice and fairness. Williams, *Existential Reasons*, 21–27.

he himself is."[10] As noted in Van den Toren's model, exposing tensions and antinomies in cultures, worldviews, and lifestyles reveals the need to explore alternatives.[11]

One of the strongest examples of the use of tension in *The Chronicles of Narnia* is how Lewis juxtaposes mortality with indifference in Susan's life in *The Last Battle*. I discuss this in detail in chapter 9 on the worldview of apatheism. The key point is that the narrative context is charged with feelings of loss, finality concerning life-defining decisions, and the frailty of life. These are tensions we often feel as human beings in the face of death, and they are mirrored to the reader through Susan's life. Funerals in the primary world naturally invite reflection about what matters in life. Encountering unexpected death through the experience of main character's lives, as the other members of the Pevensie family find they have died and gone to Aslan's Country, invites the captive reader to reflect on mortality as well.

KEY FIVE: CONCERN

Another key for narrative apologetics is *Concern*, offering a narrative response to relevant concerns or objections to Christianity, such as evil, exclusive religious claims, skepticism about the goodness of Christianity, divine hiddenness and the like. In traditional apologetics concern fits within the framework of defensive apologetics. In a narrative context, it may show the limitation of a given perspective, such as Digory's despair over his mother's cancer vis-à-vis the love and goodness of Aslan. The narrative can, for example, imaginatively show the coexistence of suffering and one who has mysterious plans, yet who is clearly present and loves deeply.

KEY SIX: CALL

Call is the lens that considers how narrative or *The Chronicles of Narnia* advocates Christian belief and truth. In traditional apologetics, call fits within the framework of offensive apologetics. Call recognizes the resources of narrative in any form (e.g., narrative experience, metaphor, image, a larger story) to persuade or help a reader to see, understand, or

---

10. Schaeffer, *Complete Works*, 93.
11. Van den Toren, "Challenges and Possibilities," 64.

believe, often without making an explicit claim. One example of how a story calls the reader to belief is the unfulfilled longing in Reepicheep's desire for the utter East. This also fits key four, tension. Reepicheep's longing recalls Lewis's own belief that our unfulfilled longings are hints that we were made for another world. By mirroring the unfulfilled longing that is satisfied in Aslan's Country, Lewis calls his readers to consider whether they feel a similar tug and to seek the source like the courageous mouse. Moreover, the atmospheric qualities of Narnia add to the wooing that the reader feels. Another example that is more direct is Aslan telling the children that in their world, he goes by another name.

In addition to recognizing key narrative or atmospheric qualities that woo the reader toward Christian truths (see Treasure mentioned previously), this category includes narrative forms or supposals of arguments (e.g., ontological argument—see chapter 7), aspects of the moral argument, argument from desire, and many others. It also naturally relates to other keys (translation, transformation, treasure, tension). A conversation partner or apologist could, in principle, use what is categorized as call to help translate a given concept or make a more explicit claim. For example, I could ask if you have ever felt a longing like Reepicheep, a longing that nothing in this world seems to satisfy? This could open up discussion about how Lewis thought such longings are a kind of signpost pointing us to God.

WORLDVIEWS, NARNIA, AND THE SIX KEYS

In part two, I use these keys to explore how the *Narnia* stories can function as narrative apologetics, engaging with some of the most influential belief systems globally and cross-culturally. This is done in three segments:

1. I explain the contours of a particular belief system, drawing particularly on James Sire's classic worldview profiles in *The Universe Next Door*.[12]

---

12. Now in its sixth edition, Sire's work was selected because his profiles are considered classic categories in the field. Because worldview beliefs vary widely among individuals within a given belief system, Sire's categories provide the right balance of tradition, simplicity, and rigor for this project's purposes. Because Sire only briefly mentions apatheism in his naturalism profile, other primary sources are used to articulate and assess this increasingly relevant belief system.

2. Next, I identify some of the most important needs and barriers within that profile for apologetic engagement.

3. Finally, I show how *The Chronicles of Narnia* advocates Christian belief to a given profile through the six keys.

I explain the contours of four major belief systems: Islamic theism, naturalism, Eastern pantheistic monism, and apatheism, which roughly correspond to the most prominent religious groups of the world.[13] Although worldview is not the same as religion, worldviews are expressed in various religions.[14] Sire defines *worldview* as follows:

> A commitment, a fundamental orientation of the heart, that can be expressed as a story or in a set of presuppositions (assumptions which may be true, partially true, or entirely false) that we hold (consciously or subconsciously, consistently or inconsistently) about the basic constitution of reality, and that provides the foundation on which we live and move and have our being.[15]

Each worldview profile is identified according to its answer to eight fundamental questions. Sire's questions are:

1. What is prime reality—the really real?
2. What is the nature of external reality (that is, the world around us)?
3. What is a human being?
4. What happens to a person at death?
5. Why is it possible to know anything?
6. How do we know what is right and wrong?
7. What is the meaning of human history?
8. What personal, life-orienting core commitments are consistent with this worldview?[16]

---

13. These worldviews roughly correspond to the largest religious groups of the world as categorized by Pew Research Center's 2010 study: naturalism/apatheism (Unaffiliated, 16.3 percent); Eastern pantheistic monism (Hindus, 15.0 percent, and Buddhists, 7.1 percent); Islamic theism (Muslims, 23.2 percent). Hackett and Grim, *Global Religious Landscape*, para. 2.
14. Sire, *Universe Next Door*, 4.
15. Sire, *Universe Next Door*, 6.
16. Sire, *Universe Next Door*, 8–9.

Second, after explaining the contours of a given belief system, I next identify some of the essential needs and barriers to Christian belief within that specific profile. These needs and barriers are founded on insights from cross-cultural apologetics, relevant insights from specific conversion stories, and research about the nature of conversion from a given worldview.

Third, I show how *The Chronicles of Narnia* advocates Christian belief to a specific belief system through the lens of six keys: translation, transformation, treasure, tension, concern, call. In chapter 5, I explore Narnia's challenge to Islamic theism based on *The Lion, the Witch and the Wardrobe*. In chapter 6, I focus on Narnia's challenge to naturalism based on *The Voyage of the Dawn Treader*. In chapter 7, I take a slightly different approach and look at how Lewis treats the ontological argument in *The Silver Chair*. In chapter 8, I analyze Narnia's challenge to Eastern pantheistic monism based on *The Magician's Nephew*. Finally, in chapter 9 I consider Narnia's challenge to apatheism based on *The Last Battle*.

My hope is that this exploration will equip and inspire you to recognize ways that stories like *The Chronicles of Narnia* can help communicate and advocate the Christian story across worldviews. I also hope it will unlock some of the doors that are naturally open for conversation about what matters most when talking about *The Chronicles of Narnia* or any story that contains elements touched by the six keys of translation, transformation, treasure, tension, concern, and call. I begin with the first story Lewis wrote in the series, *The Lion, the Witch and the Wardrobe*.

PART TWO

Other Watchful Dragons

How Narnia Speaks to Different Worldviews

5

Engaging Islam

with *The Lion, the Witch and the Wardrobe*

INTRODUCTION

The Lion, the Witch and the Wardrobe was the first Narnia book that C. S. Lewis wrote. In this story, the Pevensie children first enter Narnia, and very quickly hearts are revealed as Edmund offers to exchange his own family for something as trivial as Turkish Delight. The price of Edmund's betrayal to the White Witch is his life, and yet Aslan willingly chooses to give his own life to set Edmund free and satisfy the Emperor's Deep Magic. Miraculously, Aslan does not stay dead. Through the Deeper Magic from before the dawn of time, as an innocent victim, Aslan's death works backward, and he is restored to life. In this story, Lewis gives a powerful translation of the quality of Christian grace and Jesus's death and resurrection.

The first worldview profile that I consider is Islamic theism.[1] Jesus's incarnation and humiliating death are particular barriers for Muslims.

---

1. It is worth noting that some criticisms have been made of Lewis in terms of his depiction of Calormene culture as being offensive to Muslims and Middle Eastern cultures, particularly in *The Horse and His Boy* and *The Last Battle*. Accordingly, the fact that the Calormenes worship Tash, who is physical and repulsive, is found to be offensive and distinctly at odds with Islamic monotheism. But it should be noted that one could equally argue that *because* the Calormenes worship a physical god like Tash, this is evidence that Lewis was not intending it to represent Islam. In Islam, Allah is

As we will explore further, they challenge the Islamic understanding of God's transcendence. In this chapter, I first briefly explain the contours of Islamic belief. I will then explore some of the most critical barriers and needs for apologetic engagement. Finally, I show some of the ways that Narnia advocates Christian belief to this worldview and how *The Lion, the Witch and the Wardrobe* has particular power and relevance for helping Muslims engage with Jesus's sacrificial death.

WHAT DO MUSLIMS BELIEVE?

Islam shares common ground with Christianity in its belief in one God, but has a very different conception of God in key respects. God's fundamental nature, relationship to human beings, and beliefs about end times vary significantly from those of Christianity. Matthew Bennett's book, for example, notes that this difference establishes a different trajectory from Christian theism, and he surveys Islam's theology using the categories of sin, salvation, and end times.[2] Others explain the differences based on Islam's answers to questions about our nature, the world, the brokenness of the world, and our end.[3] Winfried Corduan's work is beneficial because it uses Sire's eight classic worldview categories to highlight Islam's essential beliefs. This will help provide a thorough but general picture of Islam before looking at how narrative can help with cross-cultural apologetics in Islam.

First, Islam is decisively monotheistic: "The fundamental reality of Islam is God (Allah), described as monotheistic, infinite, personal, transcendent, immanent, omniscient, sovereign, and good. Of these attributes Islam emphasizes his oneness, transcendence, and sovereignty."[4] But as Corduan explains, "Islam did not so much define itself internally as externally" to contrast itself with other beliefs of the time, especially "polytheism" near Mecca, "Jewish monotheism," and "trinitarian monotheism."[5] Corduan says that Islam's "comparative impulse" comes from a phrase that is repeated in the call to prayer five times a day: "Allahu

---

transcendent and never physical. See Ahmad, "Narnia in the Eyes."

2. Bennett, *40 Questions About Islam*, 107–50.
3. Anderson et al., *Introduction to Christian Worldview*, 293–307.
4. Corduan, "Islamic Theism," 236.
5. Corduan, "Islamic Theism," 237.

Akbar."[6] This phrase, he explains, is normally translated "God is great"; however, in this context it implies "'God is greater than all others,' or 'God is the one and only supreme being.'"[7]

Accordingly, the worst sin in Islam is the sin of *shirk*. Corduan explains *shirk* this way: "Anything that could conceivably be construed as detracting from his greatness must be considered to be false.... *Shirk* means to conjoin Allah with any of his creatures, to ascribe a partner to him, or to understand him to possess limitations that are characteristic of his creatures but not of him."[8] Corduan observes that this has significant implications for how Muslims see the incarnation in Christianity, but it also means that any attributes that are given by Allah "cannot be measured by human standards."[9]

Similar to other forms of theism, Corduan explains, Islam maintains that Allah is both transcendent and immanent, but for Islam, "God's transcendence far outweighs his immanence . . . any notion of a possible relationship to Allah must recognize this boundary."[10] Corduan continues, Allah's immanence is best understood as how he "acts in the world."[11] He does note that Muslims hold to some aspects of general revelation (see Qur'an 2:164), but they also condemn anyone who sees signs and ends up "worshiping them rather than Allah."[12]

Second, in Islamic theism, "God (Allah) created the universe *ex nihilo*, and all creatures are responsible to him. However, the world is a closed system insofar as nothing happens in the world outside of his divine decrees."[13] Qur'an 3:191 and 1:2 suggest that Allah is the creator, cherisher, and sustainer of the worlds. This includes the unseen realm, including angels and *jinn* (spirit beings who can be good or evil). Furthermore, he continues, according to the doctrine of *Qadr* ("power"), Allah is "the creator and owner of the universe," and consequently, "nothing happens" that is outside of his plan (see Qur'an 57:22–23).[14] Ultimately,

---

6. Corduan, "Islamic Theism," 238.
7. Corduan, "Islamic Theism," 238.
8. Corduan, "Islamic Theism," 238–39.
9. Corduan, "Islamic Theism," 239.
10. Corduan, "Islamic Theism," 239.
11. Corduan, "Islamic Theism," 239.
12. Corduan, "Islamic Theism," 241–42.
13. Corduan, "Islamic Theism," 244.
14. Corduan, "Islamic Theism," 245.

Corduan explains, Islamic theism is "a closed universe," meaning Allah's will "sets the boundary for what any creature can do as a causal agent."[15]

Third, "Human beings are the pinnacle of God's creation. They have been given abilities of which other creatures, such as angels and jinn, are not capable. However, their high standing also brings with it the responsibility to live up to God's standards."[16] In the Qur'an, when Allah decided to create mankind, he announced his plan to the angels. They questioned whether human beings would be prone to "mischief" and bloodshed (Qur'an 2:30). Allah replied that he knows something that the angels do not, and "[Allah] personally educated Adam in how to identify the many creatures of the earth (presumably plants, animals, and objects in nature)."[17] Corduan continues: in a later meeting with the spiritual beings, Allah invites these beings to tell him the names of things, but they cannot do it. Allah then invites Adam to do the same, and he is able. Corduan writes, "In order to drive home this point, Allah commanded all the angels to bow down before Adam."[18]

With the exception of an angel called Iblîs, the angels all bowed down (Qur'an 2:34). In his rebellion, Corduan explains, Iblîs, who becomes Satan (*Shaytan*), refuses and becomes one who rejects "Faith." Unlike the Biblical account, the fall of Satan is related to the angel "refusing to demonstrate the superiority of human beings over him."[19] As the story unfolds, Corduan explains, Allah puts Adam and his wife in the garden and commands them not to eat of a certain tree; but Satan persuades them to disobey, so they are expelled from the garden.[20] Corduan notes that one significant difference from Christianity is that Allah restores Adam to fellowship (Qur'an 2:37), and there is no transference of "original sin" or permanent curse.[21]

Corduan maintains that in Islam, humans are Allah's "representatives on earth, higher than any other living creatures ... with a nature that is not corrupted by Adam's fall."[22] This also means that humans are born innocent and "Muslim." Corduan explains, it is the human's responsibility

---

15. Corduan, "Islamic Theism," 247.
16. Corduan, "Islamic Theism," 247.
17. Corduan, "Islamic Theism," 248.
18. Corduan, "Islamic Theism," 248.
19. Corduan, "Islamic Theism," 248.
20. Corduan, "Islamic Theism," 248.
21. Corduan, "Islamic Theism," 261.
22. Corduan, "Islamic Theism," 249.

to "remain pure," and "to live one's entire life in submission" to Allah (see Qur'an 2:21).[23] He continues: human life is a test of obedience to Allah, and the consequence of failing the test is hell.[24]

Fourth, "Death is a time of transition between this life and our eternal state, which will consist of either paradise or hell."[25] At death, two angels, Munkar and Nakir, test the faith of the dead in their tombs. The *Shahadah*, an Islamic creed and one of the five pillars of Islam, is often confessed immediately prior to death, or if they are not able, by those gathered at an individual's funeral. Most Muslims believe that all dead will be raised to face judgment, but there is debate over whether the intermediate state is one of soul sleep or a kind of purgatory.[26]

"All human beings," Corduan continues, "will be called to stand before the divine tribunal" in judgment of every action and attitude in one's life. Moreover, "Every human being will have accumulated a book of their deeds, both good and evil, during their mortal lives. No one can be fully sure that they have enough good to outweigh any bad, and so be assured of going to paradise."[27] Assurance is regarded as presumptuous in Islam. Corduan explains, "To claim assurance for salvation implies that one can dictate to Allah what he must do, and this attitude is considered to be inappropriate."[28]

Corduan continues, "As soon as Allah has established his verdict, one of the angels will come up to the person and hand him the book of his deeds"—to either the right hand or the left.[29] If the book is placed in the right hand, one has received Allah's mercy and can enter paradise. If placed in the left, a person's judgment is living forever in hell (see Qur'an 69:13–37). Moreover, with the exception of "martyrs, children before puberty, and those who are mentally impaired," all are held accountable for their actions. Hell is depicted in the Qur'an as a place of intense suffering in fire and boiling water, while heaven is described as an oasis of delight (see Qur'an 13:23).[30]

---

23. Corduan, "Islamic Theism," 249.
24. Corduan, "Islamic Theism," 250.
25. Corduan, "Islamic Theism," 250.
26. Corduan, "Islamic Theism," 250.
27. Corduan, "Islamic Theism," 251.
28. Corduan, "Islamic Theism," 251.
29. Corduan, "Islamic Theism," 251.
30. Corduan, "Islamic Theism," 251–52.

Fifth, "Allah has endowed human beings with the capability of knowledge by means of reason and the senses. Thereby, they can also know God's revelation. However, God's sovereign decrees limit human knowledge."[31] In Islam, Allah has created human beings such that their senses provide reliable sources for reasoning and discerning truth from error (see Qur'an 2:256). Reason and knowledge are also supported by divine revelation via prophets, but due to their evil, not a lack of information, humans often fall to temptation and unbelief.[32]

Among the prophets, there is a more distinguished group called messengers, including Moses as bringer of the Law, David as bringer of the Psalms, and Jesus as bringer of the Gospel.[33] But a problem remained, Corduan explains; "The same unbelieving people who did not listen to them in person corrupted their writings in order to suit their idolatrous preferences." He continues, Muhammad's message, preserved in the Qur'an, was considered "free from error or human interference."[34] Accordingly, there is no need for additional prophets. Furthermore, according to Islam's doctrine of *Qadr*, those who reject Muhammad and the Qur'an are predestined to do so (see Qur'an 6:25, 111, 125).[35]

Sixth, "Right and wrong are based on the teachings of the Qur'an, as amplified by the hadith and interpreted by the schools of law, the shari'a."[36] Muslims are obligated to follow five pillars: (1) "to recite the confession (there is no God but Allah)," (2) "pray five times a day" facing Mecca, (3) "fast during the month of Ramadan," (4) give annual alms to the poor, and (5) make a pilgrimage to Mecca (*hajj*) at least once in their lifetime. In addition to the five pillars, there are three other categories for moral action in Islam: (1) "those directly commanded (*fard*)," (2) "those permitted (*halal*)," and (3) "those that are prohibited (*haram*)."[37]

Seventh, "Human history has significance in demonstrating the absolute sovereignty of God but, even more so, as the opportunity for

---

31. Corduan, "Islamic Theism," 252.
32. Corduan, "Islamic Theism," 253.
33. Corduan, "Islamic Theism," 254.
34. Corduan, "Islamic Theism," 254.
35. Corduan, "Islamic Theism," 255–56.
36. Corduan, "Islamic Theism," 257.
37. Corduan, "Islamic Theism," 258. Corduan importantly notes, "When everything is riding on one's actions, and when there is no assurance of God's indulgence, let alone any grace, avoiding the potentially negative consequences of any sin is bound to become the primary incentive for one's actions rather than the positive motivation of keeping the rules out of gratitude." Corduan, "Islamic Theism," 258–59.

people to demonstrate their submission to him."[38] In classical interpretations of Islam, the goal of history is to "subsume the entire world under the *umma*, the Islamic community," which is understood as both a political entity (an Islamic state) and a "congregation of believers" (see Qur'an 2:143).[39] However, it is important to recognize that interpretations of this ideal vary widely among Muslim thinkers and communities.

Eighth, "A devout Muslim is grateful to Allah for providing the opportunity to serve him and will strive to follow the divine instructions in even the smallest part of life."[40] A devoted Muslim will sometimes express gratitude that Allah has offered a chance to enter paradise, reference the Qur'an's teaching as "good news," and consider any chance at salvation to be an act of mercy by Allah.[41] Corduan notes that only one *surah* does not include the expression "in the name of Allah, the most gracious and most merciful," and Muslims see the need to live up to divine standards for salvation as an opportunity rather than a burden.[42] With this said, the sobering fact is that assurance is ultimately not available to the Muslim. Corduan writes, "All the compliance by a human being notwithstanding, the will of Allah can always override all the good works a person may have accumulated."[43]

With this general outline of Islamic beliefs in place, we are better positioned to observe the similarities and differences that naturally exist between Islam and Christianity. The next step is to identify some of the most important needs and barriers for cross-cultural apologetics to Islamic theism.

WHAT ARE THE NEEDS AND CHALLENGES IN APOLOGETICS TO MUSLIMS?

There are a number of needs and challenges in engaging apologetically with Islamic beliefs and with Muslims. I will focus on seven. First, *the incarnation is one obstacle for Muslims since it commits the sin of shirk*. Shirk is similar to the Biblical concept of idolatry. It is one of the seven major

38. Corduan, "Islamic Theism," 259.

39. Corduan, "Islamic Theism," 259–60. Corduan notes that many believe the Mahdi will appear before the last judgment, with some believing that Jesus is the Mahdi.

40. Corduan, "Islamic Theism," 260.

41. Corduan, "Islamic Theism," 260.

42. Corduan, "Islamic Theism," 261.

43. Corduan, "Islamic Theism," 262.

sins of Islam, and it is generally considered unpardonable (see Qur'an 4:48, 116). There is no hope for those who associate anything with Allah. In Islam, Allah is absolutely one, and there is no portion in paradise for those who commit *shirk*. This obstacle is significant in that there are Quranic passages that suggest that the Christian doctrines of the incarnation and the Trinity are forms of *shirk* (see Qur'an 112:1–4).

A second related obstacle is *the Christian doctrine of the Trinity*. Islamic theology condemns the doctrine of the Trinity as the sin of *shirk* and warns that severe judgment awaits anyone believing it (see Qur'an 9:30; 5:72–73). The Trinity stands at odds with Islam's most fundamental doctrine, Allah's absolute oneness (*tawhid*). Muslim writer Reza Aslan remarks, "If *tawhid* is the foundation of Islam, then its opposite, *shirk* is Islam's greatest sin."[44]

A third obstacle is *Jesus's identity*. In Islam, Jesus is believed to be a prophet, not God. Sarmad Qutub and Musa Qutub's adherent essay as Muslims in *The Handbook of Religion* is illustrative:

> The ascription of divinity to other than God is an act of disbelief, which automatically takes one out of the mercy of God into eternal damnation if one does not repent before death. Muslims certainly believe that those who followed Jesus as a prophet of God as his early disciples did were Muslims (meaning submitted to the will of God) and will be in the eternal bliss of paradise. However, those who took Jesus Christ as their Lord instead of the One True God or made Jesus to be the Son of God (and died in this belief) will have no share of that divine mercy and will receive God's wrath on judgment day.[45]

The belief that Jesus is God rather than a prophet commits *shirk*. This Muslim conviction draws on passages such as Qur'an 5:116 and 4:157.

Christianity's belief that Jesus is God directly challenges the Islamic doctrine of *tawhid*. Some passages in the Bible are explicit about Jesus's divinity (John 1:1, 14; 10:33; 20:28; Titus 2:13; Heb 1:8). Jesus's own self-understanding includes frequent claims to be the Son of Man, corresponding to the human eschatological figure of Dan 7.[46] Jesus claims to be the unique Son of God (see Matt 11:27). Furthermore, Jesus exercises prerogatives that belong to God. For example, Jesus claimed authority over the Sabbath, a day that was prescribed as holy to the Lord (Gen

---

44. Aslan, *No god but God*, 153.
45. Qutub and Qutub, "Islam: Adherent Essay," 178.
46. Moreland and Craig, "Trinity," 575.

1—2:3; Exod 20:8-11; Luke 6:1-11); Jesus displayed authority over demons and disease (Luke 4:38-41); Jesus had power and authority over nature (Luke 5:1-11); and most significantly, Jesus displayed authority over sin (Luke 5:17-26).[47] In *Mere Christianity*, C. S. Lewis discusses how shocking it would have been to the Jewish people to hear Jesus talking as if he were God, and the same applies to Muslims: "God, in their language, meant the Being outside the world Who had made it and was infinitely different from anything else. And when you have grasped that, you will see that what this man said was, quite simply, the most shocking thing that has ever been uttered by human lips."[48]

A fourth barrier for Islamic theists is *the crucifixion of Jesus*. Most Muslims do not believe that Jesus was crucified, based on Qur'an 4:157, and the theological emphasis on the transcendence and glory of God make the idea of God suffering and dying offensive. This is despite a widely accepted case for the historical crucifixion of Jesus even among skeptical historians.[49]

A fifth barrier for Muslims is *misunderstandings about Christianity*. There are several sorts of misunderstandings. Misunderstandings can relate to the history between Islam and Christianity. The Crusades are a common example, which are seen as acts of aggression carried out by Christianity toward Muslims. The historical reality is much more nuanced. Christians must also acknowledge the genuine harms done in the name of Christianity, while clearing away misunderstandings.[50] Daniel Janosik fittingly counsels, "Christians need to be open with their Muslim friends about the failures on the part of the Christians, but they also need to be able to respond to the false representations."[51]

Like other belief profiles, Islamic theists also struggle with *misunderstandings about what Christians actually believe*. For example,

---

47. For an excellent and accessible book on this topic, see Bowman and Komoszewski, *Putting Jesus in His Place*. Or, for an updated and thorough treatment, see Bowman and Komoszewski, *Incarnate Christ*.

48. Lewis, *Mere Christianity*, 51.

49. As an example, John Dominic Crossan, a New Testament scholar well known for skepticism about many classical Christian beliefs, remarks, "Jesus' death by crucifixion under Pontius Pilate is as sure as anything historical can ever be. For if no follower of Jesus had written anything for one hundred years after his crucifixion, we would still know about him from two authors not among his supporters. Their names are Flavius Josephus and Cornelius Tacitus." Crossan, *Jesus*, 145.

50. Janosik, *Guide to Answering Islam*, 230-32.

51. Janosik, *Guide to Answering Islam*, 234.

Qur'an 5:116 is sometimes taken to represent the Christian doctrine of the Trinity, and Mary is considered divine. On this view the Godhead is "Father-*Mary*-Son." This interpretation is sometimes debated, but it is representative of the kinds of misunderstandings that exist.

A sixth barrier is *misrepresentations of Christianity by Christians*. Janosik identifies five barriers to Muslim conversions. Most of these barriers fit within the category of misrepresenting biblical Christianity: (1) *contentious Christians* (Christians are divided among themselves—see John 13:35; Christian fear and hatred of Muslims); (2) *Christian legalism* (Muslims already know the burden of religious legalism); (3) *Christian violence* (Christians must avoid violence, even if responding to Islamic violence); (4) *Christian justice* (Christians need to address injustices appropriately, especially because many Muslims have left Islam because of religious injustices); and (5) *Christian apathy* (lukewarm Christianity is an obstacle).[52]

A final barrier that exists is the *cost of Christian belief for many Muslims*. Persecution is a well-known cost. The Muslim community and even family members of Christian converts from Islam have been known to ostracize and even harm those leaving Islam. There is the perceived cost of forfeiting paradise in the afterlife. Even in contexts where persecution may not be a risk, there is also the high social cost of losing one's community that Van den Toren noted in his model.

THE LION, THE WITCH AND THE WARDROBE'S CHALLENGES TO ISLAMIC THEISM

While there is some common ground in Islam and Christianity's monotheistic beliefs, because Islamic theology excludes the possibility of the Trinity and incarnation, the two religions are fundamentally in contradiction. Because the fundamentals of Islamic theology are so contrary to Christian theism, Lewis's effort to get past watchful dragons to convey the potency of Christianity may be especially helpful for engaging Muslims. Based on the needs and obstacles that have been identified, I focus on seven challenges that can help to communicate Christian beliefs to Muslims through *The Lion, the Witch and the Wardrobe*. Of course, many of the challenges that I identify here apply to persons from all worldviews, but I will focus on their applicability to Islamic theism.

52. Janosik, *Guide to Answering Islam*, 302.

The Challenge of Walking Myths

In *The Lion, the Witch and the Wardrobe*, Lewis translates some of the feelings that the Christian faith involves through the experiences of a young girl named Lucy. Lucy and her siblings are evacuees from London in the 1940s because of the Second World War and the ongoing threat of air raid bombing. They arrive at a very large country home with an old professor, an irritable housekeeper, and three servants. On their first night at the house, the children are hurt with the wound of separation from their parents. Like a child-run household, they also struggle to define their family pecking order, though adults are distantly present. Their transitional home is full of the unknown, consisting of empty rooms, long hallways, and unfamiliar noises.

In wandering, the children come upon a somewhat neglected and empty room with a wardrobe. "Nothing there!" is Peter's appraisal, and everyone but Lucy keeps exploring. Lucy, however, is curious about the wardrobe and wants to see inside. Cautiously, she leaves the wardrobe doors open and inches slowly toward the back, with her hands stretched out. The back of the wardrobe seems much deeper than expected, and the wardrobe gets darker with each step. She finds herself in a snowy wood lit by a lamppost, which makes little sense in the middle of the woods.

A few moments later, she can hear the approach of feet, but the person who appears is unlike anyone she knows—he is a living, breathing faun. Lucy introduces herself. After recovering from his own shock, the faun introduces himself as Tumnus. Following the awkward beginning, Mr. Tumnus explains that the land they are in is Narnia, and it has been winter for a long, long time. Mr. Tumnus becomes much warmer and invites Lucy to come to his home to get out of the snow. Though Lucy feels like she should probably get back to her family, she accepts his offer, but she can only stay for a moment.

Mr. Tumnus leads Lucy to his quaint home in a cave, which Lucy finds pleasant and welcoming. As Lucy waits for Mr. Tumnus to make tea, she looks around the home. She sees the picture of an old faun with a gray beard on the mantel and sees a shelf full of books such as *Nymphs and Their Ways* and *Is Man a Myth?*[53]

There are several aspects of the story that are worthy of note in how they bring myth to life. First, Lewis is able to convey certain mythic qualities in the scene. Charlie Starr explains, "We feel we are entering a world

---

53. Lewis, *Lion*, 173.

that has already been going on for a very long time. With a light, subtle touch, Lewis achieves the same quality by giving us some of the titles on Mr. Tumnus's bookshelf. We don't know the content of the books, but the titles hint at a larger world."[54] Some of the relevance for the Muslim reader is that Narnia is *experienced* as real (translation). Lewis woos the reader into this mysterious, though foreign world, and invites a brief suspension of disbelief (translation).

Second, Lucy finds that a real world and history exist that she knows nothing about (translation, tension). This world is unexpected and unlike where she is from, but it is every bit as real. This challenge is considerably strengthened as we learn more about Narnia and Aslan. From a cross-cultural apologetic standpoint, this helps to separate some Western associations that sometimes come with Christianity in the East and allows the Muslim reader to experience a world that is similar to the Christian story (concern, translation).

Finally, Lewis mirrors the colloquial concept of myth, but in reverse. In England, fauns are mythological creatures. In Narnia, humans are mythological creatures. Human beings are the long-anticipated objects of legend, and yet Mr. Tumnus is making tea for this gracious young girl named Lucy. Could there be stories in our own world that seem implausible but are true? Could it be that God became man, as the Christian story says? What if myth became fact, as Lewis thought? (Translation, treasure.)

The Challenge of Kidnapped Innocence

In Mr. Tumnus's house, he prepares a wonderful tea, complete with an egg, sardines on toast, toast with honey, and sugar-topped cake. After Lucy is done eating, the faun shares wonderful stories of life in the forest, including about the creatures such as dryads and dwarfs and visits from Silenus and Bacchus. Lucy learns that this world is old and enchanting. It is a place with a history full of feasting and celebration. But the cheer is curiously subdued: now, it is always winter. Mr. Tumnus starts to play a flute that makes Lucy drowsy.

When Lucy insists she must go home, Mr. Tumnus unexpectedly tells her it is too late. He becomes very emotional, bursting into tears. Lucy is confused and asks what is wrong. The faun is distraught that he is

---

54. Starr, *Faun's Bookshelf*, 12.

such a bad faun. Lucy doesn't agree and says as much. He is a very good faun, the nicest she has met. Mr. Tumnus laments that his father, the faun pictured on his mantelpiece, would never have done what he is doing. Mr. Tumnus is in the pay of the White Witch, he explains. The White Witch is also the reason the land is always winter, "never Christmas."[55] Lucy tries to understand. What exactly does he do for the White Witch? Mr. Tumnus confesses that he is a spy for her. Since the beginning, he has been luring Lucy in so that he can capture her and take her to the witch.

There are several noteworthy features in this scene. First, notice that the context is thick with mythic qualities. Mr. Tumnus's memories are marked with beauty, celebration, and nostalgia (treasure). In Tolkien's words, Tumnus longs for Eden. Tolkien once wrote to his son, "Your obstinate memory of this 'home' of yours in an idyllic hour (when often there is an illusion of the stay of time and decay and a sense of gentle peace) are derived from Eden."[56] Human longing exists across cultures and worldviews, including Islam. As discussed earlier, Lewis maintains that this longing is ultimately satisfied in God. In Narnia, longing is satisfied in Aslan and his country.

Notice second that Mr. Tumnus says that in the old days of the woods, even Bacchus himself would visit (transformation in a negative sense, the woods are void of joy now). When Bacchus visited, the streams would turn to wine and there would be weeks of celebration. There is no mention of debauchery; the forest is blessed by his presence, and joyful (treasure). But notice that the water turns to wine, which also recalls Jesus's miracle at Cana (see John 1:1–11) (treasure, translation). In his book *Miracles*, Lewis comments on this event in Jesus's life: "This miracle proclaims that the God of all wine is present. The vine is one of the blessings sent by Jahweh: He is the reality behind the false god Bacchus."[57] It is subtle, but the idea of one with creative authority to turn water into wine is something like a "good dream" in Narnia (treasure).[58] It also familiarizes the reader with the wonder of one with authority to change water to wine (translation).

55. Lewis, *Lion*, 175.
56. Carpenter and Tolkien, *Letters of Tolkien*, 110.
57. Lewis, *Miracles*, 422.
58. In *Mere Christianity*, Lewis maintains that God spoke in three ways before Jesus came in the flesh: (1) the conscience and our failure to obey it, (2) "good dreams" of dying and rising gods in heathen religions, and (3) the Jewish people that he spent centuries hammering out the kind of God he is, and the kind of conduct he expected. In this scene, Lewis subtly includes two of the three ways. Lewis, *Mere Christianity*, 50.

A related facet is that Bacchus was a corn god. Louis Markos explains that before Lewis became a Christian, Lewis read Sir James George Frazer's *Golden Bough* and learned that "every ancient culture was aware of the pervasive power of human sin and guilt, particularly as it manifests itself in terms of forbidden acts or taboos."[59] This is relevant in that Mr. Tumnus has kidnapped a vulnerable and innocent girl and is giving her to a merciless witch—an act that would be almost universally considered evil (tension, concern). Markos continues:

> In order to deal with such taboos, these cultures not only practice rituals of sacrifice and ablution, but harbored a cherished myth about a god who came to earth, died, and returned to the abode of the gods. Frazer referred to this divine, or semi-divine, scapegoat (see Lev 16:10) as a Corn-god, for his death and rebirth paralleled the seasonal cycle of the corn. . . . As the grain is harvested and milled but then returns to life in the spring, so the Corn-god . . . is killed and buried, only to be reborn and renewed.[60]

As an atheist, Lewis thought that Jesus was just another corn king until a now famous evening walk with J. R. R. Tolkien and Hugo Dyson when Lewis became convinced that Jesus was a myth that became fact. In brief, Markos explains, "the reason every ancient culture yearned for a god to come to earth, to die, and rise again was because the Creator who made all the nations placed in every person a desire for that very thing. . . . Christ fulfilled . . . all the deepest (general-revelation-produced) yearnings of the pagan peoples."[61] Markos continues, "When Christ died on the Cross, he made real and historical that which the pagan nations had long yearned for in their fantastical, and non-historical myths"[62] (treasure, concern).

Finally, a possible emotional resonance for Muslims lies in Mr. Tumnus's moral guilt and uneasy conscience (tension, translation, call). Lewis juxtaposes the goodness of his nostalgic memories and the innocence of Lucy's childhood with Tumnus's deceit by depicting the wickedness of faking friendship with a child with the sole purpose of kidnapping her (tension, call).[63]

---

59. Markos, *Myth Made Fact*, xvi.
60. Markos, *Myth Made Fact*, xvi–xvii.
61. Markos, *Myth Made Fact*, xvii.
62. Markos, *Myth Made Fact*, xvii.
63. Steven Spielberg forcefully used this prophetic application of art in his acclaimed film *Schindler's List* by sending an innocent young girl through the Jewish ghetto in a

This point is further relevant to Muslims in that forgiveness, assurance, and a clear conscience are existential graces that Muslims often lack (tension, translation, call). Thomas W. Seckler's study of Muslim conversion in Cambodia notes that the themes of sin, cleansing, heaven, and judgment were the most common themes discussed by Muslims who converted to Christianity.[64] The reality of sin and forgiveness becomes even stronger later in the story through Aslan's death, resurrection, and restoration of life.

The Challenge of the Cost of Truth

Lucy turns very white and pleads with the faun because now she is afraid. Mr. Tumnus begins crying again and explains the threat to his own life if he doesn't follow through, and the risk that the witch will turn him into a stone statue. Lucy is sympathetic with Mr. Tumnus's situation but pleads for him to allow her to go home. Thankfully for Lucy, the faun sees that, regardless of his personal cost, he must let her go free. Meeting a human being personally and getting to know Lucy has changed him, and he realizes he can't possibly give her up to the witch now. Before leaving Lucy where they met, Mr. Tumnus laments what he has done, asking for forgiveness. A picture of innocence and gentle kindness, Lucy gladly forgives Mr. Tumnus. She also shares her hope that he will not have to suffer for letting her go.[65]

There are several relevant applications of this challenge to Muslims considering Christianity. First, there is often a true cost for those who leave Islam. This is a tension that is felt and a narrative encouragement through Mr. Tumnus (tension, call). As former Muslim Nabeel Qureshi explains, "It is no understatement to say that Muslims often risk everything to embrace the cross."[66] Mr. Tumnus risks his life to do what is right. Second, there is a tension for those living against the moral law (tension). This is true within Narnia and in the reader's world. Lewis discusses the moral law in *Mere Christianity*, and the toughness of its demand to do the right thing, regardless of how difficult or painful it might be.[67] The failure

---

red overcoat. Her innocence starkly clashes with the dark backdrop of depravity and senseless genocide that is occurring all around her on her walk home.

64. Seckler, *Experiencing the Gospel*, 87.
65. Lewis, *Lion*, 176–77.
66. Qureshi, *Seeking Allah, Finding Jesus*, 253.
67. Lewis, *Mere Christianity*, 30.

to follow the moral law crushes Mr. Tumnus with shame, guilt, and conviction that he must change course at any cost (tension). Moreover, he feels compelled to ask Lucy for forgiveness, even though the threat to his own life remains (translation, treasure).

Finally, Mr. Tumnus's obedience to the moral law, nevertheless, changes his relationship from kidnapper to sacrifice—it may cost him dearly to do what is right (tension, call). While this is no direct challenge to Islam, a regular testimony heard by some who have left Islam, particularly in its radical forms, is that they experienced its rules as oppressive and see it as suppressing human rights. This intuitive anger trades on what Lewis calls the moral law. Muslims who begin to see issues with the actions of radical Islam, especially when consistent with the Qur'an's teaching, are in a situation that is similar to Tumnus (tension). It may cost them, but in the depths of their being, the moral law calls for them to pay the price (treasure).

The Challenge of Family Rejection

After leaving Mr. Tumnus, Lucy runs back to the patch of daylight that she can see at the wardrobe entrance as quickly as she can. Instead of branches and snow, she feels the softness of long fur coats and the wooden floor of the wardrobe beneath her feet. She quickly finds herself in the room where she began. She has been in Narnia for hours, so she assumes her family must be desperate to find her. Lucy shouts that she's back and runs out of the empty room to find her siblings. She reassures them that she is fine and there is no reason to worry, but they are confused. Susan asks what she is talking about, and Peter assumes she has been hiding for too short a time for anyone to notice. Edmund simply taps his head, signaling his belief she has gone mad.[68]

Lucy tries to explain the wardrobe, utterly convinced that it is a magic portal to the land of Narnia and invites them to see for themselves.[69] What she says seems like foolishness to them. Humoring her, they explore the wardrobe. But it looks just like a normal wardrobe, and they can easily point to its back wall. It looks the same to Lucy as well now, but she is unmoved. With all her heart, she assures her family that

---

68. Lewis, *Lion*, 180.
69. Lewis, *Lion*, 180.

this wardrobe took her to Narnia. Lucy's older siblings conclude that she is either not well or is making up the whole story about Narnia.

A few days later, the weather is bad, so they decide to play hide-and-seek. By this time, the disbelief of Lucy's family, combined with the fact that the wardrobe continues to look like an ordinary wardrobe, makes her wonder if she is dreaming after all. When everyone runs to hide, Lucy decides to take another look at the wardrobe before hiding elsewhere. But as she is looking at the wardrobe, she hears approaching feet, and she is forced to get inside. Unfortunately, the footsteps are from Edmund, and he sees her get in.

Edmund opens the wardrobe to smells of mothballs and fur coats, but he can't see Lucy in the dark silence. Edmund assumes Lucy is hiding, so he jumps into the wardrobe, closes the door, and makes his way to its back. He expects to find her quickly, but instead, he finds himself disoriented in the darkness. He loses track of the entrance and begins calling after her.

Instead of the muffled sound of the wardrobe, he is surprised that his voice sounds like it is in the open air. Momentarily forgetting Lucy, he moves toward the light and steps through the door. He finds that he is standing in the middle of the woods, and snow is under his feet and blanketing the trees. The sky is pale blue, and the sun is just rising—Lucy's imaginary country is real. Coming to his senses, he calls for Lucy, apologizing for not believing her. But there is no answer. She must be bitter, he thinks.

Several key features become clear as the story unfolds. First, Lewis shows what it looks like to know the truth and be rejected by those you love. She is telling the truth, and yet her belief in this other world alienates her from her family until they later see for themselves. This recalls how one might feel as a Muslim who is the first of her family to believe the gospel (tension, translation). She will not be immediately believed, and her belief may well alienate her from her family. Lewis's defense of real violence and bloodshed in children's stories against sterilized counterparts is fitting: "Since it is so likely that they will meet cruel enemies, let them at least have heard of brave knights and heroic courage. Otherwise, you are making their destiny not brighter but darker."[70] Lewis cultivates courage in the reader through Lucy, which could help a Muslim reader wrestling with belief in Christ (treasure, call).

---

70. Lewis, "Writing for Children," 47.

Second, there are glimpses of Lewis's well-known trilemma: Lord, lunatic, or a liar? (Call) In this case, the question is, Does Narnia exist, as Lucy says? She is truthful and so can't deny what she saw for herself, even though her brothers and sister think she is lying. This is compounded later after Edmund providentially enters Narnia as well. When he returns, Edmund should be defending Lucy's word; he's seen Narnia. Instead, he lies and claims he was just teasing her. This intensifies the stress for Susan and Peter because Lucy won't budge on her belief in Narnia. The situation feels beyond them, so they reluctantly go to the professor.

Surprisingly, the professor asks Peter and Susan how they know Lucy's story isn't true: "Why don't they teach logic at these schools? [Call] There are only three possibilities. Either your sister is telling lies, or she is mad, or she is telling the truth. You know she doesn't tell lies and it is obvious that she is not mad. For the moment then and unless any further evidence turns up, we must assume that she is telling the truth."[71] In *Mere Christianity*, Lewis's trilemma relates to Jesus's identity. In *The Lion, the Witch and the Wardrobe*, we discover that Narnia is real, as Lucy says, but the realness of Narnia far exceeds what Lucy knows at this stage. There is a real lion who is on the move, and he is seeking her (translation).

Lewis depicts the feelings of contested belief at the hands of family, even when one's beliefs are true (translation). This recalls the pressures of a plausibility structure. This feeling of contested belief applies to other worldviews, but for the Muslim who is starting to wonder about Christianity or who has begun to believe, Lewis shows that one can believe the truth and yet doubt because of emotional pressures like contested belief (e.g., family skepticism) or unmet expectations (e.g., if this is true, why is the other land not visible now?). Elsewhere Lewis notes that Aslan is not a tame lion, which is a good reminder that God does not operate on our timetable, nor does he always do what we expect (translation). If belief is attached to expectations alone, doubt will come. In the same way, Lewis is able to translate expectations related to walking with God as a Christian.

The Challenge of Witch's Food

When he finds himself in Narnia, Edmund doesn't hear Lucy, but he can hear the approaching sound of bells pulling a two-reindeer sled led by a fat, three-foot dwarf. In the sled was the tallest woman Edmund had

---

71. Lewis, *Lion*, 196.

ever seen. She is covered in white fur, holds a long golden wand, and wears a golden crown. She speaks with authority and condescension as she demands that Edmund tell her what he is.[72] Edmund gives his name, but as she continues to interrogate him, she is startled to realize he is a boy—a "Son of Adam."

The queen learns from Edmund that there is a door from the world of men to the world of Narnia. Though at first hostile, she appears to warm toward Edmund. She offers him a hot drink and then asks what he would most like to eat. He asks for Turkish Delight, which she conjures with magic. As Edmund devours the witch's sweet gifts, she asks questions about his family and learns about Lucy's earlier trip to Narnia when she met the faun. Edmund finishes the whole box of Turkish Delight, but he craves more, endlessly more. He doesn't realize that it is enchanted. Instead of offering him more, the witch suggests that he should get his brother and two sisters to meet her. The witch explains she could give him more Turkish Delight back at her house, but the magic only works once where they are. She also tempts him with promises of making him a prince and then king of Narnia after her, and warns of stories told about her by some of the Narnians.

After the sleigh goes out of sight, Edmund hears someone calling to him. Lucy is delighted that her older brother is with her in Narnia. She is also very happy to report that Mr. Tumnus is fine. She has just come from having lunch with him, and the White Witch hadn't found out about Lucy's earlier visit. Edmund is irritable and his face is pale as he asks who the White Witch is, but Lucy is too happy to notice. She tells him that the witch is a false queen, hated by the good creatures of Narnia, who turns people to stone with her wand and has placed Narnia under its enchanted winter. This makes Edmund deeply uncomfortable, but the taste of Turkish Delight still tugs at him stronger than anything else.

There are several important resonances to this part of the story. Notice first that Lewis introduces the question, What is the true story? Is the witch and her kingdom the true story, or is Mr. Tumnus right? For a truth seeker, this is the honest question for any worldview (translation). If Tumnus is right, then Edmund has been enticed by a Satan-like person whose magic has enslaved the Narnian world in winter and oppression. Hints are given in that it appears that the witch's kingdom is ruled by fear, deceit, and the coercion of pleasure. The witch is threatening and

---

72. Lewis, *Lion*, 184.

tyrannical. Though her food is sweet on the surface, it is addictive to death. Edmund's early intuition told him that the witch was a threat. It was after she seduced his tastes that she felt like a friend (translation).

Second, Edmund's desire for the witch's food and his likeness to her ways recall Eph 2:1–3, which describes those outside of Christ as following the course of the world and Satan's ways (translation). Edmund desires the taste of Turkish Delight above all. Here Lewis translates the strong attraction of sin, as well as its cost—sin and Turkish Delight taste sweet on the surface, but unhindered, you will exchange everything to get them and both end in slavery or death (translation, tension). This also importantly translates something of the nature of sin from a Christian point of view to a Muslim reader and reflects some of the ugliness of sin that all humans carry (translation, tension).

The Challenge of the Moral Facet of Unbelief

Edmund's heart has been on display for some time. When others try to understand what's wrong with Lucy—she keeps talking about Narnia—Edmund taunted her. When Lucy climbed into the wardrobe during hide and seek, Edmund followed her. He saw another opportunity to poke fun at his sister. When the witch invited Edmund to join her in her sled, he ignored his internal caution. After tasting the sweetness of Turkish Delight and hearing about the possibility of becoming a future king of Narnia, he was seduced. Now when Edmund returns from Narnia, instead of defending Lucy's word, he lies and says they have only been pretending. The witch's bent plan has been sown in his heart, and in the moment, Edmund wants her Turkish Delight more than anything else—and he is willing to exchange his family to get it.

Eventually, all four children find their way into Narnia together. Trying to keep out of the way of Mrs. Macready and a tour of the house, the children cram into the wardrobe. As they wait, they start to notice that it is freezing and wet, like snow. Susan notices that she is sitting against a tree, and they begin to see light in the distance. Peter realizes they have gotten into Narnia after all, apologizing to Lucy, and they begin to walk in the woods.

As they walk, Edmund accidentally forgets his earlier lie that he was only pretending to be in Narnia with Lucy and lets slip that he knows the direction they should be heading for. The lie is out, and everyone immediately stops walking and stares at Edmund. After Peter rebukes him, there is nothing more to say, so they move on, but Edmund festers in his resentment and plots to get back at them.

The children decide to explore Narnia, and they let Lucy lead. With all she has endured, the others feel she has earned that much. Lucy wants them to meet her dear friend Mr. Tumnus and is able to lead them right up to Mr. Tumnus's cave. They are, however, shocked by what they find: his home has been broken into, left dark and empty. The house was vandalized, plates were smashed, and even the picture of the faun's father was shredded with a knife. On the carpet, they find a piece of paper nailed to the floor announcing Tumnus's arrest by the witch's secret police for high treason. Tumnus is gone and in grave danger, and the kids feel it intensely.

There are several noteworthy features in these scenes. First, this world is a world of life and death, of kingdoms and high treason, and it scares the children. From a narrative apologetic perspective, Lewis engages the reader's sense of mortality, and this includes Muslim readers (tension). Being reminded of your mortality invites reflection about the truthfulness of your beliefs. Muslims do not have assurance (tension, call). Second, Edmund is skeptical. He claims he does not know who to trust. Edmund suggests that, for all they know, Mr. Tumnus is not good, though the charge of high treason for fraternizing with Humans fits the faun's story better than the witch's (translation). In kind, true Christianity is contagious and recognizable when considered honestly.

Third, the moral dimension of Edmund's unbelief invites virtuous reflection about why one believes or disbelieves. Here Lewis hints that belief has a moral component (translation, call). What if my reasons for unbelief are not innocent? What if I don't want this story of the world to be true, even if it is true? Doubt in any worldview can be an important aspect of truth seeking (tension, call). Moreover, this challenge also recalls Rom 1–2, in which the obvious truth of God is exchanged for a lie because of moral depravity (translation).

The Challenge of Aslan

Jesus's identity is one of the central differences between Islam and Christianity. Exactly who is Jesus? Is he God or merely a prophet? Aslan is one of the most important ways that *The Lion, the Witch and the Wardrobe* contributes to the narrative apologetic task for Muslim readers.[73] I focus on six ways that Lewis presents Aslan: (1) one who is unknown but profoundly desirable, (2) the coming deliverer, (3) one who is good and terrible, (4) one who rescues the prodigal, (5) one who exchanges his life for another, and (6) one who conquers death.

One Who Is Unknown but Profoundly Desirable

As the story continues, a beaver quietly motions to them. They are disoriented and afraid, and they don't understand what is going on. With hushed words, the beaver tells the children they are not safe in the open. Tumnus had instructed the beaver to meet the children should anything happen to him. The beaver then presented a handkerchief to the children as a token, the one Lucy had given Mr. Tumnus. Lucy recognizes it immediately. Mr. Beaver tells them that Tumnus arranged for him to find them if anything happened and take them to safety. Then he tells them something that has a profound effect on them:

> "They say Aslan is on the move—perhaps already landed." . . . At the name of Aslan each one of the children felt something jump in his inside. Edmund felt a sensation of mysterious horror. Peter felt suddenly brave and adventurous. Susan felt as if some delicious smell or some delightful strain of music had just floated by her. And Lucy got the feeling you have when you wake up in the morning and realize that it is the beginning of the holidays or the beginning of summer.[74]

This is the first time they have heard the name Aslan, and they will never be the same.

Several important features surface in this scene. First, Lewis gives the reader a glimpse of each child's personal experience with longing or *Sehnsucht*. Again, Lewis believed this longing was satisfied in God (treasure, call). Lewis believes that we all have this longing, so it stands to reason that Muslim people share in this.

Second, though veiled and unfamiliar, Lewis also identifies the object of longing by name (translation, treasure). This moment is evocatively framed with atmospheric qualities of fear, deceit, uncertainty,

---

73. Though my focus is Islamic theism, it should be noted that this challenge is relevant for all belief profiles.

74. Lewis, *Lion*, 210.

vulnerability, and bewilderment, yet grace unforgettably breaks into the children's despair with a name: Aslan. Dr. Fong Choon Sam, in his lecture "A Narnia Inspired Imagination in Calling and Missions," recounts an unmistakable beginning in his path to the Christian faith when he first read this as a boy in Singapore. Sam warmly reflects,

> When I read this I think a very curious thing happened to me too. And I was around the age of ten at that time. It did feel like something big had come into my small life. I, I didn't have the words for it then. Today I would say that it felt like somebody had visited me in my house. Or it also felt like somebody had invited me into something that, that I could not understand. That something big, something big had come, and had come to ask me to go somewhere, away from all that I knew. Aslan is on the move.[75]

Sam would later hear the gospel from a friend, but he believes the Lord used *The Lion, the Witch and the Wardrobe* to prepare him to receive Jesus later.

Notice a third point: the children's response to Aslan differs according to the kind of person (tension, call). There is not a single effect. For some, there is both longing and separation from the object of desire—like a dream to which you wish to return. Edmund, however, is horrified like a guilty sinner before the holy justice of God (see Isa 6; Gen 3:7; cf. 2:25) (tension, call). This is true of any reader, and this includes Muslims. Again, Lewis suggests to the reader that one's moral state also impacts one's response to God.

The Coming Deliverer

Mr. Beaver leads the children to his home. Mrs. Beaver has kindly prepared a meal, and Lucy asks about Mr. Tumnus. The Beavers explain that Mr. Tumnus has almost certainly been taken to the witch's house, most likely turned to stone. Lucy is distraught. She knows she is the reason Mr. Tumnus has been taken, and she is convinced something must be done. Mrs. Beaver's reply is kind but sobering: alone, they have no chance of facing the witch and getting out alive. Peter also feels responsible for the faun, even with this news. Although the Beavers do not believe the children can do anything, they are hopeful now that Aslan is reportedly on the move.

---

75. Sam, "Narnia Inspired Imagination," 34:47–35:30.

The children are eager to hear more about this Aslan, with the feeling of good news once more stirring in them. The Beavers can hardly believe their ears and explain he is the King, though not often in Narnia. Edmund wonders if the witch can turn him to stone, but Mr. Beaver laughs. The witch will be lucky if she can look him in the face, Mr. Beaver remarks. With that, he quotes the Narnian hopes of Aslan's coming deliverance; when the brokenness of the world will be put to order, sorrows will be no more, winter will pass away, and spring will dawn. He is the Great Lion—not safe, but good. The children are scared but also excited at the prospect of meeting him.

There are several significant features in this challenge. First, Lewis importantly distinguishes Aslan from all peers. Who is Aslan, and implicitly, who is Jesus? Aslan is greater than the witch, King of the woods, Son of the Emperor-Beyond-the-Sea, and King of the beasts (translation, treasure, tension, concern). This also quietly subverts the sin of *shirk* in some tacit ways because, according to Aslan in *The Voyage of the Dawn Treader*, he goes by another name in our world (tension, concern).[76] It also sets Jesus's name above Muhammad and anyone else. Second, though unsettling and terrible in power, Aslan is also good and desirable (treasure, tension). This facet also distinguishes Aslan and, correspondingly, Jesus from his peers (translation, concern, call). Third, Aslan is the long-anticipated deliverer in a way that recalls Jesus. Aslan's arrival cosmically thaws the witch's sway over Narnia. Similarly, in Jesus's first coming, miracles revealed his authority to restore the brokenness of the world, and his deliverance from the demonic shows his authority over Satan. Jesus was and is the long-anticipated deliverer (Luke 1:26–5; 7:18–23) and promises a day is coming when all will be made new (Rev 21:1–8) (translation, transformation, treasure, tension, concern).

One Who Is Good and Terrible

As the Beavers tell the Pevensie children about Aslan, Lucy notices that Edmund is not with them. They call out for him, but they can't find Edmund anywhere. As the children frantically search, Mr. Beaver alarms them by telling them he must have betrayed them and gone to the witch.

Mr. Beaver asks if Edmund had ever been to Narnia before and, if so, whom he had met. The children know Edmund had come; they did

---

76. Lewis, *Voyage*, 779.

not know he had met anyone. Mr. Beaver tells them he sensed that their brother had the look of someone who had joined the witch's side.

Mr. and Mrs. Beaver eventually bring Peter, Susan, and Lucy to Aslan. He is standing at the center of a crowd of creatures. When the Beavers and Pevensie children first see Aslan, they don't know what to do. The narrator explains that the children were cured of any idea that something cannot be both "good and terrible at the same time" when they first saw Aslan's face. The group struggles to decide who should approach Aslan. Peter concludes that he should speak, but he is nervous. Aslan welcomes them all by name, and they feel a sense of peace in his presence. Aslan next asks about Edmund. They explain his betrayal, and Peter confesses to some of the blame, admitting that his anger helped push Edmund away. Lewis potently conveys Aslan's response: "Aslan said nothing either to excuse Peter or to blame him but merely stood looking at him with his great unchanging eyes. And it seemed to all of them that there was nothing to be said."[77]

Notice that in this challenge, Lewis once again distinguishes between two kingdom types: there are those who belong to Aslan, long for Aslan, and manifest his ways, and there are those who belong to the witch and manifest her ways (see Eph 2:1–10) (translation, treasure). This is relevant for all readers. Second, Lewis brings to life something of what it looks like to stand before the all-seeing eyes of truth and justice (tension, call). There are no excuses. There can be grace, but there are no excuses. This is familiar to Islam in one sense, but the holy judge is not Allah in this world. Aslan has another name. Third, Lewis helpfully translates the surprising attractiveness of holiness, and this is relevant for any worldview (treasure, translation).

One Who Rescues the Prodigal

As the story continues, Lucy is heartbroken for Edmund and pleads with Aslan to help. Can Edmund be saved? Aslan's reply is sobering but hopeful and authoritative. Aslan reassures her that everything will be done, but the cost will be high.

As the story develops, Edmund's hopeless state is much worse than he can imagine. He has grossly misjudged the witch. Instead of giving him Turkish Delight, Edmund is enslaved and forced to walk further than he

---

77. Lewis, *Lion*, 250.

thought a person was capable of walking. As her magic winter comes to an end and spring bursts forth, the witch becomes increasingly desperate. As she contemplates the prophecies of four thrones in Cair Paravel, it occurs to her that killing Edmund would stop the prophecy; there would only be three occupied thrones. She sharpens her knife, ready to cut his throat. But a rescue party from Aslan arrives just in time. They spare his life and bring him to safety.

The next morning, Edmund has a weighty private conversation with Aslan. After they speak, Aslan brings Edmund to his siblings, telling them there is no need to discuss what is past. Edmund is apologetic about the way he has behaved, and makes it clear that they are friends again.

Almost immediately, news comes that the witch requests an audience with Aslan. She is claiming her right to Edmund's life as a traitor under the Deep Magic, established by the Emperor-Over-the-Sea at the dawn of time. She has a claim on every traitor, a right to take their life. Astonishingly, Aslan affirms the witch's words, and rebuffs with a frown Susan's suggestion that they could work against the Emperor's Magic. Aslan speaks to the witch alone in what feels like hours. After the lengthy discussion, Aslan says that he has settled the matter and the witch has agreed to relinquish her claim on Edmund's life.[78]

There are several features to note. First, Lewis helpfully translates sin and accountability (translation, tension). There is true moral guilt and accountability for sin. The Deep Magic does not bend. Notice second that Aslan is Edmund's advocate (treasure, translation). Without compromising the Deep Magic, Aslan delivers the prodigal (translation). Third, notice that Edmund does nothing for his own deliverance, in contrast to Islamic salvation. He does not perform his way to forgiveness, and the scales of his life are entirely weighted toward guilt, but Aslan sets him free (translation, treasure). This recalls the gospel (see Rom 5:8; Eph 2:8–9). We will later see Aslan's personal cost. Assurance of forgiveness is not something that Islam promises. Moreover, these themes are repeated in Muslim conversion stories as points of relevance. Edmund's forgiveness is at odds with the burden of self-salvation in Islam (tension, treasure, translation, call).[79] The scales of righteousness are tipped by grace.

---

78. Lewis, *Lion*, 261.

79. See Khalil and Bilici, "Conversion Out of Islam"; Sidlo, "Deconversion Narratives"; Seckler, *Experiencing the Gospel*, 87.

One Who Exchanges His Life for Another

At this point in the story, what no one knows yet is that Aslan has agreed to exchange his own life for Edmund's freedom. In a later scene, Aslan's mood is abnormally melancholy. The camp has moved in preparation for the witch's coming siege. With counsel from Aslan, Peter prepares the centaurs and others, but Peter is surprised to hear that Aslan might not join them in the battle. Aslan seems burdened and depressed. Susan and Lucy are concerned too and find that they can't sleep that night. They are certain that either something is going to happen to him, or he is about to do something. The girls catch a glimpse of Aslan slowly walking away into the woods, looking tired and burdened, and follow him. Eventually, they can no longer hide, and Aslan asks why they are following him. The girls explain that they can't sleep and ask permission to stay with him. After some pause, Aslan agrees. The night is heavy, and he can use the company.

As they walk along, Aslan looks increasingly frail and weak. Susan and Lucy ask what's wrong, and he admits to being lonely and sad. He asks them to put their hands in his mane for comfort. As they walk, they see that he is leading them up the hill where the Stone Table stands. Aslan stops and bids farewell to the girls, telling them to stay hidden.[80]

At the top of the hill, a great crowd of wicked creatures is standing around the Stone Table with burning torches, led by the witch. Afraid at first, the witch is delighted that Aslan has come and orders him bound. Aslan goes willingly, patiently, and bravely, allowing himself to be shaved and muzzled. After muzzling and tying him, the crowd begin kicking, hitting, spitting, and jeering at him. Struggling, they then hoist him to the Stone Table, while the witch prepares her stone knife, just as she had begun to do when she tried to kill Edmund.

As the witch approaches Aslan's head, her face twitches with passion, but Aslan remains quiet and looks up at the sky. The witch's voice quivers as she stoops to deride Aslan to his face:

> And now, who has won? Fool, did you think that by all this you would save the human traitor? Now I will kill you instead of him as our pact was and so the Deep Magic will be appeased. But when you are dead what will prevent me from killing him as well? And who will take him out of my hand then? Understand that you

---

80. Lewis, *Lion*, 266.

have given me Narnia forever, you have lost your own life and you have not saved his. In that knowledge, despair and die.[81]

She then kills him.

This is a powerful scene, echoing Jesus's sacrificial death in the place of sinners. First, Aslan dies (translation, tension). This is consistent with the historical record about Jesus's death on the cross, but it is at odds with the common belief of Muslims that Jesus did not die on the cross. Second, this contagiously illustrates the goodness of Aslan and, correspondingly, Jesus by showing the cost he paid to deliver a prodigal (treasure, translation, call). Unlike Muslim salvation, this is an alien righteousness. Edmund brings nothing to tip the scales of justice in his favor. Notice third that Aslan's death "appeases" the Deep Magic (treasure, translation, tension, call). This is consistent with true forgiveness, and it is part of assurance. As discussed before, assurance is a true tension for the Muslim faith. Muslims do not believe assurance is fitting, yet this prodigal has it. Furthermore, Aslan tells Edmund's siblings that there is no need to talk about Edmund's offense; Aslan is taking care of it (treasure, translation, tension, call).

One Who Conquers Death

After killing Aslan, the witch immediately turns her attention to Aslan's camp. With Aslan dead, the witch is convinced she and her people can make light work of the humans and Aslan's followers. After the witch and her savage people have departed, Lucy and Susan immediately go to the hilltop, where they can see Aslan's body lying dead. The girls kiss Aslan's face, which is now cold, and affectionately stroke his fur. The girls are undone and cry until they have no more tears. They struggle to untie his body, but unexpected help comes as mice nibble away the cords surrounding Aslan's body.

By this time, it is very early in the morning, and it is slowly getting lighter. The girls decide to walk some to see if they can get warmer. As they are looking out to the east, the girls hear a deafening crack over their shoulders, but they are scared to look back. It sounded like a giant had broken an enormous plate, and Lucy clutches Susan's arm. The Stone Table is broken in two, and Aslan is gone. The girls can hardly believe it. Now they've taken Aslan's body. Susan wonders if it is more magic.

---

81. Lewis, *Lion*, 269.

Unexpectedly, a great voice behind Susan and Lucy answers, "Yes!" It is Aslan himself, restored to life. Susan can barely speak and wonders if she sees a ghost. But Aslan stoops to her and licks her forehead, and a rich smell from his mane surrounds her. The girls fling themselves on Aslan and cover him with kisses. The girls are still confused about what they have seen, but Aslan unforgettably explains:

> Though the Witch knew the Deep Magic, there is a magic deeper still which she did not know. Her knowledge goes back only to the dawn of time. But if she could have looked a little further back, into the stillness and the darkness before Time dawned, she would have read there a different incantation. She would have known that when a willing victim who had committed no treachery was killed in a traitor's stead, the Table would crack and Death itself would start working backward.[82]

This challenge has several key features. First, this scene helpfully translates the hopelessness of despair and the hope of Christ's resurrection (treasure, translation). This is at odds with Islam's view of Jesus and his life. It also baptizes one's imagination with a taste of the gospel. Second, there is a clear glimpse of sovereign purpose and plan, one that existed before time began (translation). Third, it translates and reemphasizes the innocence and love of Christ—Aslan is the innocent and willing one who exchanges his life for the traitor (treasure, translation, tension, call). Again, this is at odds with Islamic soteriology. Greater still, this is another taste of the gospel: sinners like us have an innocent and willing Savior who exchanged his life to deliver us from our treachery (treasure, translation, tension, call).

CONCLUSION

Frances, an Iranian diaspora Muslim, studied literature at the University of Nottingham in the 1970s, ultimately obtaining an MPhil and PhD in literature.[83] Although not the only factor that influenced her, Narnia played a significant role in her becoming a Christian. She read and reread the *Narnia* books many times and was intrigued by the figure of Aslan. Around age ten or eleven, she began to understand that Aslan represented Jesus. She describes meeting Aslan in Narnia like passing through a

---

82. Lewis, *Lion*, 274.
83. Miller, "Secret World of God," 5.

doorway of the wardrobe that she could not return from. Her impression of Islam was that there was a distinct sense of fatalism, whereas Jesus was human and accessible: "He understands, he is there."[84] It wasn't until she was in her twenties that her Christian faith was solidified through interactions with Christians and regular church attendance, but *The Chronicles of Narnia* also contributed to her journey.

C. S. Lewis once wrote, "Let us suppose that there were a land like Narnia and that the Son of God, as He became a Man in our world, became a Lion there, and then imagine what would happen."[85] This is how Lewis wrote *The Chronicles of Narnia*. With his imagination, Lewis explored what it might be like for the Son of God to enter a land of talking beasts. Using *The Lion, the Witch and the Wardrobe*, I have shown several ways Narnia can communicate Christian truth at relevant points of need and concern identified in the literature for Muslims. Others are possible, but I highlighted seven challenges: (1) walking myths, (2) kidnapped innocence, (3) the cost of truth, (4) family rejection, (5) witch's food, (6) the moral facet of unbelief, and (7) Aslan.[86]

As I note elsewhere, after former atheist Holly Ordway became open to the existence of God, she still struggled to accept the concept of God becoming a man. This is doubtless a problem for some Muslims as well (as a Muslim, Frances struggled with the title "Son of God"). *The Chronicles of Narnia* helped Ordway and Frances see, and may help future Muslims know, the wonder of the incarnation. God's greatness exceeds transcendence alone; he is also Immanuel.

---

84. Miller, "Secret World of God," 5.
85. Lewis, *Collected Letters*, 3:480.
86. Some relevant challenges from other worldview profiles include the challenge of: coming judgment (*Last Battle*), no greater love (*Magician's Nephew*), forgiveness (*Magician's Nephew*), and Aslan's kingdom (*Magician's Nephew*).

6

Engaging Naturalism

with *The Voyage of the Dawn Treader*

INTRODUCTION

IN *THE VOYAGE OF the Dawn Treader*, Eustace Scrubb providentially finds himself breathing the air of a world he doesn't believe in, and he wants no part of it. He is a man of information, a man of science and progress. For him, the real world is a world of cause and effect, explainable by the laws of nature. He has no time for make-believe worlds of talking beasts and unseen creatures. It doesn't matter if he hears animals talking or if the make-believe ocean splashes his face; what is certain is that the physical world he knows in England is all there is. As Carl Sagan famously quipped, "The Cosmos is all that is or ever was or ever will be."[1] Eustace embodies much of the spirit of the age in any context where naturalism reigns.[2]

The second worldview profile that I explore is naturalism. In one sense "naturalism" is not an obvious cross-cultural worldview for those in Western cultures, since the outlook of scientific materialism is so much a part of the air we breathe. But naturalism is cross-cultural to many living

---

1. Sagan, *Cosmos*, 1.
2. Non-Western naturalists have naturalistic "traits" that could also be affected by this. Amita Chatterjee distinguishes between methodological, ontological, and moral aspects of naturalism that appear in Indian philosophy. See Chatterjee, "Naturalism in Classical Indian Philosophy."

in the West. Furthermore, it is important to note that there are naturalistic worldviews globally, both indigenous, such as certain schools of Indian philosophy, and under Western influence, such as the dialectical materialist Marxist worldview that is the politically dominant ideology of China. So Christians face the challenge of engaging naturalism throughout the world. Like the previous chapter, this chapter begins by briefly explaining the contours of naturalism, based in part on Sire's classic worldview profile. Next, I identify some of the most critical barriers and needs for apologetic engagement with this belief system. Finally, I use the six keys to show how Narnia advocates Christian belief to naturalism through *The Voyage of the Dawn Treader*.

WHAT IS NATURALISM?

Naturalism is broadly understood as the belief that there is nothing like God or the supernatural and that reality is "exhausted by nature."[3] In this view, everything that exists operates by natural, unguided causes: reality is "nothing but" the material. Unlike atheism, which maintains that God or gods do not exist, naturalism focuses on the nature of the world. James Sire's profile of naturalism is a helpful overview of this worldview. Sire highlights eight core features of naturalism in response to the worldview questions previously identified.

1. "Prime reality is matter. Matter exists eternally and is all there is. God does not exist."[4] In this view, there is nothing beyond the physical world. The history and story of the world can be explained in physical terms alone. Sire points to astrophysicist Carl Sagan's famous words as an apt summary of this fundamental belief: "The cosmos is all that is, or ever was, or ever will be."[5]

2. "The cosmos exists as a uniformity of cause and effect in a closed system."[6] This means naturalism denies the possibility of miracles, creation, divine intervention, and ultimate purpose. As atheist Richard Dawkins argues, "The universe we observe has precisely the properties we should expect if there is at the bottom, no

---

3. Papineau, "Naturalism," para. 1.
4. Sire, *Universe Next Door*, 57.
5. Sire, *Universe Next Door*, 57.
6. Sire, *Universe Next Door*, 59.

design, no purpose, no evil and no good. Nothing but blind pitiless indifference."[7]

3. "Human beings are complex machines; personality is an interrelation of chemical and physical properties we do not yet fully understand."[8] The key point that Sire makes is that human beings are "part of the cosmos," and are, thus strictly speaking, "matter."[9] Again, Dawkins illustrates this: "DNA," he writes, "neither knows nor cares. DNA just is. And we dance to its music."[10]

4. "Death is extinction of personality and individuality."[11] Sire explains that when the matter that constitutes an individual "is disorganizes at death," that person "disappears."[12] Accordingly, based on the Humanist Manifesto II, Sire notes, the only sense of "immortality" that one can hope for as a naturalist is the influence one has on others.[13]

5. "Through our innate and autonomous human reason, including the methods of science, we can know the universe."[14] Sire explains that the "faculty of reason and the thoughts human beings come to have are taken as a givens" that developed by the "contingencies of natural evolution."[15] Human knowledge, he explains, is the "product of human reason grounded in its perceived ability to reach the truth about human beings in the world."[16]

6. "Morality is related only to human beings."[17] Although naturalists and theists often share many moral values, such as justice and compassion, when examining the Humanist Manifesto II, Sire notes that the "*basis* for these norms is radically different."[18] Sire explains, "For the naturalist, values are constructed" by humans based on what

---

7. Dawkins, *River Out of Eden*, 133.
8. Sire, *Universe Next Door*, 61.
9. Sire, *Universe Next Door*, 62.
10. Dawkins, *River Out of Eden*, 133.
11. Sire, *Universe Next Door*, 63.
12. Sire, *Universe Next Door*, 63.
13. Sire, *Universe Next Door*, 64.
14. Sire, *Universe Next Door*, 64.
15. Sire, *Universe Next Door*, 65.
16. Sire, *Universe Next Door*, 65.
17. Sire, *Universe Next Door*, 65.
18. Sire, *Universe Next Door*, 66.

the Humanist Manifesto II calls "human need and interest."[19] Accordingly, there was no sense of right and wrong prior to human consciousness and existence.[20]

7. "History is a linear stream of events linked by cause and effect but without an overarching purpose."[21] According to Sire, history for the naturalist is "what we make it to be," and "the only meaning" for human events is the meaning humans ascribe to these events.[22] Sire explains, "When we go, human history disappears, and natural history goes on its way alone."[23]

8. "Core commitments are adopted unwittingly or chosen by individuals."[24] Naturalism does not have any defined core commitments. Instead, individual naturalists choose their goals and commitments. Although naturalists often conform to "the norms of their community" and advocate "secular human flourishing," there is nothing in the naturalist worldview that requires this.[25]

Sire's eight distinctives provide some important background for cross-cultural apologetics to this worldview. Next, I will consider some of the needs and barriers for cross-cultural apologetics to this general worldview.

WHAT ARE THE NEEDS AND BARRIERS IN APOLOGETICS TO NATURALISTS?

There are a number of significant needs and barriers to Christian belief for naturalism that are identified in the literature.[26] On a naturalistic

19. Sire, *Universe Next Door*, 66–67.
20. Sire, *Universe Next Door*, 66.
21. Sire, *Universe Next Door*, 70.
22. Sire, *Universe Next Door*, 73.
23. Sire, *Universe Next Door*, 73.
24. Sire, *Universe Next Door*, 73.
25. Sire, *Universe Next Door*, 73.
26. For example, Tawa J. Anderson, W. Michael Clark, and David K. Naugle note that naturalism understands: (1) humans as the outcome of accidental collocations of atoms, (2) that the world is self-existing, (3) that knowledge is best discovered through science via observation, experimentation, and rational analysis, (4) that the world just is the way it is, (5) that human value is nothing higher than the human race, (6) that religion is destructive, (7) that peace and harmony are found away from religion, (8) that there is no ultimate purpose in life, (9) that human life ends in death, and (10)

view, religion is often seen as irrational, divisive and harmful. Faith is frequently seen as "blind faith," in the absence or even face of observable evidence, and in conflict with science and reason. Religion is seen as causing wars, violence, and division, pointing to the Christian Crusades and Islamic holy wars as examples. Religious morality is seen as oppressive and harmful to minorities, especially women and individuals who identify as LGBTQ+.

Engaging naturalism also faces a particular challenge in the contemporary West, that of "paradigm dominance." Naturalism is culturally embedded in the dominant assumptions of Western culture. This overriding obstacle is important to understand before seeing how narrative apologetics addresses some of naturalism's more specific objections and barriers.

How Paradigm Shifts Happen

Many thinkers have recognized the power of dominant mental and cultural frameworks, or "paradigms," in shaping our beliefs. Philosopher of science Thomas Kuhn explored this idea in his famous work, *The Structure of Scientific Revolutions*. Kuhn challenged the common belief that scientific progress moves forward in a simple, objective, step-by-step way. Instead, he argues that science often goes through periods of calm, marked by the consensus of the dominant scientific community, until they hit a time of crisis and sudden change, a "paradigm shift." Paradigm shifts happen from time to time following the build-up of significant anomalies, of new facts that do not fit the existing model. Under the weight of mounting data, scientists grow discontented with the prevailing model, and a revolutionary paradigm emerges, taking the place of the old dominant model. Kuhn even uses the language of "conversion experience" to describe *suprarational* factors of paradigm shifts in scientific thought.[27]

---

that history is linear but has no purpose. Anderson et al., *Introduction to Christian Worldview*, 242–52. Similarly, Steve Wilkens and Mark L. Sanford note: (1) that religion is understood as destructive and dividing, (2) that unity and peace can be had without religion, (3) that technology has great potential, (4) that naturalism is the best explanation of the world, (5) that it has the best means of achieving the highest aspirations of life, (6) that the laws of nature are orderly and predictable, and (7) that naturalists are generally on a quest for the good life. Wilkens and Sanford, *Hidden Worldviews*, 100–19. Also see Detzler and Potter, *Cross-Cultural Apologetics*, ch. 9; Moreland, *Scientism and Secularism*.

27. Kuhn, *Scientific Revolutions*, 204.

Suprarational factors are elements that go beyond reason, such as imagination, intuition, and personal or cultural values—the very areas that narrative apologetics seek to engage. Kuhn illustrates his understanding of these suprarational aspects of paradigm shifts with a scientist who now finds himself "fully persuaded by a new view but unable to internalize it and be at home in the world it helps to shape."[28] Kuhn writes,

> Intellectually such a man has made his choice, but the *conversion* required if it is to be effective eludes him. He may use the new theory nonetheless, but he will do so as a foreigner in a *foreign environment*, an alternative available to him only because there are natives already there. His work is parasitic on theirs, for he *lacks the constellation of mental sets* which future members of the community will acquire through education.[29]

The scientist's lack of mental sets, in Kuhn's work, is consistent with an underdeveloped imagination. To deeply consider a truth, one must be able to *imagine* it. Kuhn's scientist is a "foreigner in a foreign environment"; he "lacks the constellation of mental sets," even though "natives" (those who already indwell the new paradigm) are already there. The scientist has trouble imagining the new model in an existentially compelling way.

Around the same time that Kuhn's book was published, sociologist Peter Berger coined the term *plausibility structure*.[30] Berger defines this structure as "the social context in which any cognitive or normative definition of reality is plausible."[31] Elsewhere Berger explains that beliefs are socially constructed and maintained, so a dominant paradigm in a given context goes nearly unchallenged.[32] If you live within a specific cultural paradigm, you experience an ongoing though often unspoken pressure to conform, both internally in your beliefs and externally in how you speak and act. Berger illustrates this belief structure in the Catholic principle "*Extra ecclesiam nulla salus*—'There is no salvation outside the church.'" In earlier times, Rome was much less tolerant of other faiths. At that time, there was "no doubt as to *which* church was meant."[33] Increased tolerance and the prevalence of other faith traditions have had the result that "the

---

28. Kuhn, *Scientific Revolutions*, 204.
29. Kuhn, *Scientific Revolutions*, 204; emphasis added.
30. Berger and Luckmann, *Social Construction of Reality*; Berger, *Sacred Canopy*.
31. Berger, *Many Altars of Modernity*, 31.
32. Berger, *Sacred Canopy*, 45.
33. Berger, *Many Altars of Modernity*, 31.

believing individual finds him- or herself facing the possibility of doubt, on whatever level of sophistication."[34] Berger explains, "It was easy, indeed almost inevitable, to be a self-assured Catholic in an Austrian mountain village a couple of centuries ago. It is much less easy, and definitely not inevitable, to be so today in Vienna."[35] Both Kuhn and Berger see the influence of your context or culture as the dominant paradigm or plausibility structure, as a significant factor in what beliefs you accept.

Dominant Barriers and Dispositions

Communicating Christianity, particularly in the West, must engage naturalism as a dominant paradigm. The ethos of naturalism directly challenges theistic belief, both societally and personally. In his influential monograph *A Secular Age*, philosopher Charles Taylor observes that five hundred years ago, nonbelief in God was nearly unthinkable, but that is no longer the case today.[36] There was a significant shift of focus away from belief and dependence on the "enchanted world," where God was believed to be involved in the world, to what Taylor calls the "immanent frame," where we tend to think and live as if this world is all there is, even for those who profess belief in God.[37] In addition to this, scientific advances have given scientific thought a high degree of prestige, challenging domains of thought previously dominated by religion.[38] As missiologist Lesslie Newbigin observes, Western culture is a pagan culture born out of a *rejection* of Christianity. Drawing on Berger's concept of plausibility structure, Newbigin notes that because of its roots, Western culture's disposition is exceptionally hostile to Christian truth claims. It thrives on what is empirically verifiable and balks at the notion of divine revelation.[39]

Several other naturalistic cultural dispositions are barriers to Christian belief: a general spirit of humanism or optimism about scientific progress; a sense of autonomy from the need for supernatural intervention; a spirit of intellectual superiority over theists who are seen as being

---

34. Berger, *Many Altars of Modernity*, 31.
35. Berger, *Many Altars of Modernity*, 31.
36. Taylor, *Secular Age*, 556. See also 25.
37. Taylor, *Secular Age*, 25.
38. See DeWitt, *Worldviews*, 148; Plantinga, *Where the Conflict*, 3–8.
39. Newbigin, *Foolishness to the Greeks*, 14.

self-deceived; a tendency toward reductionism; a belief that the laws of nature are without telos or inherent purpose; a reliance on what we can see; and a general trust in the impartiality of reason within the dominant paradigm.[40]

As we saw earlier, before his conversion, Lewis was an atheist and resonated with these general dispositions. In a letter to his close friend dated October 12, 1916, when Lewis was nearly eighteen he rejected all religions as lacking proof. He saw them as myths invented by humans, and Christianity as a cult that had sprung up to elevate Jesus from philosopher and teacher into a god. Not many years later, Lewis expressed words that sound like a different person: "I believe in Christianity as I believe that the Sun has risen, not only because I see it but because by it, I see everything else."[41] So, what changed? The short answer: a lot.

IMAGINATION AND A CLIMATE OF FAVORABLE CONDITIONS

Lewis's autobiography describes how George MacDonald's book *Phantastes* broke through and "baptised" his imagination. Imaginative literature made a significant difference to one who once described himself as the most reluctant convert in all England.[42] Lewis reflected that he got far more than he bargained for when he bought and read *Phantastes*.[43] MacDonald went past Lewis's watchful dragons, and he didn't see it coming. Once he could see, Lewis stood in awe of grace, and likened himself to a prodigal who didn't even walk home himself, but had to be brought in by a Love that carried him to salvation, kicking and resisting.[44]

Lewis's experience certainly gave him an appreciation for the fertile soil of the imagination, even in a time of religious decline. As we saw in chapter 1, Lewis recognized in his essay "The Decline of Religion" the role of the "intellectual climate" in creating "favorable conditions" for belief.[45]

---

40. Dawkins, *God Delusion*; also see Barbour, *When Science Meets Religion*.
41. Lewis, "Is Theology Poetry?" 164–65.
42. Lewis, *Surprised by Joy*, 279.
43. Lewis, *Surprised by Joy*, 222.
44. Lewis, *Surprised by Joy*, 279.
45. Lewis, "Decline of Religion," 221.

Lewis's experience with the transforming force of literature is echoed more recently in the life of former atheist English professor Holly Ordway. Ordway writes, "I was an atheist, and a hostile one, who agreed with the New Atheists that Christianity was not just false, but irrational and harmful."[46] She writes that although historical apologetics eventually played a role in her conversion, "I was so firmly an atheist, I found the very idea of faith to be so repellent that I *would not have listened* to the arguments that ultimately convinced me."[47]

As a literary scholar, Ordway was reading seventeenth-century metaphysical poet John Donne's sonnet "Batter my heart, three-person'd God." She recalls that she didn't believe intellectually what he believed, but on the other hand, she recognized Donne was no fool. She was moved deeply by the words, "Batter my heart three-person'd God . . . and bend / Your force to break, blow, burn, and make me new."[48] Ordway was gaining, in the face of her intellectual beliefs, the imaginative experience of a relationship with the living God—imagination awoke her. For the first time, she thought, "I would like to know something more about this thing called faith, because maybe it is deeper and more interesting than I thought."[49]

Ordway says that imagination stirred her, historical apologetics convinced her, but then *The Chronicles of Narnia* helped her to grasp the difficult notion of the incarnation of God.[50] Lewis and Ordway, both formerly hostile atheists, and both academics, are witnesses of literature's potential to subvert naturalism.

The Dragons of Zeitgeist and the Lewisian Supposal

Much of Lewis's fiction quietly challenges the dispositions and plausibility structure of the naturalistic worldview. *The Chronicles of Narnia* is one such place, but we should keep in mind that Lewis did not create Narnia as an allegory of Christian truths. As we saw in chapter 1, Lewis started creatively with images, and wrote fairy tales because, as a genre, they allowed him to express his ideas best. Lewis then realized that fairy tales could "steal past watchful dragons"—inhibitions or dispositions that blocked thoughtful

---

46. Ordway, *Apologetics*, 9.
47. Ordway, *Apologetics*, 9.
48. Donne, "Batter," lines 1, 3–4.
49. Biola, "Imagination in Service to Truth," 11:42.
50. Ordway, *Apologetics*, 9.

consideration of Christian belief—so that the ideas could, for the first time, "appear in their real potency."[51] This happened to Lewis while reading *Phantastes*, and it is something that he evokes in his writing.

THE VOYAGE OF THE DAWN TREADER'S CHALLENGES TO NATURALISM

There are at least six significant ways *The Voyage of the Dawn Treader* challenges naturalism.[52] None of these guarantees a change in belief. However, they invite a kind of imaginative baptism for the reader who enters the story with wonder.

The Challenge of Displacement

A first way that Lewis challenges the adequacy of naturalism is by *displacement*. Lewis creates a character and transports him to a vivid, lifelike world where he has real experiences that do not fit his categories or beliefs. In *The Voyage of the Dawn Treader*, Eustace Scrubb is taken on an unexpected trip, against his will, to a world he *does not believe in*. Eustace and the enchanted reader experience an intense feeling of the loss of control, and a bombardment of sensory data that *should not* exist.

Eustace is transported from a mid-twentieth-century England, one that is consistent with the reader's primary world, to Narnia, an unknown world that is also real. Eustace, along with Lucy and Edmund, providentially enter Narnia through a painting in Eustace's spare bedroom. They are unexplainably transported into the untamed waters of a real sea, with wind blowing, waves crashing, and the smell of the ocean.[53]

Eustace's frailty and overwhelming loss of control are felt deeply as he finds himself thrown into the sea.[54] The scene is intensified by the fact that Eustace cannot swim, and the water is frigid. The three children emerge in an unexpected world with a sea quest underway. Eustace, Lucy, and Edmund are hoisted out of the salty water by ropes from the crew of the ship *Dawn Treader*, under the authority of King Caspian. Because Lucy and Edmund Pevensie have been to Narnia, they know Caspian and

---

51. Lewis, "Sometimes Fairy Stories," 58.
52. There is some interdependence in these categories.
53. Lewis, *Voyage*, 616.
54. Lewis, *Voyage*, 616.

recognize the Narnian world, but Eustace is shocked by his environment and is in denial. Through tears, Eustace demands to be taken home, to the confusion of Caspian, who only sees the Narnian world. Bewildered, Eustace tries to find the way back, looking for the picture frame and doorway back to his world, but sees only the ocean.[55] Lewis's art intensely portrays Eustace's disorientation as he tries to get his bearings in a world that should not exist. All the emotions evoked by fears of drowning, scratching for air, unexpected rescue as a rope pulls the children to safety, and even the subtle description of the sea's salty air, form a real world to be inhabited by the reader. This is a world that Eustace does not believe should exist, yet all his experiences disagree. He is like Kuhn's scientist—Eustace is a foreigner in a foreign environment. He lacks the constellation of mental sets, but the natives are already there. These sentiments are familiar in yet another way. Lewis describes his own reluctance to believe as an atheist in his *Surprised by Joy*. He writes of feeling pursued by God, but fearing to meet him, and also strongly resisting, eventually giving in as a "reluctant convert," only recognizing, looking back, God's grace in accepting him even in his reluctance.[56] Like Eustace, belief was foreign to Lewis, but a new paradigm was at hand.

This challenge of displacement offers a translation of the experience of a paradigm shift by casting Eustace into a world that he does not believe in. This recalls the naturalist experiencing the Christian worldview. It is foreign, unfamiliar, something he does not believe in, but it is real (translation). In Van den Toren's terms, it "retains its strangeness," but becomes "bit by bit more familiar."[57] The fact that Eustace is taken against his will recalls Lewis's own experience of conversion. Lewis was brought in kicking and struggling, looking for an opportunity to escape, which resembles Eustace's attitude on being brought into Narnia.[58] Eustace is providentially carried in against his will (translation). An existential angst is also created by the feelings of drowning. The weight of mortality and fear of death are pressures that invite naturalists to seek a sure foundation (tension, call). That Eustace will not believe in the world in front of him raises a mirror to the possibility of willful unbelief (call, tension).

55. Lewis, *Voyage*, 618.
56. Lewis, *Surprised by Joy*, 279.
57. Van den Toren, "Challenges and Possibilities," 51.
58. Lewis, *Surprised by Joy*, 279.

The Challenge of an Alternative Plausibility Structure

Lewis also helps the reader to experience through Eustace's eyes a world with an alternative plausibility structure, one where unbelief and an unrelenting passion for "progress" is in the minority, and belief in Aslan and the enchanted world of medieval cosmology are the controlling zeitgeist. In mildly suggestive ways, Eustace personifies certain features of the progressive man of science. Eustace is said to be good at botany, likes pinning beetles down on cards, and he likes books of facts and figures (in implied contrast to stories).[59] Eustace comes from a trendy modern family who are vegetarians, nonsmokers, and teetotalers.[60] Even after arriving in the medieval Narnian world, Eustace awkwardly asks for "Plumptree's Vitaminised Nerve Food," and requests that it be made with distilled water.[61] Eustace bemoans the inferior technology of the *Dawn Treader* itself, comparing it to modern ships, planes, and submarines, and complains about the *Dawn Treader*'s lack of modern conveniences like a saloon, radio, bathrooms, and deck chairs.[62]

Eustace's challenged plausibility structure is most clearly conveyed by his unbelief in the face of what is obvious to others. Before arriving in the Narnian world, Eustace mocks Edmund and Lucy's belief in Narnia as a silly game. In his journal labeled August 7, Eustace wonders if he is dreaming, and his conceit magnifies his blindness. He insists to himself that a storm is raging (rather than him being unused to travel at sea) and in an ironic twist, accuses everyone else of shutting their eyes to facts.

Similarly, Eustace insists on regarding Reepicheep as a well-trained rodent, even though in Narnia he is the most courageous of Talking Beasts. When Eustace first sees Reepicheep, he is disgusted and dismisses him as a performing animal.[63]

Moreover, Eustace incessantly demands English justice in Narnia: he claims he could "bring an action" against Caspian to have Reepicheep destroyed, claims he will "lodge a disposition" against them all with the British Consul, and regularly wonders when he will finally have access to the British Consul, as though he is not in Narnia but in some far-flung part of his own world.

59. Lewis, *Voyage*, 612.
60. Lewis, *Voyage*, 611.
61. Lewis, *Voyage*, 618.
62. Lewis, *Voyage*, 629.
63. Lewis, *Voyage*, 619.

Even after Eustace undergoes a kind of conversion (which we will come to), he retains a shadow of his former plausibility structure. In a later scene, Eustace is puzzled by a star named Ramandu, who has human features. "In our world," said Eustace, "a star is a huge ball of flaming gas."[64] Eustace's words echo the reductionism of a naturalist plausibility structure. Ramandu's reply is both a gracious rebuke and a subtle challenge to the adequacy of such a system: "Even in your world, my son, that is not what a star is but only what it is made of."[65] Remember, Eustace's world is representative of the reader's world. Ramandu's distinction recalls Aristotle's four causes. Eustace's world, and the naturalist's world, is often fixated on the material cause. Ramandu informs Eustace that reality is more than material, even in England.

Next, Ramandu immediately points to personhood—he tells Eustace he already knows a star, because he has met Coriakin. In this way, Lewis juxtaposes a kind of personhood with materialism. In one sense, Lewis contrasts the "discarded image" of the medieval world, where the sky teemed with life, against the reductionism of modernity—dispositions consistent with naturalism.[66] In another sense, perhaps unintentionally, Ramandu and Coriakin evoke images of what the late theologian Francis Schaeffer called "the mannishness of man"[67]—persons are much more than biochemical makeup. This point is amplified by the context, since Coriakin's morality and the consequences of his actions are in view.[68]

There are several observations in this challenge. First, Lewis challenges the sentiment of progress and self-deceit that is sometimes presented by Western society. The mirror in this context, however, shows that the unbeliever is the one who is self-deceived (translation, tension, call). Lewis's appeal to something greater than a material cause invites the reader to imagine reality as more than matter and suggestively challenges naturalism's explanatory power (tension, call).

---

64. Lewis, *Voyage*, 752.

65. Lewis, *Voyage*, 752.

66. Lewis, *Discarded Image*. A medieval literature expert, Lewis maintains that an image or model of the universe stands behind the writers of the period. They viewed the world as charged with life.

67. Schaeffer, *Complete Works*, 24.

68. Lewis, *Voyage*, 752.

The Challenge of Teleology

A third challenge is to the disposition that rejects teleology in the natural world, rejecting any inherent purpose in nature.[69] Providence and purpose are especially evident in Lucy and Edmund's lives. One such thread stretches from the children's first time in Narnia through the end of the work. As the book begins, Lucy and Edmund sit in their room in England. The children have traveled to Narnia twice, and nostalgia fills their minds. Lewis writes that while most of us have a secret country that is only an imaginary country, theirs was real.[70] Their longing is compounded by the fact that they were given a near promise that they would one day return to Narnia, but magic is the only way of getting in.[71] Also, in their room, there is a lifelike picture of a ship on the wall, which looks distinctively Narnian in style, and evokes longing for Narnia in them. Lewis's contagious use of cosmic promise, magic, longing, and other-worldly existence press against assumptions of blind forces and reductionism. When Lucy first arrives on the ship, juxtaposed with Eustace's horror, Lucy finds herself at home and expects they will have a lovely voyage.[72] Lucy's anticipation draws on her belief in providence and recent experience, in contrast to the cynicism of Eustace's disenchanted, naturalistic outlook.

This challenge presents several features. First, the world, though unbelievable to Eustace, is also desirable and good (translation, treasure). Moreover, it is real (tension). Lewis suggests that this world is providentially governed; it is not a world of chance. Furthermore, naturalism as a worldview struggles to account for ultimate purpose (tension, call).

The Challenge of Un-Dragoning

A later part of the story powerfully conveys the thread of providence and purpose through Eustace's experiences. Eustace becomes an actual dragon after taking enchanted treasure on one of the islands they discover,

---

69. Oxford scientist and outspoken atheist Richard Dawkins expresses the sentiments of some naturalists regarding the question of providence and purpose in the world: "All appearances to the contrary, the only watchmaker in nature is the blind forces of physics, albeit deployed in a very special way." Dawkins, *Blind Watchmaker*, 5.

70. Lewis, *Voyage*, 613.

71. Lewis, *Voyage*, 613.

72. Lewis, *Voyage*, 620.

due to his dragon-like, greedy desires.[73] Imprisoned by dragon skin, like someone who suddenly loses all hearing, Eustace is overwhelmed with hopelessness, and he begins to cry large, hot dragon tears.[74] There is nothing Eustace can do, and as days slowly drag by, he discovers that there is nothing Lucy, Edmund, or anyone else on the *Dawn Treader* can do for him either. Worse yet, because of his size, weight, and even hunger, Eustace is now a significant obstacle to continuing their voyage.

But one night, a huge lion unexpectedly and slowly approaches him. Even though he is a dragon, Eustace is afraid of the lion in a way that recalls encountering God's holiness. The lion calls Eustace to follow him and leads him to the top of a mountain he has never seen, where there is a garden, and in the middle of the garden, a well. Eustace has an injury to his leg, so he wants to bathe to ease the pain in his leg, but the lion tells him that to enter the water, he must undress his dragon skin. With futile desperation, Eustace tries multiple times to cast his scales off, with only limited success. The lion indicates he will have to undress him. Eustace submits, and though it feels like he is being torn to his very heart, he emerges a boy again and is thrown into the water.[75] Eustace returns to shore, clothed and "un-dragoned," where he meets Edmund.[76] Edmund replies to Eustace's account that he has seen Aslan.[77] Eustace no longer hates hearing Aslan's name but instead apologizes for how he has behaved all along.[78] As the book unfolds, Eustace reflects a substantial change of heart and character. Later, after returning to his own world, others remark how much he has changed for the better.[79]

Eustace is imprisoned in a way that reflects the perversity of his heart. He can only change himself in inconsequential ways (translation). Eustace requires an outside intervention; specifically, he requires Aslan (translation, treasure). Eustace's encounter with Aslan is deeply painful; it pierces his heart, but it also sets him free from his dark, beastly flesh (translation, treasure). Eustace is un-dragoned and now clothed physically and metaphorically in Aslan-wrought clothes and skin (translation, transformation, treasure, call).

73. Lewis, *Voyage*, 670.
74. Lewis, *Voyage*, 669.
75. Lewis, *Voyage*, 682.
76. Lewis, *Voyage*, 683.
77. Lewis, *Voyage*, 683.
78. Lewis, *Voyage*, 683.
79. Lewis, *Voyage*, 780.

Eustace's deliverance is also more than natural, so it challenges a disposition that is opposed to purpose and providence (tension, call). Transformation is not merely social rehabilitation; it is significantly imputed by Aslan (translation, transformation, tension, call). Aslan approaches Eustace—he is active in this world. With regal authority, Aslan looks directly into Eustace's eyes. Although physically larger, Eustace feels dread under Aslan's gaze, and he closes his eyes in fear. Aslan remains. Eustace must follow. At the well, Aslan is present but patient; he waits for Eustace to recognize his own need and fitting despondency. Aslan knows that he is the solution, but Eustace must acknowledge his own futility (translation, tension, call). Lewis challenges the spirit of autonomy, sense of control, the feeling that God is uninvolved, and again hints that some blindness is self-imposed (translation, tension, concern, call).

The Challenge to the Primacy of Sight

"Seeing is believing," the saying goes, and the primacy of sight is a common objection to theism by naturalists. If God is real, why can't we see him? Why doesn't he make himself more obvious?[80] Lewis challenges this general disposition in *The Voyage of the Dawn Treader*. In the Island of Voices, Lucy is forced by an invisible people, the Duffers, to go to the magician's home to break their invisibility spell. She is to find the book of spells to make everything visible. After reading the spell, it occurs to her that the effects may be much greater than she thought. She realizes that there might be many other unseen things, and she is not sure she wants to meet all of them.[81]

Several features challenge the primacy of sight in this scene. First, Lucy is sent to this house by an invisible people. The people have been made invisible, which suggests a power or magic that exceeds natural functions. Additionally, Lucy's concerns about others within the unseen world highlight both her belief in the likelihood of unseen creatures and the real possibility that some may be beyond her control, or even undesirable (translation, transformation, tension).

---

80. This is reflected in John Wisdom's well-known parable of the Invisible Gardner. Antony Flew famously asks, "Just how does what you call an invisible, intangible, eternally elusive gardener differ from an imaginary gardener or even from no gardener at all?" Flew et al., "Theology & Falsification," 13.

81. Lewis, *Voyage*, 716.

Next, having cast the spell, Lucy expects that she will see the now-visible magician. Instead, she sees Aslan himself standing calmly in the doorway with kingly grandeur. Lucy runs to him, delighted that he has come, but Aslan says he was present all along.[82]

Here Lewis intimately depicts Aslan's nearness and hiddenness, against the primacy of sight. Moreover, the deeper laws ordained by Aslan reflect purpose, not capriciousness. It is no accident that Aslan is concealed. The world is haunted with Aslan's nearness, though he has chosen to remain unseen. The story creates a plausibility structure supporting the reality of the unseen and that is antithetical to an undue dependence on sight. It even cultivates a measure of warmth toward the unseen (translation, transformation, treasure, tension, concern, call).

Added to this, the story suggests the nature of personal autonomy and the limitations of finite minds as reasons for Aslan's hiddenness. In a later scene, the magician asks Aslan if he intends to show himself to the Duffers after they have all been made visible. Aslan declines, so that he will not terrify the Duffers. It will be a long time before they are ready to see him.[83] Although Aslan's purposes are beyond our ken, invisibility is only for a season (translation, concern).

A little later in the scene, Aslan informs Lucy and the magician that he must leave, but promises Lucy they will meet again soon. She asks when that will be: "I call all times soon," says Aslan, before vanishing. "It's always like that, you can't keep him; it's not as if he were a *tame* lion," observes the magician.[84] Although Aslan's kingly independence quite naturally creates mystery for those who know him, Aslan is still clearly good. Furthermore, he is the unseen object of deep desire for both Lucy and the magician (translation, transformation, treasure, tension, concern, call).

The Challenge of Longing

Lewis believes that if you look intently into yourself, you will discover a deep-seated want or longing, a signpost, for something that the natural world cannot fulfil—something that exceeds the naturalist paradigm.[85] Stronger still, Lewis believes this desire points to God and where God

---

82. Lewis, *Voyage*, 717.
83. Lewis, *Voyage*, 720.
84. Lewis, *Voyage*, 720.
85. Lewis, *Mere Christianity*, 137.

resides.[86] It is something he calls *Joy* or *Sehnsucht*. Joe Puckett explains *Sehnsucht* as "the aching, and yet pleasurable, intense longing for a life that we cannot yet have but naturally and universally crave. It is the feeling of having lost something that we once had—giving us a sense of homesickness and discontentment with the less-than-ideal world we currently find ourselves in."[87] This joy baptized Lewis's imagination while he read MacDonald's *Phantastes* as an atheist. In kind, Lewis threads images that both evoke and depict joy throughout *The Voyage of the Dawn Treader*. Lewis knew firsthand the kind of challenge that *Sehnsucht* could have on one who is closed to the supernatural.

Reepicheep's life is saturated with *Sehnsucht* in *The Voyage of the Dawn Treader*. When he is introduced, longing and hope are already characteristic of his life. Reepicheep lives under a numinous promise, spoken over his life by a dryad when he was still young: "Where sky and water meet, Where the waves grow sweet, Doubt not, Reepicheep, To find all you seek, There is the utter East."[88] Reepicheep does not know what it means, but has been under its spell all his life.[89] Reepicheep is captured by longing and urgency for the eastern horizon. He always feels that the ship is moving too slow, and he loves to sit at the front of the vessel, looking eastward and singing the dryad's song.[90] Although Caspian has great hopes for the voyage to find the seven lost lords of Narnia, Reepicheep has a higher goal: to reach the utter East, and with it, Aslan's Country.[91]

In a final scene, at Aslan's command, Reepicheep, Edmund, Lucy, and Eustace are to proceed east, while the *Dawn Treader* must go west. The children and Reepicheep are surrounded by miles and miles of the sweet, enchanted water of the Last Sea. The air and water are charged

86. Philosopher Peter Kreeft notes that the cost of denying the premise "If nature makes nothing in vain, the One who can sit in this chair must exist" is the price of a meaningful universe in which desires and satisfactions match. By this Kreeft suggests that God can be avoided by embracing the "vanity of vanities"—exchanging "Everything" for "Nothing," in what he calls a "fool's bargain." Kreeft, *Heaven*, 209–10. That said, the conclusion that God satisfies this desire as conceived by Lewis is challenged. For some who oppose the conclusion and/or the general interpretation of Lewis's thought, see Smilde, "Horrid Red Herrings"; Bassham, "Con"; and Beversluis, *Search for Rational Religion*. For some who affirm Lewis's conclusion, see Sloan, "As If Swallowing Light"; Williams, "Pro"; and McGrath, *Intellectual World*, 137–46.

87. Puckett, *Apologetics of Joy*, 26.

88. Lewis, *Voyage*, 623.

89. Lewis, *Voyage*, 623.

90. Lewis, *Voyage*, 630.

91. Lewis, *Voyage*, 623.

with mystery. A current moves them rapidly toward what appears to be a thirty-foot wave, though they are not afraid. As they near the wave, they also see beyond it. The sun brightens substantially, yet they are inexplicably able to see behind it. A range of mountains rises beyond sight and seems to reach outside the world. A sudden but brief breeze strikes them from the east, bringing a scent and a music-like sound that they would never forget—a heartbreakingly beautiful glimpse into Aslan's Country. It is here that Reepicheep goes on alone, leaving his sword behind.

Reepicheep's life presents the reader with a peculiar person who is kind, noble, and adventurous. He is not afraid of death; yet he deeply longs for something that cannot be satisfied in the Narnian world—Aslan's Country.

Lucy's longing echoes Reepicheep's desire. In a closing scene of *The Voyage of the Dawn Treader*, Lucy asks Aslan when they will be able to return to Narnia from England.[92] Aslan replies that she and Edmund will not return to Narnia, which devastates the children. Lucy asks how they can bear never seeing Aslan again, but he reassures them they will, telling them, "But there I have another name. You must learn to know me by that name."[93]

Lewis presents the reader with the longing that he experienced, that his atheism was inadequate to explain or satisfy. If Lewis is right about *Sehnsucht*, the object of this longing transcends the impersonal laws of naturalism. Although embodied in fantasy, *Sehnsucht* enchants our world and points explicitly to Aslan—he just goes by another name.

There are several things that are worth noting in this challenge. First, Lewis's use of atmosphere is contagious and powerful. The atmosphere allows him to cultivate longing in the reader for both Aslan and his country (treasure, call). This challenge is important because longing is satisfied in Aslan and his country (treasure, translation, call). Longing is something that led Lewis to Jesus. In *Mere Christianity*, Lewis argues that our desires point to the reality of the thing desired, such as hunger pointing to the reality of food.[94] But there are some desires that don't have fulfillment in the physical world. In *The Weight of Glory*, he says, "If I find in myself a desire which no experience in this world can satisfy, the most probable explanation is that I was made for another world."[95] These

---

92. Lewis, *Voyage*, 779.
93. Lewis, *Voyage*, 779.
94. Lewis, *Mere Christianity*, 136.
95. Lewis, *Weight of Glory*, 34.

whispers of longing mirrored in Reepicheep's life are like faint calls of our greater country.

CONCLUSION

I have identified six significant ways that *The Voyage of the Dawn Treader* challenges naturalism: (1) the challenge of displacement, (2) the challenge of an alternative plausibility structure, (3) the challenge of teleology, (4) the challenge of un-dragoning, (5) the challenge to the primacy of sight, and (6) the challenge of longing. More are certainly possible.

Lewis creates favorable conditions for belief by inviting the reader to enter a secondary world where a supernatural worldview is the dominant plausibility structure. It is a world that feels different than the Western world, where naturalism is a dominant paradigm. Although some will not appreciate Lewis's challenge, its force is felt strongest in the reader who enters Narnia. Starr explains a deeper facet to this otherworldly knowing:

> If the author whose book I'm reading has done his job, my experience of the work will cause me to respond emotionally to it. If he has taken me through an experience which tells something of the true nature of *my own* world, and if I am drawn by the aesthetic pleasure of my encounter, then he has inspired in me not just a sentiment—a subjective emotional response—but a just sentiment, an emotional response that corresponds with the way things really are.[96]

Lewis invites his reader to a world much like he experienced while reading *Phantastes*, a world that baptized the imagination of an atheist and naturalist who in time became one of the twentieth century's most influential Christian voices. The one who encounters something of the true nature of the world in Narnia returns to the primary world with the "veil of familiarity" faintly torn, and Lord willing, with a subtle longing stirred up for the one who un-dragons twisted hearts.

---

96. Starr, "How *Should* We Teach English?" 74.

7

Engaging the Ontological Argument

in *The Silver Chair*

INTRODUCTION

THIS CHAPTER IS DIFFERENT: rather than focusing on a particular worldview, I want to take a side-step to explore another way C. S. Lewis challenges naturalism, which is the ontological argument for God's existence. This philosophical argument seeks to offer a proof of God's existence based on the definition of God and nature of being. A version of it can be found embedded in the narrative of *The Silver Chair*, with Lewis bringing it to life imaginatively. His deployment of this argument quietly but forcefully challenges the naturalist worldview and makes a case for belief in God to receptive readers. This challenge is more formal than other examples, but while the format is different from other challenges, it still features aspects of several of the narrative keys we have been examining (call, concern, tension, treasure).

TOWARD THE CREATION OF FAVORABLE CONDITIONS IN PLATO'S CAVE

The Silver Chair is the sixth novel according to Narnian chronology. Jill Pole and Eustace Scrubb are called from England by Aslan into Narnia to find Prince Rilian, who has been missing for ten years. Rilian has been kidnapped by the Lady of the Green Kirtle, a witch who is queen of the Underland. But she has bewitched him, causing Rilian to believe that she is good. Each night Rilian's enchantment subsides momentarily. The problem is that he thinks these are psychotic episodes, so he freely confines himself to the silver chair to protect himself and others from his "maddened state." He is only released when the witch's enchantment controls him again.

Jill, Eustace, and their guide, Puddleglum, a peculiar Marsh-wiggle, are led to the underworld from Narnia. Providentially, the queen is away, and following the signs given to them by Aslan, the three release Rilian from the bondage of the silver chair. Their operation is, however, thwarted when the queen arrives just as they are making their escape. She is silently enraged and has murder in her eyes. She attempts to re-enchant Rilian as well as Jill, Eustace, and Puddleglum, and to convince them that Narnia, the sun, and Aslan do not exist in reality—those are the pretend beliefs of children. Her magic engulfs the air like a thick fog, and the truth becomes nearly impossible for them to see. The enchantment is almost complete.

ANSELM IN PLATO'S CAVE

It is this context, a dark world of shadows, doubt, glimpses of truth, and challenged belief that Lewis weaves a narrative form of an ontological argument through an unlikely figure, Puddleglum:

> Suppose we have only dreamed, or made up, all those things—trees and grass and sun and moon and stars and Aslan himself. Suppose we have. Then all I can say is that, in that case, the made-up things seem a good deal more important than the real ones. Suppose this black pit of a kingdom of yours is the only world. Well, it strikes me as a pretty poor one. . . . I'm on Aslan's side even if there isn't any Aslan to lead it. I'm going to live as like a Narnian as I can even if there isn't any Narnia.[1]

There are two significant ways that Lewis challenges the naturalist worldview and advocates theism here: (1) through a kind of Platonic cave and (2) through an ontological argument.

First, Lewis's story recalls Plato's cave in *The Republic*, where prisoners are shackled and can only see shadows on the wall from a fire behind

---

1. Lewis, *Silver Chair*, 908–9.

them. These prisoners falsely believe the shadows exhaust reality.[2] Paul Tyson notes that in Plato's dialogues, Socrates frequently "existentially, religiously, and relationally embodies that which the dialogue is concerned with."[3] Tyson continues, "The rich dramatic structure of Plato's dialogues makes the kind of openings possible that allows the careful reader to 'see' more than can be simply said (or written)."[4]

In Lewis's story, a Socrates-like voice is *sent* into a cave-like shadowland. Puddleglum is the Socrates figure, sent to a bewitched underworld that struggles to believe in the transcendent reality beyond the cave. Those who recognize Plato know that those who are in the cave falsely embrace a world of shadows rather than reality. Only those who escape the bondage of the underworld can see the truth and understand what is Real.[5] In this way, Lewis challenges a Western plausibility structure that religiously clings to the empirical and is skeptical of the transcendent. Furthermore, this context skillfully surrounds and complements an even more forceful challenge to the atheistic worldview, one that explicitly advocates theism to Lewis's readers.

A second way that Lewis challenges the naturalistic worldview is through an ontological argument. In responding to a letter by Nancy Warner on October 16, 1963, Lewis commends her son for his keen observation of his veiled argument: "He must thank Anselm and Descartes for it, not me. I have simply put the 'Ontological Proof' in a form suitable for children. And even that is not so remarkable a feat as you might think. You can get into children's heads a good deal which is quite beyond the Bishop of Woolwich."[6] Lewis contrasts a child's potential grasp or at least recognizes a seminal form of the ontological argument with what he regarded as a profound inadequacy in John A. T. Robinson's thought ("the Bishop of Woolwich").[7] An adaptation of Stephen Davis's

---

2. Plato, *Republic*, 240–48.

3. Tyson, *Returning to Reality*, 130.

4. Tyson, *Returning to Reality*, 130.

5. David Schindler argues, "Many modern readers of Plato emphasize the unity of form and content in his dialogues. But they do not often point to the connection between this philosophical 'style' and the figure of Socrates himself, who embodied philosophy for Plato. . . . Socrates breaks open the cave allegory and descends into it, form and content converge in an extraordinary manner." Schindler, *Plato's Critique*, 168.

6. Lewis, *Collected Letters*, 3:1472.

7. Lewis, *Collected Letters*, 3:1422. Why the hostility? Lewis believed John A. T. Robinson's writing subverted the Christian faith. Michael Gehring explains, "Lewis did not vacillate on what he believed was required of clergy, bishops, and theologians if

formulation based on the text of Anselm's *Proslogion II* helps appreciate Lewis's Anselm-like argument in *The Silver Chair*.[8]

1. God is understood or defined as a being "than which nothing greater can be conceived" (the Greatest Conceivable Being, or GCB). Even the fool possesses this concept.
2. Things can exist in only two ways: in the mind and in reality.
3. The GCB can possibly exist in reality—i.e., is not an impossible thing.
4. Whatever exists only in the mind and might possibly also exist in reality might have been greater than it is.
5. The GCB exists only in the mind.
6. The GCB might have been greater than it is.
7. The GCB is a being than which a greater is conceivable.
8. It is false that the GCB exists only in the mind.
9. Therefore, the GCB exists both in the mind and in reality.

Reminiscent of Anselm's Fool, Puddleglum can and does *conceive* of Aslan despite significant pressure to disbelieve premise 1 (above). In Anselm's words:

> Indeed, we believe You to be something than which nothing greater can be thought. Or is there, then, no such nature [as You], for the Fool has said in his heart that God does not exist? [Pss 13:1 and 52:1] But surely when this very same Fool hears my words "something than which nothing greater can be thought," he understands what he hears. And what he understands is in his understanding, even if he does not understand [i.e., judge] it to exist. For that a thing is in the understanding is distinct from understanding that [this] thing exists.[9]

Puddleglum is a kind of "anti-Fool." Unlike Anselm's Fool, Puddleglum *believes* in Aslan. The queen tries to deceive Puddleglum (her enchantment echoing the power of a plausibility structure to pressure us to embrace certain beliefs), while Anselm's Fool is self-deceived.

---

they departed from orthodox Christianity. There was no gray. Abide within the lines of orthodoxy or, if you transgressed them and are an honest man, you should resign from your teaching office." Gehring, *Oxbridge Evangelist*, 207.

8. Davis, "Ontological Argument," 95. Note: premise 1 draws on Douglas Groothuis's formulation. See Groothuis, *Christian Apologetics*, 184.

9. Anselm, *Philosophical and Theological Treatises*, 93–94.

Puddleglum's character, though sincere in many ways and faithful to Narnia, is depicted as socially awkward and a deeply pessimistic simpleton of sorts—he is like a fool. In one scene, when Eustace and Jill ask Puddleglum his name, he awkwardly offers it, while dolefully expecting the children to forget it so that he will need to tell them again.[10] Later, when Puddleglum and the children meet the Gentle Giants, a people Puddleglum strongly distrusts, he is offered a drink. Because he is skeptical of the giants, the children and the reader expect him to reject it, in case it is poisoned. Instead, mindlessly, Puddleglum sips and sips, commenting as he drinks that it is probably unsafe, but he does not stop. He becomes so drunk that he can barely walk.

This same Puddleglum answers the queen's patronizing skepticism about Aslan in a way that recalls premise 1. Delimited by the restraints of a children's fairy tale, Puddleglum possesses the imaginative equivalent of a GCB in his *mind*: "Suppose we have only dreamed, or made up, all those things—trees and grass and sun and moon and stars *and Aslan himself*."[11] Lewis's stated intent combined with the genre-restrictive nature of children's fantasy provide good reason to recognize a seminal or informal version of this argument. In personal correspondence, Greg Welty, philosopher at Southeastern Baptist Theological Seminary, helpfully explains how Lewis's argument could be valid:

> If (1) Lewis's concept of Aslan is that he is "the greatest being," *and* (2) Lewis's unstated conception of what it takes to be "the greatest being" is that *he is the greatest conceivable being*, then what we have in Lewis just is a valid ontological argument. Since Lewis is only stating an "informal" version of this argument in a children's fantasy book, he doesn't have to explicitly state (2), even if he believed that (1) implies it. Rather, he only communicates (1) (Aslan is the greatest), but he regarded it as implying (2) (Aslan is the greatest conceivable). Most informal statements of an argument have enthymematic premises like this.[12]

Welty continues, "I do think you have to have (2) to have a valid ontological argument, or at least Anselm's version of it. But that doesn't mean that Lewis had to explicitly state (2). It might just be implied by his concept of 'greatest.'"[13]

10. Lewis, *Silver Chair*, 830.
11. Lewis, *Silver Chair*, 908; emphasis added.
12. Greg Welty, email message to author, December 15, 2022.
13. Greg Welty, email message to author, December 15, 2022.

The immediate context presupposes the question of Aslan's existence. Lewis inserts a subtle, though significant, distinction between Puddleglum's mental conception of the abundant goodness of the created order vis-à-vis "Aslan himself"—Aslan is greater. To appreciate the contrast, consider how Puddleglum had just described the created order when the witch's enchantment began. Puddleglum is fighting the witch's enchantment as he speaks: "But I know I was there once. I've seen the sky full of stars. I've seen the sun coming up out of the sea of a morning and sinking behind the mountains at night. And *I've seen him up in the midday sky when I couldn't look at him for brightness.*"[14] Puddleglum remembers the wonder and beauty of the Narnian world; stars, and the brightness of the midday sun shining in all its brilliance, but Aslan is greater still.

The immediate context says more about Aslan. The witch-queen cynically questions the four captives about Aslan. Though Puddleglum is present, Eustace tells her that Aslan is the great Lion who called them out of England, in order to find Prince Rilian.[15] Notice Aslan exercises authority and providence in England as well as Narnia. This is even more significant for the reader because England most naturally represents the reader's world throughout *The Chronicles of Narnia*.[16] Moreover, we see that Aslan is the ultimate deliverer of Rilian. While others believe Rilian to be dead, Aslan knows precisely where and how Rilian is captive. It is Aslan who initiates the rescue mission that is guided by Puddleglum, and he possesses knowledge that is consistent with him being all-knowing and all-present, like Christ.

In an earlier scene, Puddleglum talks about the ancient ruins they find themselves in using language reminiscent of the foreknowledge, power, and providence normally attributed to God in Christian thought: "There *are* no accidents. Our guide is Aslan; and he was there when the giant King caused the letters to be cut, and he knew already all things that would come of them; including *this*."[17] Aslan is in control. He existed before. He providentially leads. He knows the future. He is present before and throughout time.[18]

---

14. Lewis, *Silver Chair*, 905; emphasis added.

15. Lewis, *Silver Chair*, 905.

16. In a closing scene of *Voyage*, Edmond and Lucy desperately wonder if they will ever see Aslan again. Aslan replies that in England he goes by another name. Lewis, *Voyage*, 779.

17. Lewis, *Silver Chair*, 887.

18. This reflects Lewis's understanding of Aslan as a supposal of how Christ might

The inhabitants of Narnia seem to have an oral tradition that includes prophecies as well as the general awareness of Aslan's ways in *The Chronicles of Narnia*, such as the prophecies the Beavers tell the children in *The Lion, the Witch and the Wardrobe*.[19] In this vein, we can infer that Puddleglum would know about Aslan's actions and attributes from the stories handed down about him. These include Aslan's *ex nihilo* creation of Narnia and the talking animals in *The Magician's Nephew*; and from the events of *The Lion, the Witch and the Wardrobe*, Aslan's goodness, death, and resurrection as a gracious ransom for Edmund; Aslan's authority over the dominion of evil depicted cosmically via thawing ice and the coming of Christmas; and that Aslan is not safe or tame but he is good.

Curiously, Puddleglum's belief is also implicitly affirmed by the witch's questions. She suggests that his belief of Aslan in his mind as a dream does not equal his existence in reality. Donald Williams proposes that the witch's reductionism could be taken as a rebuttal aimed at a superficial version of the ontological argument: "Just because you have imagined Aslan does not mean that he exists."[20] Taken as a whole, within the language and parameters of children's fantasy, as well as Lewis's own admission, Aslan is a kind of GCB. Accordingly, premise 1 is presented in a seminal way that is consistent with the genre.

Premise 2 states that things can exist in only two ways: in the mind and in reality. Puddleglum's question centers exclusively on two states: reality (understood in the cave as only the witch's underworld) or in the mind (the allegedly made-up world of Aslan and Narnia). Puddleglum asks, "*Suppose* we have *only dreamed*, or made up, all those things."[21] The reader is also brought to consider the general truthfulness of something like premise 2.

Premise 3 states that the GCB can possibly exist in reality—i.e., it is not an impossible thing. The term *GCB* is not explicitly used by Lewis, though the genre again has to be taken into consideration, and as we saw, Aslan is implicitly the GCB of Narnia. That said, the witch does not challenge the coherence of Aslan as a concept, and there is nothing that seems to be incoherent or self-contradictory about Aslan from within the parameters of the imaginative world (the way a square circle or a married bachelor would be). Instead, the witch accuses Puddleglum and

---

become incarnate in a world like Narnia; see Lewis, *Collected Letters*, 3:480.

19. Lewis, *Lion*, 217.
20. Williams, "Anselm and Aslan," 37.
21. Lewis, *Silver Chair*, 906; emphasis added.

the others with a kind of childish Freudian projection: "You have seen lamps, and so you imagined a bigger and better lamp and called it the sun. You've seen cats, and now you want a bigger and better cat, and it's to be called a *lion*."[22] In virtue of Puddleglum's prima facie belief about Aslan's existence (the point under debate) and his own mental conception of Aslan (one cannot conceive of a married bachelor or a square circle), it is appropriate to conclude that Puddleglum regards Aslan as possible. Again, the reader, in kind, is invited to recognize that Aslan (a kind of GCB) is a possibly existing thing.

Premise 4 states that whatever exists only in the mind and might possibly also exist in reality might have been greater than it is. There are two ways this is broadly affirmed. First, as noted before, the witch describes the sun as an imagined "bigger and better lamp," and lions as a "bigger and better cat."[23] Although she is mocking, she also implicitly affirms that to exist in reality is greater than to merely exist in the mind. Puddleglum intimates this kind of value judgment about reality. The premise is affirmed in a second way through Puddleglum. He maintains that if the witch is correct, and Aslan and the Overworld are *only* in his mind, then Aslan and his created world would be even *greater* if they existed in reality. As Puddleglum expresses to the skeptical witch, "the made-up things seem a *good deal more important* than the real ones."[24] He continues, "Suppose this black pit of a kingdom of yours is the *only* world. Well, it strikes me as a pretty poor one."[25]

Finally, Puddleglum claims that if the four captives are just being childish because of such beliefs, they have somehow managed to conceive in their minds as children a world that "licks" the witch's *real* world "hollow."[26] When compared to the real existence of Aslan and Aslan's world, a world that Puddleglum *remembers*, to the world the witch is advancing, the black pit of her kingdom pales in comparison. A natural inference is that Aslan's real existence would be greater since it seems "a good deal more important." Aslan would be greater if he existed in reality *and* in Puddleglum's mind. Again, the reader is invited to consider these truth claims generally.[27]

22. Lewis, *Silver Chair*, 905.
23. Lewis, *Silver Chair*, 905.
24. Lewis, *Silver Chair*, 906; emphasis added.
25. Lewis, *Silver Chair*, 906; emphasis added.
26. Lewis, *Silver Chair*, 907.
27. It should be noted that Anselm's argument was also something of a devotional

Davis calls this Anselm's hidden premise because it is not explicitly stated by Anselm, though his argument needs it. As Davis explains, "The basic idea is that things are greater if they exist both in the mind and in reality than they would be if they existed merely in the mind."[28] For example, the legendary woodsman Paul Bunyan would be *greater* than he is if he existed in both the mind and in reality.[29] For the reader, a GCB that exists in reality and in the mind is greater than a GCB that exists only in the mind because it is more powerful, freer, and able to do things it could not if it only existed in the mind.[30]

Premise 5 states that the GCB exists only in the mind. Anselm asks us to assume that the GCB does not exist.[31] This is what the witch has been telling Puddleglum and the others all along, that the sun and Aslan are just imaginary, childish exaggerations of lamps and cats.[32]

Puddleglum *contemplates* this possibility, which invites the reader to do so too. For argument, he *supposes* all these things, even Aslan himself, are made up, and the witch's world is the only one.[33] "Suppose" is used twice for emphasis. Anselm, however, introduced premise 5 to refute it by reductio ad absurdum.[34] Douglas Groothuis explains, "If God exists merely in the understanding (existing only in the mind of the fool), then God is not the greatest possible being, since a being that existed in reality would be greater than a being that existed only in the understanding. But God is by definition the greatest possible being" from premise 1.[35] Puddleglum thus contemplates Aslan's nonexistence in a way consistent with premise 5.

Anselm believed that premise 5 combined with premises 1–4 leads to a contradiction that requires *rejecting* premise 5. If premises 5, 3, and 4 are true, then premise 6 follows, since a GCB as a *concept* is not as great as the GCB would be as an *existing* thing; "GCB might have been greater than it is."[36] Concepts have less power and abilities than existing things.[37]

---

reflection about the greatness of God.

28. Davis, "Ontological Argument," 95.
29. Davis, "Ontological Argument," 95.
30. Davis, God, Reason, and Theistic Proofs, 22–23.
31. Davis, God, Reason, and Theistic Proofs, 23.
32. Lewis, Silver Chair, 905.
33. Lewis, Silver Chair, 906.
34. Davis, God, Reason, and Theistic Proofs, 23.
35. Groothuis, Christian Apologetics, 185.
36. Davis, God, Reason, and Theistic Proofs, 24.
37. Davis, "Ontological Argument," 96.

Consider the concept of my wife versus my wife existing in reality: my wife as an existing person has powers and abilities that my wife as a mere concept does not. Similarly, Aslan (the GCB of Narnia) or the GCB as a concept has less powers and abilities than Aslan or the GCB in reality.

Premise 6 says, the GCB might have been greater than it is. As Davis explains, this is *implicitly* contradictory since it says that "the greatest conceivable being might have been greater than it is."[38] This premise is implicitly posited in Puddleglum's response to the witch's ridicule, where he says that their supposedly imaginary world "licks your real world hollow."[39] In this now old-fashioned idiom, to "lick something hollow" is to defeat or outclass as decisively as one can imagine. Puddleglum thus maintains that Aslan and his world might have been greater than it *supposedly is* (i.e., existing *only* in the mind).

To be sure, the narrative is an approximate echo of the argument, whereas Anselm identifies the contradiction explicitly and then says, "But surely this is impossible. Hence, without doubt, something than which a greater cannot be thought exists both in the understanding and in reality."[40] As Davis explains, premise 7 is entailed by premise 6, which states that the GCB is a being than which a greater is conceivable. Premise 7 is an *explicit* contradiction.[41] By reductio ad absurdum one of the premises 1–5 must be false; and premise 5 is the only plausible candidate, because the other premises are truths. Consequently, by reductio ad absurdum, the negation of premise 5 is premise 8: It is false that the GCB exists only in the mind.[42] From premises 2, 4, and 8, premise 9 follows: the GCB exists both in the mind and in reality.[43] The conclusion, following Anselm, is that the GCB exists both in the mind and in reality. Moreover, Anselm also invites the reader to consider something of God's greatness devotionally.

Lewis uses the resources of imagination in the form of children's literature to challenge skepticism about God's existence. It also shows that our ability to imagine and long for something greater, like Aslan, is not wish fulfilment, but a clue to reality in a way that recalls Lewis's argument from desire. In the process, the reader is invited to ponder the greatness of

---

38. Davis, "Ontological Argument," 96.
39. Lewis, *Silver Chair*, 907.
40. Anselm, *Philosophical and Theological Treatises*, 94.
41. Davis, "Ontological Argument," 96.
42. Davis, "Ontological Argument," 96.
43. Davis, "Ontological Argument," 96.

God. For Anselm and the psalmist, "the Fool has said in his heart that God does not exist" (Pss 14:1; 53:1).[44] Lewis's "anti-Fool" agrees—Aslan's alive.

PLOT TWIST OR PARADIGM PRESSURE?

Given the certainty of Anselm's conclusion, Puddleglum's following words appear confusing. Under the witch's sway and the dominance of her beliefs in the context of the cave, Puddleglum seems to shift from the conclusiveness of Anselm's argument to something like Pascal's wager.[45] As we read earlier, in Puddleglum's final words to the witch-queen, he says, "I'm on Aslan's side even if there isn't any Aslan to lead it. I'm going to live as like a Narnian as I can even if there isn't any Narnia."[46] A reasonable case can be made that Lewis simply uses the flexibility of the genre to now introduce something like Pascal's wager, emphasizing the infinite gain of betting on Aslan, if Aslan is real, versus the infinite loss of betting against Aslan and only gaining a life as meaningless and unfulfilling as the underworld.[47]

Another plausible scenario is that Puddleglum *feels* uncertainty under the witch's sway and the dominance of her beliefs in the context of the cave. This is much like a plausibility structure or the pressures of a dominant paradigm. The captive reader would feel some of the same. However, Puddleglum *believes* that Aslan is real with conviction that is consistent with the ontological argument.

---

44. Anselm, *Philosophical and Theological Treatises*, 93–94.

45. Pascal's wager trades on two basic possibilities about reality: either the Christian God exists, or he does not. In this context, either Aslan and the upper world exist or they do not. In a sense, we are already betting whether we like it or not.
In Pascal's wager there are two actions that are possible for everyone: wager on God or not wager on God. Philosopher Liz Jackson's summary of the wager is helpful: "In very general terms, you should wager on God because there is much to gain if you wager on God and God exists, and perhaps also much to lose if you don't wager on God and God exists. If God does not exist, whether you wager on God or not, the stakes are much lower. Given such a cost-benefit analysis, wagering on God is your best bet. Even if there's little evidence for God's existence, wagering on God may nonetheless be appropriate." Jackson, "Pascal's Wager for Christianity."

46. Lewis, *Silver Chair*, 907.

47. There are a number of ways that Pascal's wager fits: (1) two contrasting values regarding ultimate reality—atheism versus Christian theism; (2) the urgency of a decision—the clock is ticking and the decision is inevitable; (3) the inadequacy of reason to know for certain; (4) the virtuous life associated with Narnia regardless of whether or not it is real; and (5) Puddleglum's actual decision. These are all consistent with Pascal's wager.

Thomas Kuhn's celebrated book *The Structure of Scientific Revolutions* recognizes this sort of emotional aspect of belief for a scientist who moves from one dominant paradigm to another. The scientist finds himself "fully persuaded by a new view but unable to internalize it and be at home in the world it helps to shape."[48] A similar experience occurs at away games for major sporting events like soccer's World Cup. The traveling team can be winning on the scoreboard, but a loud and dominant fan base can make the winning team *feel* like they are losing. Puddleglum's true belief is proven by his choice to immediately leave the witch's court and to search for Overland, even at risk of their lives.[49] In this way, the captive reader is invited to follow along. It is after this choice that the witch's true identity is unmasked, and her spell is finally broken. Lewis creatively dramatizes aspects of the ontological argument as a choice of reality over illusion, in a way that challenges naturalism and champions belief in God.

ARGUMENT SUPPOSING

Fairy tales are not only for children. Though Puddleglum appears foolish and unhelpful on the surface, Lewis uses this unlikely hero in a way that challenges naturalism and advocates theism. He uses images that recall Plato's cave, and cleverly presents a genre-faithful ontological argument that invites more profound thoughts about God. Sent by Aslan, Puddleglum breaks the spell of the witch's shadowland and delivers the captives from its slavery. Anselm's words fit here: "For I do not seek to understand in order to believe, but I believe in order to understand. For I believe even this: that unless I believe, I shall not understand."[50] Lewis's imaginative use of a key apologetics argument ingeniously contributes to what he calls the creation of favorable conditions.

What I find especially helpful for future narrative apologetic writing is what I will call *argument supposing*. To my knowledge, Lewis did not identify his use of the ontological argument as an example of supposal. He did, however, specifically say he had put it into "a form suitable for children."[51] He also says he used supposing with Aslan. I think supposal is an especially fruitful device for writers who find that a story or a character

---

48. Kuhn, *Scientific Revolutions*, 204.
49. Lewis, *Silver Chair*, 907.
50. Anselm, *Philosophical and Theological Treatises*, 93.
51. Lewis, *Collected Letters*, 3:1472.

they are developing could suitably accommodate a relevant argument (e.g., some version of the moral argument, the argument from desire, etc.). Future works can develop this tool, but in the final chapter, I offer some preliminary ideas about themes and stories that are naturally conducive to argument supposing. It would be "in revision" in Tolkien's language (after the world and creating are largely complete), but the creative world and laws of sub-creation would need to remain fully intact and largely undisturbed.[52] I think Lewis models this here in *The Silver Chair*. Very few have noticed this argument.

BUT IS IT SOUND?

There are many arguments for and against Anselm's argument as presented. I will briefly consider two influential objections raised against the argument, though it should be remembered that Lewis's supposal was informal.[53]

In *The Critique of Pure Reason*, Immanuel Kant famously objects that Anselm improperly uses existence as a predicate.[54] As Groothuis explains, Kant argued that existence cannot serve as a predicate or property of God. Rather, a true predicate must *add* information regarding the subject.[55] Consider the difference between "The horse is horse" versus "The horse is fast."[56] If existence does not function as a true predicate (e.g., "God exists"), Anselm's argument fails because Anselm argues from the "concept of God (plus logical principles) to the existence of God" (premise 4).[57] Kant maintains that, similar to how existing is not necessary to the idea of a triangle, existing is not necessary to the idea of God.[58]

Upon closer examination, it does appear that existence can function as a predicate in the relevant sense. Groothuis gives the example of a

52. Carpenter and Tolkien, *Letters of Tolkien*, 172.
53. Another important objection that is noted by Douglas Groothuis is the intelligibility of a GCB. Groothuis argues that the notion of a Perfect Being is not "swamped in mystery." Groothuis maintains that a Perfect Being may be summarized as "a being who possesses every property it is better to have than to lack and who possesses this array of compossible excellent properties to the utmost degree (or to their intrinsic maximum value)." Groothuis, *Christian Apologetics*, 186.
54. Kant, *Critique of Pure Reason*, 563–69.
55. Groothuis, *Christian Apologetics*, 187.
56. Davis, *God, Reason, and Theistic Proofs*, 32.
57. Groothuis, *Christian Apologetics*, 187.
58. Kant, *Critique of Pure Reason*, 565; Groothuis, *Christian Apologetics*, 187.

young girl who listens to her mother read a story that includes both real and unreal animals (e.g., a real lion and an unreal unicorn). He writes, "The child may ask of any particular animal, 'Mommy, is that animal real or just in the story?'"—does the animal exist in reality or only in the understanding?[59] In this coherent question and others like it, existence functions as a predicate because it considers the "ontological status" of these animals.[60] In kind, there is no compelling reason to reject existence as a predicate that seeks to consider whether or not God exists in reality.

A second relevant objection concerns whether *existence* adds to the greatness of a thing. Atheist Michael Martin argues, "Even if it is granted that existence is a property, the ontological argument further assumes that existence adds to the greatness of a being . . . it may be the case that existence even detracts from the object's greatness."[61] Martin explains, "God is supposed to be a perfect being. This means that He is all-good, all-knowing, and all-powerful. The assumption that God does not exist does not seem to take away from His perfection, as would, for example, the assumption that He is not all-knowing."[62]

This objection, however, also fails to conclusively undermine Anselm's argument. Although Anselm does not explicitly state what he means by greatness, his intent is restricted to what he does say. *Power* is a plausible candidate.[63] Davis helpfully adds *ability* and *freedom of action* to power.[64] The GCB is uniquely able to act in the world. Greatness conceived in this way is both consistent with Anselm's thought and accomplishes three things, according to Davis: (1) it allows for *comparable greatness* (e.g., coyotes are greater—freer, more powerful, able to do things—than stones; humans are greater than dogs), but it avoids commensurability (e.g., being "more" of a prime number); (2) it *admits maximal degree* (e.g., a GCB can bring about any logically possible state of affairs); and (3) it is *intuitively a great-making property* (e.g., we intuitively feel that an alarm clock is greater than a toothpick).[65] It is in this sense that *existing* things

---

59. Groothuis, *Christian Apologetics*, 188.

60. Groothuis, *Christian Apologetics*, 189. Davis argues, for example, that "Does the Loch Ness monster exist?" functions as a predicate. Davis, *God, Reason, and Theistic Proofs*, 34.

61. Martin, *Atheism*, 81.

62. Martin, *Atheism*, 81.

63. Groothuis, *Christian Apologetics*, 189.

64. Davis, "Ontological Argument," 98.

65. Davis, "Ontological Argument," 98.

are greater than concepts that merely exist in the mind. As Groothuis correctly notes, ideas are "causally inert." When ideas do have consequences, it is because *existing* agents believe ideas and act, creating states of affairs in the world.[66] Although there have been many arguments presented for and against, there is good reason to think that this general version of the argument is sound.[67]

---

66. Groothuis, *Christian Apologetics*, 190.

67. For a thorough consideration of challenges and responses to this argument see, Davis, *God, Reason, and Theistic Proofs*, 15–45 or Davis, "Ontological Argument"; also see Nagasawa, *Maximal God*, and Sijuwade, *Rational Ontological Argument*.

8

Engaging Eastern Mysticism

with *The Magician's Nephew*

INTRODUCTION

THE MAGICIAN'S NEPHEW IS a story about Narnia's origins. In this story, Digory and Polly are privileged to witness the day that Aslan gloriously sings Narnia into existence. Aslan's young world of talking animals teems with beauty, wonder, and innocence. But the innocence is soon tainted at the hands of a son of Adam and daughter of Eve who foolishly unleash a terrible evil into Aslan's beloved world, after Digory is lured by his pride to ring an enchanted bell. The sweeping effects of this single act also lead to relevant themes such as the concept of a personal Creator, the reality of evil, and the love of God.

Because *The Magician's Nephew* presents a Christian view of reality in terms of the Creator-creation distinction and of evil as a distinct yet derivative aspect of reality, it serves as a natural bridge for narrative apologetics to the third worldview I consider, Eastern mysticism. More specifically, I explore Eastern pantheistic monism (hereafter EPM). In this chapter, I first provide a brief overview of EPM, drawing on Sire's classic worldview profile.[1] Next, I identify some of the critical barriers and needs for apologetic engagement with this belief system. Finally, with

---

1. Although there are various Eastern belief systems, I focus on one representative expression, as it overlaps with Hinduism and Buddhism.

special emphasis on *The Magician's Nephew*, I show how Narnia advocates Christian belief to this belief system.

WHAT IS EASTERN PANTHEISTIC MONISM?

Pantheism is, broadly speaking, the belief that God is everything, while monism is the belief that reality is essentially one. As Sire explains, EPM is the basic worldview underlying the Hindu Advaita Vedanta system of Shankara, the Transcendental Meditation of Maharishi Mahesh Yogi, and much of the Upanishads.[2] Because of its similar emphasis on the "singularity of primal reality," Sire includes Buddhist monism in this category, though, as we will see, it is significantly different in seeing ultimate reality as emptiness rather than as monistic being as a "thing."[3] He notes that there are important differences among the various expressions of Eastern thought that are better explained in works of comparative religion.[4] Nevertheless, Sire's worldview profile is helpful for us to get a general understanding of a key strand of Eastern thought.

Using the same worldview questions as we have seen in previous chapters, Sire focuses on eight significant beliefs in this profile:

1. "Atman is Brahman."[5] Atman is understood as the "true inner self of each person," and it is "identical with Brahman, the infinite divine

---

2. Sire, *Universe Next Door*, 137.

3. Sire, *Universe Next Door*, 150.

4. Sire, *Universe Next Door*, 139. As an example, the word *pantheism* is rejected in some Hindu schools of thought. In a round table discussion with Christian scholar Timothy Tennent, a representative of Ramanuja Hinduism explains, "Pantheism is generally used to express a cosmology of total immanence. In other words, Brahman and the universe are regarded as identical: Brahman equals the universe. However, this kind of complete immanence is not what is affirmed in the identity position, for that would mean Brahman is another word for the universe and would completely contradict the body-soul analogy that serves as the basis for a true I-thou devotional relationship of the worshipper with Brahman." Tennent, *Christianity at the Religious Roundtable*. Anderson, Clark, and Naugle write, "Ramanuja agreed with Shankara that there is only one entity that exists, but he argued that it was Saguna Brahman—that is, Brahman with attributes—which he equated with the Hindu god Vishnu. Ramanuja's qualified nonduality reflects the belief and experience of most Hindus because it has supplied the 'intellectual framework' for Hindus who worship a personal god." Anderson et al., *Introduction to Christian Worldview*, 270. Also see, Corduan, *Neighboring Faiths*, 267–311, 313–57.

5. Sire, *Universe Next Door*, 139.

reality behind all existence."⁶ In pantheistic terms, "God is the one, infinite-impersonal, ultimate reality," so anything that appears to exist as a distinct object, including inanimate objects and human beings, are *maya*, which means "illusion."⁷ The implication is that even *maya* does not ultimately exist since everything is Brahman.⁸

2. "Some things are more one than others." According to Sire, this means that reality is a "hierarchy of appearances," ascending from matter "(the least real)" to vegetable life, animal life, and human life (the most real). Humanity, he explains, is also "hierarchical," which means that some people are "closer to unity."⁹ He elaborates: "The Perfect Master, the Enlightened One, the guru are the human beings nearest to pure being... when one is one with the One, consciousness completely disappears and one merely is infinite-impersonal Being."¹⁰

3. "Many (if not all) roads lead to the One." According to Sire, this means that there are "many paths from *maya* to reality." Regardless of the path, Sire explains, we need to be "oriented correctly," which is more "technique" than doctrine. Sire continues, "Almost all these techniques, however, require quiet and solitude. They are methods of intellectually contentless meditation . . . to turn one's soul to the harmony of the cosmos . . . [and] this is the Eastern monistic way of achieving salvation." He explains, one common technique involves chanting the "intellectually contentless" word *Om*—which is only "understood" when a person is "one with the One, when 'Atman is Brahman.'" Sire clarifies, this is not, however, an "epistemological statement," it is an "ontological realization" of "becoming real."¹¹ In this sense, it is based on experience rather than propositional knowledge.

4. "To realize one's oneness with the cosmos is to pass beyond personality." Sire explains that because "Brahman is one and impersonal . . . Atman is impersonal," and consequently, human beings in their

---

6. Peterson et al., "Upanishads," 266.
7. Sire, *Universe Next Door*, 139.
8. Anderson et al., *Introduction to Christian Worldview*, 276.
9. Sire, *Universe Next Door*, 140–41.
10. Sire, *Universe Next Door*, 141. Although Sire does not develop this point, it should be noted that one's caste and gender are impacted by one's karma in Hinduism. This is relevant to questions of worth and meaning for human persons. See, for example, Anderson et al., *Introduction to Christian Worldview*, 273–75, esp. 290–91.
11. Sire, *Universe Next Door*, 141.

"truest, fullest being—are impersonal." Sire clarifies this based on the Mandukya Upanishad. "Atman," he writes, has four progressive conditions or states: "waking life, dreaming life, deep sleep, and 'the awakened life of pure consciousness.' . . . But this 'pure consciousness' is not consciousness; it is pure being."[12] Sire continues, this is why "meditation is the main route to being," and it is characteristically depicted by a Hindu guru "sitting cross-legged on a lonely ledge of a Himalayan peak in rapt contemplation."[13]

5. "To realize one's oneness with the cosmos is to pass beyond knowledge. The principle of noncontradiction does not apply where ultimate reality is concerned." Sire explains it this way: "Knowledge, like personality, demands duality—a knower and a known. But the One is beyond duality; it is sheer unity." Accordingly, Sire continues, this system is non-doctrinal: "No doctrine can be true ["language requires. . . speaker and listener, subject and predicate"]. . . . If there can be no true statement, neither can there be a lie. In other words, truth disappears as a category."[14]

6. "To realize one's oneness with the cosmos is to pass beyond good and evil; the cosmos is perfect at every moment." Sire notes the tension with belief in karma and reincarnation. "Karma," Sire explains, "is the Eastern version of you reap what you sow." He continues, the problem is that "this sounds very much like the description of a moral universe. People *should* do the good. If they do not, they will reap the consequences, if not in this life, in the next. . . . As popularly conceived, a moral universe is what the East in fact has."[15] Even more problematic, Sire explains, "all actions" are illusory because all is Brahman.[16]

7. "Death is the end of individual, personal existence, but it changes nothing essential in an individual's nature."[17] Sire explains the significance of this point in relation to the value of human life: in Eastern thought, "Only Atman is valuable. So death is no big deal."[18]

12. Sire, *Universe Next Door*, 144.
13. Sire, *Universe Next Door*, 145.
14. Sire, *Universe Next Door*, 145–46.
15. Sire, *Universe Next Door*, 146; emphasis added.
16. Sire, *Universe Next Door*, 146–47.
17. Sire, *Universe Next Door*, 148.
18. Sire, *Universe Next Door*, 148.

8. "To realize one's oneness with the One is to pass beyond time. Time is unreal. History is cyclical."[19] Sire notes that because of this, facts in history are of little concern. He explains: "To be concerned with such stuff would be to invert the whole hierarchical order. The unique [like an unrepeatable space-time event] is not the real; only the absolute and all-encompassing is real."[20]

Buddhist Distinctives

Sire next contrasts Advaita Vedanta (nondualist Hinduism) with Buddhism. In Hindu monism, "The One has or, better, *is* Being itself—the single undifferentiated final 'whatever.' It makes sense to name this Brahman or to speak of the One." Conversely, "Buddhist monism holds that final reality is the Void." Sire clarifies that, unlike Brahman in nondualist Hinduism, the Void "cannot be named or grasped." He continues, "The Hindu One is still a thing among things, though it is the chief among things. The Void is not a thing at all. It is instead the origin of every thing."[21]

There are also differences related to the nature of human beings. In Hinduism, Sire writes, "an individual person is a soul (Atman) and thus has substantial (spiritual, not material) reality because it is an emanation of Brahman (reality itself)." Moreover, "in death an individual soul loses its bodily residence but is reincarnated in another individual." Conversely, Sire explains, in Buddhism, a person is a "not-soul," which means there is no "namable nature at the core of each person." Instead, a person is an "aggregate of previous persons."[22]

Religious practices also differ in kind. Sire explains, "Hindus will commonly repeat a mantra, like Om, and thus induce a trance or trance-like state that is taken to be an ascent toward godhood. Buddhists may likewise repeat a mantra, but their goal is to reach a state of realizing their root in nonbeing."[23]

In addition to the eight beliefs already discussed, a ninth can be added: "Core commitments among individual Eastern pantheistic monists may vary widely, but one consistent commitment is, by the

---

19. Sire, *Universe Next Door*, 148.
20. Sire, *Universe Next Door*, 150.
21. Sire, *Universe Next Door*, 150–51.
22. Sire, *Universe Next Door*, 151.
23. Sire, *Universe Next Door*, 151.

elimination of desire, to achieve salvation, that is, to realize one's union with the One (Hinduism) or the Void, pure consciousness (Buddhism)." Sire notes that the path for Hinduism focuses on meditation; Buddhism has an eightfold path: "right view, right intention, right speech, right action, right livelihood, right effort, right mindfulness, and right consciousness." These differ significantly with Christian salvation. Sire notes, "Unlike a Christian who receives salvation as a gift of God's grace, the pantheist is on his or her own."[24]

Sire's nine distinctives for EPM give us a helpful introductory framework as background for cross-cultural apologetics to this worldview. Next, we will identify some of the key needs and barriers for cross-cultural apologetics to people who subscribe to this version of Eastern mysticism.

WHAT ARE THE NEEDS AND BARRIERS IN APOLOGETICS TO EASTERN PANTHEISTIC MONISTS?

Several needs and barriers have been identified in the literature for individuals who broadly affirm some form of the EPM worldview.[25] First, there is a need to translate the gospel and the general Christian story of the world. K. Michael Hilderbrand, for example, shares the account of a former Theravada Buddhist from Thailand:

> One participant in the study recounted hearing about the teachings of Jesus for the first time in a university class. The students were studying the Bible as literature and the teacher read the command of Jesus, "If anyone slaps you on the right cheek, turn to them the other cheek also." Everyone in the class laughed. The teaching sounded so absurd. Turn the other cheek. Love your enemies. Do good to those who persecute you. It was all nonsense.[26]

Dean Halverson echoes this sentiment. Halverson writes, "Most [Buddhists] have misheard the gospel"; similarly, of Hinduism, he explains,

---

24. Sire, *Universe Next Door*, 153.

25. See for example, Netland, *Encountering Pluralism*, chs. 9–10; Muck et al., *Handbook of Religion*, chs. 1, 6–15; Corduan, *Neighboring Faiths*, chs. 9–10; Yandell, *Philosophy of Religion*; Yandell and Netland, *Buddhism*; Hesselgrave, *Communicating Christ Cross-Culturally*; Halverson, *Compact Guide to World Religions*, 54–69, 87–102; Maharaj, *Death of a Guru*; Hilderbrand, *God the Evangelist*.

26. Hilderbrand, *God the Evangelist*, 32.

"Many Hindus think they must reject their culture before they can accept Christianity."[27] For this reason, many who hold to EPM need a suitable introduction to the essentials of Christianity.

Second, there is a need to *show the goodness of Christianity*. Many within this worldview, especially in the East, associate Christianity with Western imperialism. Harold Netland explains, "We live in a postcolonialist world that is acutely aware of the injustices of four centuries of Western imperialism and that believes—rightly or wrongly—that Christianity bears much of the blame for such injustice."[28] I was recently talking with Suresh Gurung, a Nepali Christian who was raised in a context where Hinduism and Buddhism are dominant beliefs. He shared that before becoming a Christian, his impression of Christianity was that it is a Western religion that is mostly concerned with political power. He thought the only reason Christians were in Nepal was to take over the country politically. This relates to the previous obstacle in that many people confuse the political associations of Christianity with the gospel itself.

Third, much like apatheists (whose worldview we will discuss in chapter 9), EPMs need a *sense of incongruence*, or tension, in the language I have used. Michael Hilderbrand has found incongruence to be a common feature of those who have come to the Christian faith from Theravada Buddhism.[29] Hilderbrand explains that incongruence is "a nagging disconsonant sense that something is not right about the world as we understand it. Our expectations of the way the world should be and reality do not seem to fit."[30]

Fourth, there is a need to *distinguish Jesus from other religious teachers*. From an evangelical perspective, we need to establish Jesus as "the way" rather than "a way." In the account of his conversion to Christianity, trained Yogi and guru, Rabi R. Maharaj describes his disgust when a Christian girl named Molli tried to share the gospel with him. Molli had peace and joy that Maharaj wanted, and he wanted to know God, but he was not at all interested in Jesus or Christianity. Maharaj reports Molli's words to him: "Joy isn't something you can produce. . . . If there isn't a genuine reason for it, then it isn't real and won't last. My joy is because my sins are forgiven, and that has changed my whole life. Peace and joy

---

27. Halverson, *Compact Guide to World Religions*, 95.
28. Netland, "Christian Theology of Religions," 26.
29. Hilderbrand, *God the Evangelist*, 37–43.
30. Hilderbrand, *God the Evangelist*, 40.

come from Christ, through really knowing him."³¹ Maharaj was outraged: "Don't keep talking about Jesus! . . . He's just one of the gods—there are millions of them—and a *Christian* god at that. I want to know the *true* God, the Creator of the universe!"³²

Fifth, EPM adherents need to understand that *forgiveness is available*. Individuals often feel trapped in the circle of karma (or samsara). Hilderbrand shares the account of a woman who had an affair with a married man. She had expected that he would leave his wife for her but that didn't happen. Instead, the disgrace and stigma this created meant she would have to leave her family and town. She lived with profound shame because there is no true forgiveness in Buddhism. No objective change in a person's moral status is available. She explains, "In Buddhism, the scar will always be with me. . . . It will be my stain forever." What attracted her to Christianity was that Jesus could "erase all of my sin." In Buddhism, she explains, "Picture a scale. All of our sins are on one side and our good deeds are on the other, but the scales never balance. We can never erase our sins." This is different than in Christianity. She continues, "God promises that he will erase everything, that my sin will no longer be my stain."³³

Maharaj expressed similar angst before becoming a Christian from Hinduism. He writes, "Throughout my conversation with Molli the conviction had gripped me that this true God must be holy and pure. How could he have anything to do with me? How well I had come to know the darkness of my heart. At last I confessed to myself, reluctantly, that all of my holy baths and *pujas* and Yoga could never change that."³⁴ He continues, "Wouldn't it be wonderful, I thought, if what Molli had said about Jesus dying for my sins were true, so that I could be forgiven and be cleansed in order to have fellowship with this holy God!"³⁵ Both of these individuals ultimately became Christians.

Sixth, there is a need to *explain evil and suffering* from a Christian perspective. Evil in this Eastern view is ultimately unreal or illusory. Although some suffering may be attributed to the nature of existence in this worldview, in some sense we are the source of our suffering because of karma. As one source poignantly explains, "We have no one to thank

31. Maharaj, *Death of a Guru*, 114–15.
32. Maharaj, *Death of a Guru*, 115.
33. Hilderbrand, *God the Evangelist*, 31.
34. Maharaj, *Death of a Guru*, 116.
35. Maharaj, *Death of a Guru*, 116.

but ourselves . . . those suffering deserve what they are experiencing. It is a result of their bad karma."[36] Karma offers a kind of theodicy, but its implications are disturbing.[37]

THE MAGICIAN'S NEPHEW'S CHALLENGES TO EASTERN PANTHEISTIC MONISM

There are a number of important ways that *The Chronicles of Narnia* can help communicate Christian belief to people who hold to this worldview. Drawing on *The Magician's Nephew*, I focus on six primary challenges: (1) the challenge of real evil, (2) the challenge of no greater love, (3) the challenge of the Benevolent Creator, (4) the challenge of innocence, (5) the challenge of the Empathetic Creator and the foreignness of evil, and (6) the challenge of Aslan's kingdom.

The Challenge of Real Evil

A key difference between Christianity and EPM is in the nature of ultimate reality. This kind of Eastern monism does not believe that ultimate reality is personal. It sees evil and suffering as ultimately illusory, since all is one. So it does not have a concept of sin as a challenge to God's moral authority, the source of alienation from God, or the cause of evil and brokenness of the world. In *The Magician's Nephew*, Lewis dramatizes questions of suffering, sin, and evil, echoing the Christian story of creation and fall. This creates an opportunity to engage with some of the obstacles and tensions of EPM.

The book opens with Digory crying in his garden.[38] Digory is so overwhelmed that he does not care that Polly, an unfamiliar girl from his London neighborhood, sees him. Digory has been torn away from his life in the country and uprooted to London. Digory's father is away in India, and he lives with his aunt and an uncle who might be insane. But the most significant source of grief to him is that his mother is ill and dying. It is easy to resonate with his despondency. Lewis understood this deeply, having lost his mother to cancer when he was a boy. This scene recalls some of his own experiences with suffering and evil.

---

36. Anderson et al., *Introduction to Christian Worldview*, 291.
37. Anderson et al., *Introduction to Christian Worldview*, 291.
38. Lewis, *Magician's Nephew*, 25.

Digory and Polly become friends, and one day, they are exploring the attics of their attached homes when they accidentally find themselves walking in on Digory's Uncle Andrew. Digory's uncle is a devious man who has been experimenting with magic. Seizing the opportunity to experiment on children, Uncle Andrew tricks Polly into taking a yellow ring, making her instantly vanish. Digory is outraged, but Uncle Andrew sees himself as beyond questions of good and evil due to his deranged sense of wisdom and personal contribution to scientific progress. Digory realizes he will have to go after her, just as his uncle has planned. Unlike the guinea pigs Uncle Andrew has sent previously, the children will be able to report what they discover. Digory agrees to go after Polly, taking a green ring for each of them so that they can both come back home. But everything feels dangerous and hopeless.

Digory finds himself where Polly is, in the Wood Between the Worlds, with various ponds. After their initial trauma passes, instead of immediately returning home, they decide they should explore first. Yellow rings, they discover, transport them, and anyone touching them, to the Wood Between the Worlds, while green rings transport them, and anyone touching them, to other worlds, depending on the magic pond they enter in the Wood. Fairly quickly, they find themselves in a cursed, dying world with a once formidable ancient city called Charn. They also discover a palace that looks like it has been deserted for hundreds, if not thousands, of years.

Inside the palace, in the hall of images, Digory and Polly find a room full of what appear to be hundreds of wax people, all seated and perfectly still. The figures look like full-sized images of past monarchs, adorned in attractive royal attire, with enormous precious stones and crowns of royalty. Though the city is decaying, the people and their clothes are perfectly intact. The world also feels thick with magic.

The final figure they notice is a great and terrible queen. The queen is intimidating and very tall, but also the most beautiful woman Digory has ever seen. In front of her is a pedestal with a little golden arch, a small bell with a hammer beside it, and an ancient inscription that they can strangely understand, inviting them to strike the bell or always wonder what would have happened had they the courage. Although Polly strongly objects and tries to leave, Digory succumbs to his lust for knowing in a way that recalls Eve's temptation in the garden of Eden (Gen 3:6). Digory takes up the hammer and strikes the golden bell. The sound that follows at first is quiet and sweet, but the reverberation, instead of stopping, grows louder and louder, to the point where the children have to yell to hear one another. The room begins to shake around them, and there are distant sounds of rain, thunder, and the unexplainable thuds of heavy objects falling. The trembling under their feet finally shakes so hard that part of the palace collapses around them. Then the bell stops ringing. As things became quiet again, they discover that the beautiful queen is awake.

Notice several features. First, Uncle Andrew presents himself as a virtuous man of science. He must explore. He must know. And yet, the value of human life is likened to that of guinea pigs. Uncle Andrew is willing to risk the lives of children for the sake of "progress." What is the value of a human life? By mirroring this absurd disregard for human life, Lewis invites the reader to treasure it (treasure). Digory's outrage at his uncle further underscores a fitting regard for Polly's life. This is something like a translation of the sanctity of human life from a Christian perspective (see Gen 9:6) (translation). Meanwhile, Uncle Andrew's rejection of the moral standard that Digory applies to him as not applying to the wise and learned echoes something of the EPM view that good and evil are illusory distinctions. Furthermore, Uncle Andrew's denial of the evil act of threatening children's lives is intuitively much less plausible than the belief that the act is not evil or merely an illusion of evil (tension).

Second, notice that a (concern) related to evil is introduced—the source of widespread evil is personal. Uncle Andrew's bent use of magic impacts others' lives. But then in Charn, and later swelling into Narnia, Digory is the source of evil. Digory's bent choice has a profound impact on his life and Polly's. Even Narnia's innocence will be tainted by Digory's act through the arrival of the queen into Narnia. Digory ignores Polly's warning and his own moral sense as well. He is fully aware that he is in a world that should not be toyed with. The world is charged with magic, yet it is his pride that calls him to "adventure." It is subdued, but Lewis is able to introduce some preliminary features of the freewill defense (concern). Tawa Anderson articulates the key premise well: "If God is omnipotent, he possesses maximal power; but even an omnipotent God cannot create truly free creatures who never freely do wrong."[39] Digory chooses tragically.

As a kind of (translation), Lewis is able to introduce the reader to something like the events of Gen 3. The effects of Digory's prideful choice far exceed the seeming smallness of the decision. Everything about the

---

39. Anderson, *Why Believe*, 268–69.

temptation appears small, yet all of the effects that swell from the epicenter of this choice convey the weighty significance of personal responsibility. Lewis also translates the feeling of temptation and some glimpses of grace later in the narrative, in that Aslan does not ultimately give up on Digory. This is despite the effects Digory's choice has on Aslan's good and living creation (translation).

The Challenge of No Greater Love

As the narrative unfolds, Polly and Digory discover that although stunning, the queen is a tyrant. She gives no second thought to any measure of death toll. The queen sought, gained, and used what's called "the Deplorable Word"—a word that if used, destroys every living thing except the speaker of the word. When her powerful sister came to challenge her in Charn, the queen, with little regret, employed the dark incantation and became Charn's only survivor.[40]

When Polly hears about this day, she is repulsed by the horror of such cruelty, and protests on behalf of the innocent people and animals who suffered. The queen's response says it all: they were her possession, only there to do her will.[41] This is who Digory has set free: Queen Jadis, a merciless despot, with an insatiable yearning to rule.[42] Now that Charn is in ruins, she wants England. Although the children attempt to escape using the rings, Jadis grabs Polly by the hair, so the magic pulls the children, along with the queen, back to England.

Predictably, the queen brings havoc to England. Though her magic does not work in England, her strength and thirst for power are unchanged. The queen's plan to conquer England is thwarted when Digory and Polly attempt to take her back to Charn, taking her out of our world using the magic rings. The problem this time is that others are also making contact, so the children are surprised to find Uncle Andrew, a cabby, and Strawberry (the cabby's horse) with them, as well as Jadis. Exacerbating the situation, they find themselves in another world, but it isn't Charn.

The evil of Queen Jadis puts the goodness of Aslan in sharp relief, and the contrast between good and evil challenges a monistic outlook. This challenge has several important features. First, notice the queen's

---

40. Lewis, *Magician's Nephew*, 67.
41. Lewis, *Magician's Nephew*, 67.
42. Lewis, *Magician's Nephew*, 67.

love. Her great love is for herself. Jadis is pleased to exchange the lives of the whole world for her own life. Conversely, in the larger story of *The Chronicles of Narnia*, the great King and Creator of Narnia will exchange his life for the freedom of one in a way that strongly contrasts with the queen. This translates the gospel and God's love by inverting it—what Aslan, and correspondingly, Jesus is *not* like (see John 15:14; Rom 5:8) (translation, treasure). Furthermore, it distinguishes Aslan from all peers, which is another obstacle for monists (concern, call). J. P. Moreland and Tim Muehlhoff's words are fitting: "Buddha was powerless to negate the effects of bad karma for him or others. Yet Jesus regularly says to others, 'I forgive you.'"[43]

A second application of this challenge is tension. Recall that good and evil are ultimately metaphysically the same for EPM. But the challenge of no greater love trades on a nearly universal feature of the moral law—namely, that you should not sacrifice all living things in your world, especially innocent women and children, to preserve your own life. The monist reader who is honest lives in (tension) here—is there really no ultimate distinction between murdering all living beings to save your life versus giving your life to save them all? Is there no difference between someone who would give their life for you and someone who would murder you?

In addition to dramatizing this narratively, it opens up a talking point for Christian apologetic dialogue. Following Van den Toren's model, this is a *non-peripheral belief* that invites consideration of a personal and good God because Christianity does a much better job of explaining this commonsense feature of the world than EPM—evil is real. It is not the same as good.[44]

---

43. Moreland and Muehlhoff, *God Conversation*.

44. Andrew Loke's article argues for God's existence based on the existence of objective moral truths, e.g., it is wrong to use the deplorable word on a world of innocent people to save your life (my example, not his). His premises are as follows: (1) A number of objective moral truths exist (e.g., "a person should not torture babies for fun," "Hitler should not have killed 6 million Jews," etc.). (2) These objective moral truths are either metaphysically grounded in an impersonal entity, a non-divine personal entity, or a divine personal entity i.e., God, or they are brute facts. (3) These objective moral truths cannot be metaphysically grounded in an impersonal entity (e.g., the nature of moral oughtness requires that moral obligations be grounded in persons). (4) These objective moral truths cannot be metaphysically grounded in a non-divine personal entity. (5) These objective moral truths can be metaphysically grounded in a divine personal entity, i.e., God. (6) These objective moral truths are not brute facts. (7) Therefore, these objective moral truths are metaphysically grounded in a divine personal entity, i.e., God (from 2 to 6). (8) Therefore, God exists (from 1 and 7). Loke argues that the alternative can be excluded based on the essential characteristics of non-God hypotheses. See

Finally, an understanding of Aslan's sacrificial death and Edmund's forgiveness is very relevant to EPM.[45] David Hesselgrave, for example, shares the account of Bakht Singh, a convert from Hinduism and Indian evangelist, concerning his starting point for sharing the gospel in India. In Singh's words, "I have never yet failed to get a hearing if I talk to them about forgiveness of sins and peace and rest in your heart."[46] The hopelessness of karma is a common sentiment, yet real forgiveness is available (tension, treasure).

The Challenge of the Benevolent Creator

As the story of *The Magician's Nephew* continues, the world they have just entered is unnervingly dark. There are no stars. The air is cold and dry, and under their feet is something flat and cool.[47] The blackness makes them wonder if they have died. It is an empty world, with nothing there.

In the darkness, they hear something: a voice singing, deeply beautiful and seeming to come from all directions. Blazing stars materialize and appear to be singing in harmony with it, and Digory is sure that the First Voice sang them into existence. It was the most beautiful sound Digory had heard in his life. The deep song evokes very different responses among the new arrivals: "'Glory be!' said the Cabby. 'I'd ha' been a better man all my life if I'd known there were things like this.'"[48] Even Strawberry the horse seems to like the song, as if he had found himself back in his childhood field.[49] Uncle Andrew and the queen have very different experiences. Uncle Andrew dislikes it and wants to escape it, while Jadis appears to understand the music, recognizing it as a magic stronger than her own. She hates it and wants to destroy it.[50]

As the voice rises, the eastern sky changes from white to pink to gold as the sun rises. The colors were exciting, Lewis says, "until you saw the Singer himself, and then you forgot everything else. It was a Lion. Huge, shaggy, and bright, it stood facing the risen sun. Its mouth was

---

Loke, "New Moral Argument."

45. Edmund's forgiveness is discussed in more detail in chapter 5 on Islam and *The Lion, the Witch and the Wardrobe*.

46. Hesselgrave, *Communicating Christ Cross-Culturally*, 249.

47. Lewis, *Magician's Nephew*, 93.

48. Lewis, *Magician's Nephew*, 95.

49. Lewis, *Magician's Nephew*, 95.

50. Lewis, *Magician's Nephew*, 96.

wide open in song and it was about three hundred yards away."⁵¹ The Lion sings this beautiful world into being, and he is somehow more wonderful.

The Lion continues to sing, causing the world to teem with all manner of sound and life, as different animals emerge from the ground and gather around the Lion. There is awe, but there is no fear. After this, the Lion, for the first time, becomes silent. He begins moving among the animals, touching them by twos. Those he touches leave their kind and begin to follow him and stand in a large circle around the Lion. Although Digory longs to speak to the Lion about curing his mother's illness, he recognizes this is too important a moment to interrupt.

The Lion next opens his mouth, but no sound comes out; only warm breath that sways the animals like wind moves the trees. Lewis continues, "The deepest, wildest voice they had ever heard was saying: 'Narnia, Narnia, Narnia, awake. Love. Think. Speak. Be walking trees. Be talking beasts. Be divine waters.'"⁵² Now the children could hear. The Lion speaks. His now living, talking creation replies in affirmation, praising Aslan. The Lion graciously addresses his creation with both tenderness and authority: "Creatures, I give you yourselves. . . . I give to you forever this land of Narnia. I give you the woods, the fruits, the rivers. I give you the stars and I give you myself."⁵³ Remarkably, in addition to giving his image-bearing creatures vice-regency of the land he has sung into being, the Lion gives them himself.

The view of creation embedded in the story here reflects a Christian understanding and challenges the EPM worldview in several ways. First, notice that Narnia is created. It is sung into existence. In contrast to EPM, ultimate reality is personal, and Aslan is the Creator (see John 1:1–3; Col 1:15–17). This beautiful world exists because it was lovingly made (translation). Harold Netland points to former Buddhist Paul Williams as someone who grew dissatisfied with Buddhism's metaphysical and epistemological claims, specifically the contingency of the universe. Williams writes, "The question 'Why is there something rather than nothing?' has become a bit like what Zen Buddhists call a *koan*. It is a constant niggling question that has worried and goaded me (often, I think, against my will) into a different level of understanding, a different vision, of the world and our place in it."⁵⁴

---

51. Lewis, *Magician's Nephew*, 96–97.
52. Lewis, *Magician's Nephew*, 110.
53. Lewis, *Magician's Nephew*, 110.
54. Williams, *Unexpected Way*, 22–30, quoted in Yandell and Netland, *Buddhism*, 191–92.

This scene suggests that the cause of the universe is a personal Creator, and he is good, honorable, and knowable (translation, treasure).

Second, notice that there is a distinct awareness of holiness and awe that is depicted before the Creator—including those from England. Lewis thus (translates) both the existence of a Creator and a sense of moral accountability to him, *despite* never seeing Aslan before. This gently invites something of a (tension) for the reader related to one's moral state.

Third, notice that one's moral disposition, conscience, and hearing are reflected in response to Aslan's existence (translation, tension, call). The cabby, for example, wishes he had been a better man all his life had he known "there were things like this."[55] Yet the cabby longs for the source. Even Digory momentarily leaves the burden of his mother's cancer aside for a moment because of this solemn event. Lewis thus conveys both the (tension) of moral accountability and (treasure) in the source of longing. Conversely, Uncle Andrew and the queen abhor the song; they can only see and hear a lion, and they hate him.

Lewis thus depicts various responses to the existence of the holy Creator. This quietly engages the (concern) that Christianity is exclusively Western and creates a (tension) of truth by suggesting that one could be blinded by self-imposed bias or moral brokenness. It recalls Rabi Maharaj's initial reaction to Jesus. He wanted Christianity to be false, and even read the famous atheist Bertrand Russell's book *Why I Am Not a Christian* in an effort to avoid Christianity, but found the arguments of no defense to him.[56]

Fourth, notice that the Creator makes a beautiful world, and Aslan is himself the object of desire and wonder (treasure). He is mysterious and mighty. As noted, some Western thinkers give the impression that the most profound questions of human existence are neatly and simplistically packaged, which is distasteful to some Eastern sensibilities.[57] God is both a truth to be known intellectually and a mystery to be experienced existentially. Lewis's evocation of beauty speaks to the desire for an experience with mystery (translation, treasure). Here, Lewis depicts a Lion who wondrously and mysteriously sings life into existence, evoking solemn awe and authority with his presence (translation, tension). The

---

55. Lewis, *Magician's Nephew*, 95.
56. Maharaj, *Death of a Guru*, 122.
57. Netland, "Toward Contextualized Apologetics," 301.

great Lion summons the stars, yet he is personal. He touches. He stares at his talking, thinking, laughing creatures (translation, treasure).

Fifth, and most striking, the Lion, after entrusting Narnia to the Talking Beasts, concludes by giving *himself* to them. Here Lewis emphasizes the (treasure) that is Aslan. Whereas Buddha taught a way of life, Jesus taught that he is the way to life (see John 14:6). Keith Yandell and Harold Netland's distinction between Buddha and Jesus is apropos:

> In effect the Buddha says, "Follow my teachings, follow the dharma and you too can experience the way leading to enlightenment." But Jesus says much more than simply that he has discovered the way to the father and that if we follow him and his teaching we too can find the way. He puts himself forward as the embodiment of the Way, and the Truth and the Life.[58]

The Challenge of Innocence

A curious thing happens next in the account. After graciously giving his creatures all things, Aslan issues a solemn warning to treat the Dumb Beasts well, not acting like them, or they will stop being Talking Beasts and become like them again. With one voice, the talking creatures solemnly declare they will not, and then everything falls silent.[59]

Clumsily, the words "No fear!" crash into this momentous quiet as the Jackdaw speaks. Now there's a new silence as the animals try to hold their laughter. Aslan tells them to laugh without fear, and laughter breaks forth.[60] The first joke of this innocent creation has been told, and Aslan's people laugh with delight. Terry Lindvall explains this insightfully: "The new creation of Narnia roars and guffaws with innocence. No malice or mean mischief mars the participants of the jokes.... Indeed, the sin of earth sours the self's ability to be laughed at. Pride protests against being an object of laughter. But not so of innocence, as the Jackdaw."[61]

Notice first that Aslan's creation is innocent. Its goodness is desirable. The laughter of innocence fills the young air. Acceptance is normal. Shame is absent. In this, we see the (treasure) of innocence. (Translation) is also given. A mirror is presented to the reader. Shame now exists.

---

58. Yandell and Netland, *Buddhism*, 191–92.
59. Lewis, *Magician's Nephew*, 110.
60. Lewis, *Magician's Nephew*, 110.
61. Lindvall, *Surprised by Laughter*, 268.

Innocence is gone. Alienation exists between self, others, and God. Yet Aslan and the kind of world that he makes is good; it is (treasured). We long for this kind of world, a world of peace and goodness, a world of innocence and roaring laughter. Furthermore, Aslan expects his talking animals to justly govern those with lesser capacities (translation, treasure).

Lewis accomplishes an evocation of beauty in line with what James Sire thinks is needed for engaging those who believe in EPM. Sire writes, "Those who would communicate the beauty of truth in Christ have a tough job, for the mists of ugly Western imperialism, war, violence, greed, and gluttony are thick indeed."[62] At a minimum, Lewis shows some reflections of the beauty of a world without sin where God walks among his people (John 1:1-5, 14; Rev 21:3; see also Gen 3:8).

The Challenge of the Empathetic Creator and the Foreignness of Evil

As the account continues, the merriment, though genuine, unfortunately lasts only a moment. Aslan warns them that evil has been brought to Narnia. The animals don't even know the word evil. They take it as Neevil or weevil. Digory is desperate, though, to ask Aslan's help for his mother's illness. The story has shown us how much her cancer weighs on his young mind, and now Digory has seen the Lion's creative power. Maybe he can help.[63]

Having witnessed Aslan's creative glory, Digory approaches the great Lion with fear but a deeper desire that exceeds his fear. He asks for a magic fruit to make his mother well, hoping for Aslan's "yes" and fearing that he will say "no."[64]

But Aslan does not answer at first. He tells Digory that because he was the one who brought the witch into Narnia, he will be part of a temporary grace in Narnia's future. He is to make a trip to retrieve an apple from a special garden. A tree that will grow from the apple's seed will repel the witch for many years to come. His mission is an expectation. Nevertheless, Digory's thoughts are consumed with desperate thoughts of his mother. He realizes that he cannot bargain with Aslan but pleads for a cure for his mother. Until now, his eyes were looking down at Aslan,

---

62. Sire, *Universe Next Door*, 154.
63. Lewis, *Magician's Nephew*, 111.
64. Lewis, *Magician's Nephew*, 122.

timidly avoiding eye contact. When he does look up to plead more desperately, Digory is shocked to see tears in Aslan's eyes as he looks at his face: "They were such big, bright tears compared with Digory's own that for a moment he felt as if the Lion must really be sorrier about his Mother than he was himself. 'My son, my son,' said Aslan. 'I know. Grief is great. Only you and I in this land know that yet.'"[65]

The story brings to life the foreignness of death and suffering, showing that not just Digory but Aslan himself is deeply moved to grief by their reality. This challenge has several significant features. First, as noted before, the source of evil is depicted as personal. This quietly engages the (concern) of the problem of evil. Aslan's good creation is tainted by foreign sin at the hands of moral persons. Second, there is (translation) in that evil is seen as foreign; the word *evil* does not make sense to the innocent creatures of Narnia (see Gen 1–3). As before, the reader is presented with the fact that our world is not like this. Evil is normal in the primary world. Third, Lewis (translates) a sense of Aslan's sovereignty in the midst of fear, as Digory recognizes his authority to send him on a mission and that he is not someone to bargain with. Yet, Lewis also subverts the common mantra (concern): "Where is God when we suffer?" Far from indifferent, Aslan feels Digory's pain and his mother's suffering acutely (translation, concern, treasure). Aslan knows people by name and situation in *all* worlds. Any sense of shame that one might have if suffering as the result of karma is absent. Aslan is sovereign and empathetic.

As the story develops, Lewis addresses some facets of our existential struggle with evil (concern). Evil and suffering are palpably real in *The Magician's Nephew*. God deeply identifies with human struggles, even if he does not always remove them on this side of eternity. Far from indifferent, God cares more deeply than we do. Yet we can struggle to trust God, and we see a version of this struggle in Digory's mission for Aslan. Upon arriving in the garden, the witch tempts Digory to question the goodness of Aslan. Digory is told that the apple is the apple of youth, but Aslan has told him to bring the fruit back to protect Narnia. Digory is not to eat it. The witch claims that Aslan only wants it to eat it himself. She tells Digory that if he eats it, he can live with her forever and rule in Narnia or his own world. Not only that, he can use the apple to save his mother. She accuses Aslan of being completely indifferent, even cruel,

---

65. Lewis, *Magician's Nephew*, 128.

and claims Aslan is merely treating Digory as "his slave."[66] Perhaps Aslan is something much worse than he thought. If Aslan is unwilling to heal, he must be very cruel indeed. Digory is sorely tempted, but the cruelty of the witch's suggestion that he leave Polly behind helps him see through the witch's temptation, and he escapes the witch, taking the apple back to Aslan.

On returning to Aslan, Digory plants the apple, which will grow into a tree of protection for Narnia. He admits to Aslan that he nearly ate one himself, and Aslan tells him that even though the apple would have healed his mother, there would have come a day when both Digory and his mother would have thought it better to die. As Aslan explains, "Things always work according to their nature."[67] The fruit of a stolen apple in Narnia would have been a merciless kingdom like Charn.

Hearing this breaks Digory's young heart: "Digory could say nothing, for tears choked him and he gave up all hopes of saving his Mother's life; but at the same time he knew that the Lion knew what would have happened, and that there might be things more terrible even than losing someone you love by death."[68] Digory has seen that Aslan is truthful, and he is good. Even in the shadow of his mother's death, Aslan can be trusted. But having trusted and been obedient to Aslan, Digory receives back as a gift what would have been spoiled if grasped through disobedience. Aslan grants him to pluck an apple from the new tree, one that will not grant eternal life but will heal sickness and bring a kind of joy back in England.[69]

On returning to our world, Digory lovingly takes the apple of life that Aslan has given him out of his pocket and gives it to his mother: "Nothing else was worth looking at: you couldn't look at anything else. And the smell of the Apple of Youth was as if there was a window in the room that opened on Heaven."[70] Piece by piece, Digory gives the apple to his dying mother. She falls asleep, and over the coming days and weeks, experiences a miraculous recovery. In time, it is clear: Aslan's power is even present in England.

We see several of the six keys at work in this part of the narrative. First, Lewis creates (tension) in the reader by convincingly highlighting

---

66. Lewis, *Magician's Nephew*, 142.
67. Lewis, *Magician's Nephew*, 151.
68. Lewis, *Magician's Nephew*, 151.
69. Lewis, *Magician's Nephew*, 152.
70. Lewis, *Magician's Nephew*, 156.

human frailty. Across worldviews, human mortality and what happens at death are a cause of existential angst that often invites more profound reflection. Rabi Maharaj recalls that prior to becoming a Christian, he was miserable. He writes, "Only my fear of what lay beyond death kept me from suicide."[71]

Second, Lewis deeply and meaningfully evokes trust in the goodness of God, while crushing hurt, despair, and mystery still abound. This is relevant for (concern) and for (translation). It subverts some of the existential problem of evil and establishes something of a fitting expectation of life "between the times."

Third, Digory gets a glimpse of Aslan's goodness and the faithfulness of his words, despite what would be a near-insurmountable temptation for a child. In doing so, children and adults are presented with a good Creator God who identifies with their sorrow, and who can be trusted in the face of overwhelming suffering (concern). This also displays (transformation) in Digory's life and celebrates the goodness of trusting Aslan, even when life is bewildering (translation, treasure). Digory overcomes this temptation. Finally, it demonstrates that Aslan possesses the authority to restore and heal in England. Greater still, glimpses of heaven that seem to break in through Aslan's apple evoke a sense of living hope in the face of death (treasure, translation). This living hope is reinforced by the touches of joy that recall Lewis's argument from desire and is satisfied in eternal life with God (call, treasure).

While the narrative does not answer all conceivable arguments made from evil, for the one who allows, it contributes to the "intellectual climate." It eases some of the existential urgency (concern) to fully understand all that is going on and reminds the sufferer of One who identifies with our sorrows.

The Challenge of Aslan's Kingdom

One common obstacle to belief for those from Eastern cultures especially, is Christianity's association with Western oppression and imperialism, although this concern is also shared by many in the West. This barrier to belief is cited by individuals across various worldviews. There are several ways in which Lewis subverts this perception of Christianity in *The Magician's Nephew*. I will focus on two.

---

71. Maharaj, *Death of a Guru*, 116.

Aslan's Kingdom People. The first king and queen of Narnia are from a surprisingly humble social status. Frank's language is unpolished, and his ways are unrefined. His heart, though flawed, is honorable. Lowly people are the first kings and queens in Aslan's newly sung world. In London, Frank was a cabby. He is a man of courage and simplicity. When Narnia's world is sung into being, his heart is stirred by its beauty. He delights in the creation and is drawn to its source. When others are afraid in the foreign land, Frank is at home and longs to hear more of Aslan's song. Moreover, the holiness of the moment makes Frank aware of his sin, and he regrets some of his past. When Frank first stands before Aslan, he humbly takes off his hat.

When Aslan asks Frank if he would like to stay in Narnia, he replies affirmatively, but explains why he can't accept—he's a married man, and his wife is back in London. Instead of closing the door to Frank, Aslan's response astonishes everyone. Aslan summons Frank's wife, Helen, to Narnia in a moment, no magic rings needed. Helen arrives disheveled and dressed as though interrupted on laundry day. She is humble and gracious, even though the world feels unfamiliar. To everyone's amazement, Aslan declares that this couple will be Narnia's first king and queen. He appoints them to rule the Talking Beasts, do justice, and protect the Narnians from their enemies. Frank is more than surprised; he feels entirely unfit. He lacks the kind of education and status he assumes is required to rule a kingdom.

Aslan's Kingdom Values. Aslan's dialogue with Frank reveals the kind of king and kingdom he truly desires: being a good farmer, a kind and fair leader without favoritism, putting himself at risk first in any battle, and passing on these values to his heirs. Despite Frank's lowly status, everything that he says shows that he is precisely the kind of king that Aslan wants. Better still, it shows the type of kingdom Aslan wants. Aslan's kingdom is intended to be a kindly and just land, and his vice-regents are to uphold his kingdom's values with justice and mercy.

As *The Magician's Nephew* comes to a close, the narrator describes the peace and prosperity that were experienced under King Frank and Queen Helen. Their kingdom is blessed with peace, joy, and even diversity as their children marry the nymphs, naiads, and dryads. This further echoes the vast diversity of free Talking Beasts.

There are three key aspects to this challenge. First, some versions of EPM see caste as the consequence of karma. A person is born into a particular caste because of their karmic debt. Conversely, Aslan, the

Creator, appoints lowly people to the positions of king and queen (tension, translation).

Second, Aslan expects that his vice-regents rule with justice and mercy (concern, translation). Once their crowns are formed, Aslan calls Frank and Helen to kneel before him and he places crowns on their heads and commissions them to justice, mercy, and courage.[72] Unlike the tyranny of Jadis, Aslan's appointed rulers are to uphold justice, but with mercy (concern, translation). This vision of a just kingdom challenges certain associations with Christianity and imperialism, reimagining what a good kingdom could be (treasure).

Third, this challenge highlights the dignity and value of human persons (and Talking Beasts as an analogue for human beings made in God's image) in a manner consistent with the Christian worldview. Lewis introduces the value of persons (translation) and points to God's value of human persons (treasure).

In *The Magician's Nephew* and throughout *The Chronicles of Narnia*, behaviors, institutions, values, and reality are marked differences between kingdoms where Aslan reigns and those where he does not (concern). Those governed by Aslan's kingdom values are commended as free and virtuous, while slavery, bondage, and fear govern anti-type kingdoms (concern, translation). Despite the abuses done in his name, Jesus loves people, and he expects his redeemed people to love them too (John 3:16; Rom 5:8; Matt 5:38–48; 22:36–40). Furthermore, he expects his redeemed people to humbly reflect him and his kingdom as salt and light (Matt 5:1–16).

Vishal Mangalwadi illustrates the significant difference between Christianity and traditional Hinduism concerning *the value of human life*.[73] Mangalwadi tells the true story of an eighteen-month-old baby named Sheela. One of four children, Sheela was born to a low-caste family in the Indian village of Gatheora. As Mangalwadi's wife, Ruth, was

---

72. Lewis, *Magician's Nephew*, 146.

73. The positive impact of Christianity on human life has been noted by others. Tom Holland's acclaimed book *Dominion*, for example, notes that Christians changed the tide on the value of children. He writes, "Lepers and slaves were not the most defenseless of God's children. Across the Roman world, wailing at the sides of roads or on rubbish tips, babies abandoned by their parents were a common sight. Others might be dropped down drains, there to perish in the hundreds. . . . Only a few peoples—the odd Germanic tribe and, inevitably, the Jews—had stood aloof from the exposure of unwanted children. Pretty much everyone else had always taken it for granted. Until, that was, the emergence of a Christian people." Holland, *Dominion*, 143.

visiting homes, she found out that Sheela was very sick and starving to death. What shocked their family, however, was that the mother and father would not seek medical attention, nor would they allow Vishal or Ruth to pursue it on Sheela's behalf. Sheela's parents offered unimaginable explanations: "But where is the time to go to the hospital?" or "We don't want to go into debt," or "We don't have the time."[74] As Christians, Vishal and Ruth could not believe this: "Are you killing this girl?" they asked.[75] The parents replied, "Of course not! But what can we do if she won't eat and will vomit everything we give her?"[76] Even more disheartening, other people in the village agreed with the parents' rationale.

Sheela's story begins hopefully but ends tragically. The parents ultimately relented and allowed Vishal and Ruth to take Sheela to a hospital and to briefly stay in their home, based on the counsel of an elderly neighbor. The sad rationale was that if the police came and took Sheela to the hospital, the family would have to pay the bill. After Sheela recovered some, she was returned to her family. The story, lamentably, repeated— Sheela became very sick again, Vishal and Ruth took her to the hospital, Sheela briefly stayed at their house, she improved, Sheela was returned home. Not much later, Vishal and Ruth heard that Sheela was dead. What happened? Mangalwadi explains the worldviews behind this tragedy:

> Sheela's parents starved her to death because they saw her as a liability. . . . Ruth and I [as Christians] could not understand Sheela's parents because our worldview was so different from theirs. They looked at children as assets or liabilities, conveniences or burdens. We looked at them as human beings with intrinsic worth. We believed that God's command, "You shall not murder," gave to every human person a fundamental right to life. We did not expect to gain anything from Sheela. We believed that loving God required loving her. We intervened because we believed that God's Word commanded us to "speak up for those who cannot speak for themselves, for the rights of all who are destitute. Speak up and judge fairly; defend the rights of the poor and needy." . . . Sheela's parents believed that, like themselves, Sheela was trapped inescapably in the clutches of poverty. They held to traditional Hindu fatalism.[77]

74. Mangalwadi, *Book that Made*, 60–61.
75. Mangalwadi, *Book that Made*, 60.
76. Mangalwadi, *Book that Made*, 60.
77. Mangalwadi, *Book that Made*, 63.

Although Mangalwadi importantly notes that Hindus who are shaped by non-Hindu thinking tend to value life more, the account juxtaposes the value of human life between these two worldviews. Through *The Magician's Nephew*, Lewis invites the reader to see the value of human life in and through Aslan and his kingdom.

CONCLUSION

As I have shown, Narnia brings Christian themes to life in ways that are relevant to engaging with EPM by subverting some of the most common obstacles to faith and advocating for faith through narrative apologetic devices. I focused on six primary challenges in *The Magician's Nephew*: (1) the challenge of real evil, (2) the challenge of no greater love, (3) the challenge of the Benevolent Creator, (4) the challenge of innocence, (5) the challenge of the Empathetic Creator and the foreignness of evil, and (6) the challenge of Aslan's kingdom.

It is worth noting that I have no reason to believe Lewis had Eastern religions or philosophies particularly in mind when writing *The Magician's Nephew*, but I think the world he created still serves narrative apologetic ends in engaging EPM. By depicting a moral universe in which good and evil are real, it challenges readers who deny this reality, whether due to pantheistic monism or a naturalistic worldview that reduces everything to matter in motion.

There are many ways that *The Magician's Nephew* can help serve the apologetic needs of engaging this kind of Eastern thought, but I find what I have termed "The Challenge of No Greater Love" to be the strongest. This is especially so when contrasted with Aslan's love. Now, the problem of "looking along and looking at the sunbeam" is especially acute in this challenge, and it matters.[78] All I can do is invite a person to imagine Lewis's story in our world, as Ellen Charry did with the doctrine of grace. It will be rough and abbreviated.

Imagine a queen in our world who had the ability to utter a single phrase that would kill every living creature, including her own family, but it would spare her life.

Now imagine her uttering the words.

Now imagine that she has zero remorse.

---

78. Lewis, "Myth Became Fact," 65–66; Lewis, "Meditation in a Toolshed," 230.

If someone were to ask the queen how she could be so cruel, she would find the question confusing. They were hers, she would think, to use up their lives for her benefit. Why the outrage?

Now imagine the all-good Creator God of our world, in the form of a first-century Jewish man from Nazareth. He is here under the banner: "Greater love has no one than this, that someone lay down his life for his friends" (John 15:13).

Now imagine him on a Roman cross in Jerusalem around AD 33.

Now imagine him saying from the cross, "It is finished" (see John 3:16; 19:30).

Now imagine someone saying, "Good and evil are the same."

This is a small glimpse of the kind of bridge that Lewis makes to Jesus.

9

Engaging Apatheism

with *The Last Battle*

INTRODUCTION

THE LAST BATTLE IS the final Narnia book, and it tells the story of the end times of the Narnian world in a kind of eschatology. The story begins in a world shrouded in deceit, with the kingdom under invasion. It is also a world of contested belief and doubt, due in part to abuses done in Aslan's name. The cumulative effect of a false Aslan and rival gods is to leave many of the Narnian world numb and skeptical. Against hope, the story culminates with awe-inspiring glimpses of the glorious future to come for those who respond favorably to Aslan. It also offers a sobering reminder of mortality, warning of the bleak fate of those who willfully reject Aslan. This Narnian chronicle is thus well-suited to address the rise of spiritual indifference toward the things of God.

For many, the most significant barrier to considering Christian belief is simply indifference: Christianity may work for you, but it's not for me. This is sometimes called apatheism, a blend of words running together, "apathy-theism." Particularly in cultures that are prosperous and secure, it can be easy to feel that God is unnecessary to a life of flourishing. Yet there will be a day when we will draw our last breath, so we must all face the question of what comes beyond. The Christian belief in final judgment means that the stakes are eternal: if Christianity is indeed true, then eternal life or eternal punishment awaits us depending on our response in this life. *The Last Battle* confronts the reader with the question of whether they have hope in the face of death and judgment.

My argument throughout the book has been that narrative apologetics, *particularly* Lewis's *The Chronicles of Narnia*, can contribute to cross-cultural apologetics by helping to translate relevant Christian beliefs, advocating for Christianity's truth and goodness, subverting the adequacy of non-Christian beliefs, and helping to respond to objections made against Christian belief. In this chapter, I consider apatheism as a fourth belief profile. Like previous chapters, I begin by briefly explaining the contours of apatheism. Next, I identify some of the most critical barriers and needs for apologetic engagement to this outlook. Finally, focusing on *The Last Battle*, I show how Narnia encourages Christian belief to those who hold to apatheism.

WHAT IS APATHEISM?

Unlike other belief systems we have considered, apatheism is not a formal worldview. Rather, it is a posture or attitude of indifference toward belief in God. It is an outlook that Christian apologetics must engage with because it is a common obstacle to considering Christian belief. The author and journalist Jonathan Rauch, in a widely referenced article in *The Atlantic*, "Let It Be," identifies himself as an apatheist. He defines the term *apatheism* as "a disinclination to care all that much about one's own religion, and an even stronger disinclination to care about other people's."[1] Rather than being "lazy recumbency," Rauch believes apatheism is a sociological achievement. Writing after the events of September 11, 2001, he explains that for much of history, religious zeal has driven division and violence, and sees the taming of religious passion not as a lapse, but as an achievement.

Philosophers Trevor Hedberg and Jordan Huzarevich echo Rauch's sentiment: "[Apatheism] is distinct from theism, atheism, and agnosticism. A theist believes that God exists; an atheist believes that God does not exist; an agnostic believes that we cannot know whether God exists; an apatheist believes that we *should not care* whether God exists (emphasis added)."[2] Hedberg and Huzarevich consider six common reasons for

1. Rauch, "Let It Be," 34.
2. Beshears, "Athens Without a Statue," 518.

valuing "existence questions" (EQs).³ With the exception of how belief or disbelief in God could impact one's afterlife, they find the normal motivation for considering such questions unconvincing, and so insufficient reason for focusing on this question.⁴ According to Hedberg and Huzarevich,

> Each of these objections posits a different reason for thinking that belief in God is practically significant. Five of these objections prove unsuccessful. The sixth, which appeals to the practical significance of belief in God with respect to our fates in the afterlife, is more promising but nonetheless encounters significant obstacles. Since the success of this objection is controversial, whether we have good grounds to reject practical apatheism should be similarly controversial, and the view should be given further examination.⁵

Hedberg and Huzarevich thus conclude, "If our answers to [existence questions] lack practical significance, then perhaps they warrant less philosophical attention, and perhaps debates concerning them should be more carefree because the stakes are not as high as most believe."⁶ They conclude that we *should not care* whether God exists.

WHAT ARE THE NEEDS AND BARRIERS IN APOLOGETICS TO APATHEISTS?

Kyle Beshears, a pastor and scholar who has written about apatheism, maintains that our present cultural milieu supports the flourishing of this attitude to faith. He identifies four related barriers to Christian belief:

---

3. Existence questions are taken to mean variants of questions about God's existence (e.g., "does God exist? Is it rational to believe God exists? Can we know whether or not God exists? What would count as evidence for God's existence?"). Hedberg and Huzarevich, "Appraising Objections," 257.

4. Hedberg and Huzarevich examine six distinct objections to practical apatheism, to include: "(1) EQs are practically significant because we cannot develop a satisfactory objective ethical system unless God exists. (2) EQs are practically significant because we cannot be motivated to behave ethically unless God exists. (3) EQs are practically significant because we cannot live meaningful lives unless God exists. (4) EQs are practically significant because of the historical prominence of philosophical positions tied to how EQs are answered. (5) EQs are practically significant because answering them correctly increases the likelihood that one will experience a miracle. (6) EQs are practically significant because how we answer them affects our fates in the afterlife." Hedberg and Huzarevich, "Appraising Objections," 258–59.

5. Hedberg and Huzarevich, "Appraising Objections," 257.

6. Hedberg and Huzarevich, "Appraising Objections," 258.

(1) contested belief and globalization, (2) existential security without God, (3) distraction, and (4) autonomy.

First, following thinkers such as Charles Taylor, James K. A. Smith, and Alan Noble, Beshears points to the way belief in the contemporary world is *contested* due to increased globalization and the regular intersection of religious belief and cultural diversity. This is reminiscent of the pressures that Peter Berger terms a plausibility structure. Because we regularly encounter many different people with wildly different beliefs, it makes it harder to believe in Christianity as the one true faith.

Second, the advances of science, prevalence of secularism, as well as increased affluence and technology have created a sense of *existential security* that did not exist in earlier times in history—times when the irrelevance of God was unthinkable. As Charles Taylor explains, in the last five hundred years, there was a significant shift of focus to the "immanent frame" away from belief and dependence on what he calls the "enchanted world," where God was believed to be involved and intervening in the world.[7] Beshears continues, "The more a society feels safe and taken care of, the less important it finds God to be. And the less motivated people are to turn to God, the less likely they will find his existence relevant."[8] Apatheists share one commonality, according to Beshears: "A sense of existential security absent God."[9]

Third, as well as self-sufficient, our world is also increasingly *distracted*. Drawing on Alan Noble's work, Beshears maintains that the "persistent distraction of our culture prevents us from asking the deepest, most important questions about existence and truth. The things that prick our souls for the sake of the gospel (e.g., death, beauty, anxiety, etc.) can be numbed quickly by an eight-hour dose of binge-watching."[10] Beshears continues, "We effortlessly avoid asking the biggest, most difficult questions of life because we are so busy."[11] It is in this soil of "contestability, diversity, comfort, and distraction—that apatheism not only grows but flourishes."[12]

Finally, Beshears argues that the primacy of personal *autonomy* is the ultimate cause of apatheism. He writes, "The core reason why

7. Taylor, *Secular Age*, 25, 556.
8. Beshears, *Apatheism*, 33.
9. Beshears, "Athens Without a Statue," 523.
10. Beshears, *Apatheism*, 35. See also Noble, *Disruptive Witness*.
11. Beshears, *Apatheism*, 35.
12. Beshears, *Apatheism*, 38.

apatheism exists" is that "we do not *want* to care about God. We've developed an antipathy toward spiritual contemplation because we don't want what inevitably follows, a fundamental change in who we are and how we live. To sacrifice autonomy is too high a cost, so we protect it through apathy."[13] It recalls what Francis Schaeffer termed "idols of personal peace and affluence" some years ago. People want to be left alone and to live untroubled by others' needs, whether close by or across the world.[14] "Personal peace," Schaeffer explains, "means wanting to have my personal life pattern undisturbed in my lifetime. . . . Affluence means an overwhelming and ever-increasing prosperity—a life made up of things, things, and more things."[15] Lived without measure, both are at odds with the lordship of Christ.

These four obstacles—contested belief and globalization, existential security without God, distraction, and autonomy—are essential targets for apologetics among apatheists.

APATHEISM: A PRELIMINARY ASSESSMENT

Before we consider ways that Narnia engages this belief system, there are a number of important observations and issues for apatheism that we should note. First, although apatheism is not a developed belief system, it is a belief. As Beshears argues, "Ask an apatheist why they are uninterested in God, and their response will likely be that they don't *believe* God is relevant to their life."[16] The problem is that they also do not believe questions about God are worth asking to know whether or not this is true, despite much of the world having been positively impacted by Christian theism, and particularly being crucial in shaping Western culture and society.

Second, rather than being virtuous, there are good reasons to see apatheism as intellectually and morally harmful. Tawa Anderson argues, "Apatheism leads to the vices of acedia (failure to care sufficiently about things that deserve close consideration) and misology (hatred of reasoned argumentation)."[17] Paul Copan is similarly critical: "From

---

13. Beshears, *Apatheism*, 41.
14. Schaeffer, *Complete Works*, 211.
15. Schaeffer, *Complete Works*, 211.
16. Beshears, "Athens Without a Statue," 520.
17. Anderson, "Big Questions," quoted in Beshears, "Athens Without a Statue," 518.

a spiritual, rational, and moral perspective it's like not caring about having cancer. Or it's like a child who doesn't see the point of a good education."[18] Lewis's words are fitting: "Christianity, if false, is of no importance, and if true, of infinite importance. The only thing it cannot be is moderately important."[19]

Third, apatheism's sense of "progress" is what Lewis called "chronological snobbery." As Lewis defines it, chronological snobbery is the uncritical belief in the superiority of one's own time and culture, and the viewing of the past as discredited.[20] Lewis felt he had blindly embraced chronological snobbery until Owen Barfield challenged him, and it had been an obstacle to him becoming a Christian. Lewis argues that you have to be aware of your own cultural context with its fashions and look at the arguments around particular beliefs: "Was it ever refuted (and if so by whom, where, and how conclusively) or did it merely die away as fashions do? If the latter, this tells us nothing about its truth or falsehood."[21]

This can be applied to Hedberg and Huzarevich's article. It is doubtful that the article has "conclusively refuted" or displaced the theistic worldview's explanatory power for objective ethical systems or the grounding of the objective meaning of life with secular models.[22] Other points under consideration seem trivial from a Christian perspective (e.g., believing to have answered prayer) or misapplied (e.g., being ethically motivated without theism). The issue for nontheistic ethics is not whether one can be motivated ethically without belief in God—Christians believe that nontheists can be moral without theism. The question is whether naturalism as a worldview makes better sense of moral values and duties than theism, or whether Christianity gives a better grounding and justification for objective standards of morality.

Fourth, the *possibility* of God as the Greatest Conceivable Being demands the attention of the morally and intellectually sensitive mind. An unwillingness to entertain such questions may suggest that the perceiver's faculties are not appropriately sensitive or ordered as they should be. For example, a person may have little regard, or even complete disregard, for

18. Copan, *Loving Wisdom*, 35.
19. Lewis, *Mere Christianity*, 101–2.
20. Lewis, *Surprised by Joy*, 254.
21. Lewis, *Surprised by Joy*, 254.
22. See for example Baggett and Walls, *God and Cosmos*, where they compare the explanatory power of various secular systems against theism for moral data; also see Moreland et al., *Debating Christian Theism*.

human life, but this does not diminish the actual value of a human being. In such cases, the person's emotions or intellect are in some sense morally deficient. Apatheism's indifference to God and questions about him recalls Lewis's surprising admission in *The Abolition of Man*—particularly as author of the Narnian septet—that he did not enjoy the presence of children. But Lewis recognized this as a defect in himself when judged against the Tao (the doctrine of objective value), which is the belief that certain attitudes are really true and others really false, to the kind of thing the universe is and the kind of things we are.[23] Emotions, on this view, are recognitions of objective value. When rightly ordered, virtuous emotions like what ought to be approved. Adam Pelser notes that this view is increasingly supported in the fields of philosophy and psychology. Pelser explains, "Emotions are perception-like experiences of objective values. On perceptual accounts, emotions, like sense perceptions, can get things right or wrong and the wise and virtuous person will not only make the appropriate moral and aesthetic judgments, she will also 'see' the value in the world accurately through her emotions."[24]

Lewis and ancient thinkers across cultural and religious contexts believed that sentiments could and should be cultivated through exemplars. Pelser explains,

> By "irrigating" our students' arid hearts . . . we can make them free . . . to experience or "see" the injustice of apartheid, the inhumanity of genocide, the beauty of a Beethoven symphony, the elegance of the physical laws of the universe, the dignity of human persons, our own sinfulness, and even the grace and goodness of God through well-formed emotional perceptions—through, in particular, indignation, moral horror, aesthetic awe, wonder, love, contrition, and gratitude, respectively.[25]

Unlike Lewis, who recognized that his lack of affection was a moral deficiency, apatheists are content, and in some cases proud, of their indifference about the One whom Anselm fittingly adored as "that than which nothing greater can be conceived."

---

23. Lewis, *Abolition of Man*, 18–19.
24. Pelser, "Irrigating Deserts," 31.
25. Pelser, "Irrigating Deserts," 32.

WHAT ARE THE PATHWAYS TO ENGAGING APATHEISTS?

Beshears identifies several key pathways for engaging apatheism. Four ways are especially relevant: the tension of livability for non-Christian worldviews, doubt, interest, and self-reflection. First, much like Francis Schaeffer, he recommends presuppositional methods of worldview analysis accompanied by penetrating questions to stoke curiosity. Following Schaeffer, Beshears writes, "Non-Christian beliefs necessarily hold presuppositions that do not agree with the real world. Consequently, unbelievers are 'far from reality,' and this distance can be demonstrated to them by uncovering 'points of tension' in their beliefs."[26] He continues, "All people, as image bearers of God, are pulled toward his objective sense of love, beauty, meaning, significance, and truth. But, because we desire autonomy from him, we create our own myopic and disoriented sense of love, beauty, meaning, significance, and truth."[27]

Schaeffer used the metaphor of a self-constructed roof that people erect to avoid dealing with the truth about the kind of world God has made. The apologist or evangelist's job is to lovingly, and sometimes painfully, pull down the false shelter so that the light of God's world can shine. Beshears sees this as anticipating Charles Taylor's "buffered self."[28] He explains, "If we remove the roof, then the apatheist's buffered self is no longer buffered. And when we push on points of tension, we expose the inconsistency with the way the apatheist lives and how things really are."[29] By removing the false shelter, a key ingredient appears—doubt. Doubt thus correctly exposes the fragility of the apatheist's existential insecurity.[30] Inspired by Søren Kierkegaard's *Johannes Climacus*, a figure Kierkegaard created to explore and critique prominent philosophical

---

26. Beshears, "Athens Without a Statue," 528.
27. Beshears, "Athens Without a Statue," 528.
28. Beshears, "Athens Without a Statue," 528.
29. Beshears, "Athens Without a Statue," 528. James K. A. Smith explains Charles Taylor's language well: "Buffered self—In the modern social imaginary, the self is sort of insulated in an interior 'mind,' no longer vulnerable to the transcendent or the demonic. Contrast with the porous self . . . in the ancient/medieval social imaginary, the self is open and vulnerable to the enchanted 'outside' world—susceptible to grace, possession." Smith, *How (Not) to Be Secular*, 140, 142.
30. Beshears, "Athens Without a Statue," 528.

ideas, Beshears commends engaging apatheism by using what he calls "a triad of anti-apathy—doubt, interest, and objective thinking."[31]

Beshears believes these pressures can compel the apatheist toward a sustained self-reflection that holds their interest long enough to allow objective thinking about God.[32] He quotes Kierkegaard as arguing that "doubt is a higher form than any objective thinking, for it presupposes the latter but has something more, a third, which is interest or consciousness."[33]

Finally, Beshears maintains that we need to show the desirability of the Christian faith. He writes, "Essentially, when it comes to apatheism, instead of presenting Christianity primarily as *rational*, we ought to present the faith as *desirable*."[34]

THE LAST BATTLE'S CHALLENGE TO APATHEISM

Based on what has been discussed thus far, there are several important ways that Narnia can help advocate Christian belief to apatheists. As noted, some of the key obstacles for apatheists include: insensitivity due to contested belief caused by religious diversity and globalization; a sense of existential security without God; distraction; a strong desire for autonomy; and a general indifference about God and ultimate questions. With these in mind, I will focus on six ways that *The Last Battle* can help to subvert some of these obstacles and encourage Christian belief among apatheists. These are: (1) the challenge of the true story in a place of contested belief, (2) the challenge of mirrored indifference, (3) the challenge of fleeting satisfaction, (4) the challenge of mortality, (5) the challenge of approaching judgment, and (6) the challenge of heaven.

The Challenge of the True Story in a Place of Contested Belief

As discussed, the diversity of belief options, particularly those resulting in religious fanaticism, is a significant obstacle for apatheists engaging with Christian belief. This forms part of the conviction that religious indifference is a cultural advancement. The problem is, this insensitivity

---

31. Beshears, "Athens Without a Statue," 528.
32. Beshears, "Athens Without a Statue," 528.
33. Beshears, "Athens Without a Statue," 528.
34. Beshears, "Sharing with Apatheist Friends," para. 15.

shuts the apatheist off from the one true gospel, and something needs to wake them from their slumber.

Narnia provides something like a mirror of self-reflection for the apatheist. Narnia in *The Last Battle*, much like the contemporary world, is a world of contested belief. There are at least six different kinds of religious belief presented in the story: (1) belief in Aslan, which is true and life giving—e.g., King Tirian, Jill, and others who believe and ultimately reside in Aslan's Country; (2) belief in Aslan, but poorly understood—e.g., the masses who believe in Aslan but are easily manipulated; (3) belief in Tash, who is real but enslaving—e.g., Tash is depicted as a real but life-taking being, despite the sincere affection some followers have for him; (4) belief in Tash as sincere but misplaced or incorrect—e.g., Emeth is a sincere believer in Tash, but his heart's desire is ultimately found in Aslan; (5) religious syncretism, which is used cynically as a tool for manipulation—e.g., Shift and the chief Calormene use religion to control the masses for personal gain; and (6) rejection of Aslan as false or irrelevant—e.g., the Dwarfs will not be taken in again, and Susan Pevensie no longer believes.[35]

Notice how Lewis depicts the reality of a single true story in the context of contested belief. In the final book of the series, a desperate battle is underway. Although Narnia has lived in peace for many years, a manipulative ape named Shift has managed to convince a somewhat foolish and impressionable donkey named Puzzle to impersonate Aslan, and he does it effectively. By fitting Puzzle with a lion's skin and exploiting confusion about Aslan's mysterious ways, Shift convinces many that Aslan has returned to Narnia and that he speaks for him.[36]

Hope that initially saturates Narnia with the joy of Aslan's advent turns to bewilderment. As a kind of anti-Christ, Shift uses Aslan's name as an opium of the people. In Aslan's name, Shift begins to amass self-serving power, and he orders acts that are confusing to those who are loyal to Aslan. In Aslan's name, Shift orders felling holy trees, murdering

---

35. From an evangelical perspective, Emeth's conversation with Aslan has fittingly come under scrutiny for its apparent inclusivism; see Lewis, *Last Battle*, 1082–83. In a letter to Mrs. Johnson dated November 8, 1952, Lewis explains his view further in reply to a question about what happens to Jews who are still waiting for the Messiah, suggesting that sincere prayers by those in false religions are accepted by God, and arguing from the parable of the sheep and the goats that some who are saved seem to be unaware they have served Christ. Lewis, *Collected Letters*, 3:245–46.

36. "He's not a tame lion" or a derivative phrase is used at least seven times in *The Last Battle*.

dryads, partnering with the Calormenes to enslave Narnians, and he imprisons King Tirian. And in Aslan's name Shift proclaims that Tash, the Calormene god, is just another name for Aslan. The effects are widespread and myriad.

This challenge aligns with the (translation) motif by depicting a world of contested beliefs in which many stories are being propagated, yet there is also a genuine Aslan. This is important in a world where the call to treat all religious claims as equal is mistakenly considered peaceable and virtuous, while simultaneously rejecting the non-peripheral truth claims of most religious systems dogmatically. Furthermore, abuses done in the name of religion are contrasted with the real Aslan, who is nothing like the deceiver; Aslan is good and truthful. This challenge also fits the (concern) motif. The intersection of diverse cultures and the presence of religious fanaticism are present, and yet the real Aslan still exists in the larger context. Abuses in this situation are done in the name of religion, but culpability is rightly laid at the deceiver's feet, not at Aslan's. Identity theft occurs in Narnia, just as it does today.

The Challenge of Mirrored Indifference

One effect of Shift and Puzzle stealing Aslan's identity is seen in the impact on the faith of the Dwarfs. The Dwarfs eventually come to see that they have been "taken in" by Shift and Puzzle. This phrase is repeated in *The Last Battle*. Having seen through Shift's con, the Dwarfs are embittered by any talk of Aslan from King Tirian or Jill. Griffle, the Black Dwarf, demurs the suggestion that Aslan has helped in any way and will not believe Jill when she says that she has seen him for herself, dismissing this and her claim to have come from another world as obvious brainwashing.[37] He continues, "We're on our own now. No more Aslan, no more Kings, no more silly stories about other worlds. The Dwarfs are for the Dwarfs."[38] "The Dwarfs are for the Dwarfs" recalls the people in the book of Judges who did what was right in their own eyes. The problem is because the Dwarfs refuse ever to be taken in by anyone again—they reject the *real* Aslan. They cannot see nor will they accept Aslan. They have misjudged him. And they cannot see or recognize the good gifts that

---

37. Lewis, *Last Battle*, 1010.
38. Lewis, *Last Battle*, 1011.

he offers, no matter what Aslan does—they are willfully blind, and the foolishness of their pride is obvious.

Moreover, Lewis helpfully teases out that although there can be many beliefs in a given context, there is one truth. Instead of arguing for the falsity of contrary beliefs, Aslan's truthfulness is shown through the testimony of grateful witnesses. In this context, it is Jill, Lucy, and Edmund. Furthermore, the reader is privy to the truth. Aslan's goodness is seen in his willingness to reach out to the obstinate (e.g., Aslan gives a feast that the Dwarfs willfully interpret as stable food and dirty water). Moreover, Lewis shows that there are losses with willful blindness. If Aslan is real and as good as others claim, I am missing him. Have I allowed abuses in the name of religion to keep me from the one for whom I was made? Have I mistaken gracious gifts for stable food? Is it really wisdom to avoid this question? Is God moving and wooing me?

This mirroring invites a virtuous apatheist to see and self-reflect (call) confidentially. As Lewis argued elsewhere, Christianity must be believed or rejected based on its truthfulness, not how helpful it might be.[39] Do I hope that I am right or wrong? If so, why? Would I reject his call willingly if he existed? If so, I am somewhat like the Dwarfs.

There are several significant ways that Lewis subverts apatheism in this context. The reader is presented with a chance for self-reflection and missing goodness. The reader is made conscious of self-imposed blindness (tension). The reader is presented with the callousing of deceit left by anti-Christ figures (concern). The reader is presented with doubt: What if Aslan is real (tension)? Moreover, the reader is made aware of the virtue of seeking and finding truth, and about the danger of missing something like divine goodness (tension, treasure, call).

The Challenge of Fleeting Satisfaction

As I noted, existential security without God is a consistent disposition for apatheists. In many ways, Susan Pevensie surprisingly embodies this temperament. One of the most disturbing and unexpected scenes in the whole Narnian series is Susan's fate in *The Last Battle*. Matthew Alderman calls the scene "one of childhood's great narrative shocks."[40]

---

39. Lewis, "Man or Rabbit," 109.
40. Alderman, "Whatever Happened to Susan Pevensie?" para. 1.

In the course of the final battle, Tirian ends up going through the stable door, not knowing what is on the other side. The door is dark and mysterious, evoking dread and finality. Much like death, it also feels inevitable, as though everyone must pass through it. Unexpectedly, Tirian finds himself in Aslan's Country. As Tirian stares in amazement, he is introduced to the High King Peter, Lady Polly, Lord Digory, Queen Lucy, and King Edmund. He is also surprised to see that Jill and Eustace are there as a queen and king, transformed from when he last saw them, covered in dirt and tears. But something still feels off to Tirian, and he wonders where Queen Susan is.[41] What follows is worth reading in full:

> "My sister Susan," answered Peter shortly and gravely, "is no longer a friend of Narnia." "Yes," said Eustace, "and whenever you've tried to get her to come and talk about Narnia or do anything about Narnia, she says 'What wonderful memories you have! Fancy your still thinking about all those funny games we used to play when we were children.'" "Oh Susan!" said Jill. "She's interested in nothing nowadays except nylons and lipstick and invitations. She always was a jolly sight too keen on being grown-up." "Grown-up, indeed," said the Lady Polly. "I wish she would grow up. She wasted all her school time wanting to be the age she is now, and she'll waste all the rest of her life trying to stay that age."[42]

This passage is startling and controversial among readers. As the second-oldest Pevensie sibling, Susan was often a voice of reason and measure among the children. Susan was gifted a bow and quiver of arrows from Father Christmas, along with an ivory horn that later summoned the Pevensies to Aslan's How—the place where the Stone Table once stood. Susan had reigned as Queen Susan of the Horn. Susan was present for Aslan's death and had felt the horror and sadness of Aslan's loss. On that day, she, along with Lucy, had kissed Aslan's face as it grew cold, stroked his marred fur, and cried until she could cry no more. Susan had heard the deafening crack of the Stone Table over her shoulder and trembled at what could be behind her. She had seen the empty Stone Table and wondered if Aslan's body had been stolen, only later to hear his great voice explain the Deeper Magic from before the Dawn of Time.[43] With Lucy, Susan felt the rush of joy replace her despair, and she too flung herself on

---

41. Lewis, *Last Battle*, 1059.
42. Lewis, *Last Battle*, 1059.
43. Lewis, *Lion*, 274.

the now living Aslan and covered him with kisses.[44] Susan was also there when Aslan's roar bent the trees like grass before riding his strong, tireless back to reclaim Narnia from the witch. Now, Susan is "no longer a friend of Narnia." Her priorities as a young woman have changed. Her interests now lie in nylons, lipstick, and invitations. These are novelties of affluence that diminish in significance during hardship. More disheartening, she considers her former faith a game she played as a child. In a word, Narnia and Aslan are now irrelevant. In apatheist terms, she has existential security without Aslan. She has socially advanced, while her siblings cling to an antiquated faith. Moreover, Susan is distracted by her youthful present. Contrary to criticisms that Lewis objected to Susan growing up, Polly laments Susan's naïveté for clinging to a fleeting life of trendy fashion.[45] Susan freely exchanges Aslan for this.

There are a number of ways that Lewis subverts obstacles that are relevant to apatheism. He translates betrayal and accountability in ways that are consistent with his view of violating the moral law (translation, call). If you notice, Susan's betrayal is greater than Edmund's—she was there at Aslan's death, saw him alive, and knew why Aslan gave his life. In Susan's life, we witness transformation in the reverse (transformation). A girl who once knew the goodness of Aslan exchanges him—the one who is repeatedly called the "heart's desire"—for lipstick and parties. Lewis identifies and contrasts Susan's short-lived treasures against a world of cosmic and deadly battle (treasure, tension, call). Her desire is fixed on fleeting pleasures and an unattainable fountain of youth. While the final king of Narnia is willing to lay down his life for the kingdom, Susan is unwilling to release her self-serving vanity; and she considers the world of Narnia a children's game (treasure, tension, call). The atmospheric qualities of the scene are saturated with fleeting time. This creates tension in the reader and recalls the force of Pascal's wager—we are *already* betting (tension, call). Albeit unknowingly and in vain, Susan is betting on the Shadowlands, and the apatheist is too. But what if there is more? Is my life pursuit satisfying? One thing is clear: we cannot stay the hand of time.

---

44. Lewis, *Lion*, 274; Tolkien calls this sudden joyous turn, when hope appears after all hope is lost a *eucatastrophe*, as discussed in chapter 1.

45. Lewis, *Last Battle*, 1059.

The Challenge of Mortality

Mortality is one of the most important resources for subverting apatheism. *The Last Battle* is especially well suited to remind the apatheist about her mortality and to awaken her from a false sense of existential security. The larger context is a world that is at war. Many of the characters anticipate their coming death as they face the battle for Narnia. Poggin foresees that they will all end up going through the mysterious stable door and is almost crippled with dread.[46]

The teeth of Lewis's challenge to existential security are felt even more fiercely because Lewis intersects the Narnian world with England. Choices in England, death in England, and even open choices with grave consequences push the apatheist to wake up to seek a sure foundation. In the *Chronicles*, that security is only found in Aslan and Aslan's Great Father, the Emperor-Over-the-Sea—in England, Aslan goes by another name.

As the narrative unfolds, Tirian continues talking with the kings and queens of Narnia, finding that they are in a new country. The fruit of the land is unfamiliar yet somehow sweeter and far better than any fruit they had ever tasted. More curious, it feels like a place where everything is allowed.[47] Eustace, meanwhile, is trying to figure out how everyone ended up in this land. Peter explains that he and Edmund saw the train carrying Lucy and their parents coming in too fast toward them. There was then an alarming roar and a bang, before they found themselves here. Polly and Digory were on the train and had a similar experience. They describe being "unstiffened," meaning they stopped feeling old, yet everyone felt about the same age in this land.

Later, as the book closes, Lucy explains that she's afraid of being sent back to their world, and she desperately wants to stay. But Aslan gently explains that she does not need to fear that now: "'There was a real railway accident,' said Aslan softly. 'Your father and mother and all of you are—as you used to call it in the Shadowlands—dead. The term is over: the holidays have begun. The dream is ended: this is the morning.'"[48]

There are several ways in which the challenge of mortality subverts apatheism. Consistent with the tension motif, the atmospheric qualities of the scene are saturated with fleeting time. This creates tension in the

---

46. Lewis, *Last Battle*, 1054.
47. Lewis, *Last Battle*, 1062.
48. Lewis, *Last Battle*, 1097.

reader and recalls the force of Pascal's wager—we are all betting right now. Albeit unknowingly and in vain, Susan is betting on the Shadowlands, and the apatheist is too. Intentional or not, Lewis subverts Susan's false sense of existential security, as well as those who find themselves in her life (tension, call).

Ecclesiastes 7:2 says, "It is better to go to the house of mourning than to go to the house of feasting, for this is the end of all mankind, and the living will lay it to heart." The writer wisely notes that death is a place that can awaken an appropriate sense of doubt about our existential security and what truly matters in life, while a party often distracts us. Death reminds us of the frailty of life. Death reminds us about what matters. Death is the ultimate equalizer—rich or poor, kind or terrible; we will stand before the Lord and give an account for our lives. At parties, we don't usually think about life beyond the party. At death, we are forced to ask: "Is there more? Is there actual hope beyond the grave?"

Lewis also translates the reality of life after death (translation). It is a place where Aslan reigns, and it is good. This is developed more in what I call the challenge of heaven. Lewis uses transformation and treasure to show that those who love Aslan go to a better life (transformation, treasure). Even their bodies are feeling better. Life after death is a life that is just beginning—"the holiday has begun." Tension is created by the intersection of Narnia with the real world of England. Death touches both worlds (tension). This invites self-reflection in the reader and, fittingly, creates doubt about one's existential security.

The narrative force of Susan's exclusion from Narnia is reflected in comments made by readers. Setting aside those who erroneously focus on Susan's gender rather than her shortsighted vanity, Lewis once responded to a concerned child's letter asking about Susan. In that letter, Lewis explained that Susan was still alive in our world, with the potential to reach Aslan's Country eventually.[49] The seriousness of Susan's state is further amplified by the challenge of approaching judgment (tension, call).

The Challenge of Approaching Judgment

The Last Battle also vividly depicts Narnia's end and final judgment. With a deafening roar, Aslan wakens Father Time, a great giant who Jill and Eustace once saw asleep underground north of Narnia and were told he

---

49. Lewis, *Letters to Children*, 67.

would awaken at the end of the world.[50] The giant raises a horn to his mouth, and after some time, the sound travels to their ears. This causes a downpour of stars from the sky, creating a blackness and void that steadily grows.[51] As the dark cosmic shift unfolds in what feels like slow motion, stars cast enough light for those watching to see movement as monstrous creatures, including dragons and bat-like, featherless birds, to descend on Narnia.[52] Then come all the creatures from across the world of Narnia, men and beasts, dwarfs and giants, and every strange creature from the ends of the earth.[53] All of these creatures come before Aslan and the door. The door imperceptibly changes size, or the creatures do. This is clear because the door is somehow closer to scale with the crowd of living creatures.

As each creature approaches Aslan, they look straight in his face, and it does not appear that they have a choice about it. They all come before him in a way that recalls giving an account to one who knows you completely. Responses to Aslan's face differ dramatically. Some show fear and revulsion, and vanish into his shadow, but others look to Aslan and love him, though some of these still show fear that recalls Isaiah's encounter with the holiness of God (Isa 6:1–5). Talking Beasts who despise Aslan suddenly cease to be Talking Beasts and become ordinary animals, while those who revere him enter the Door.

Cosmic changes continue. The sun dramatically increases in size and becomes dark red—it is dying. The great Time giant also turns red, and the moon follows suit. Then Aslan commands the end.[54] The giant extinguishes the sun, and there is total darkness. Ice-cold air blows through the doorway, and Aslan calls on Peter, as high king of Narnia, to shut the door, which Peter does, locking it with a golden key. Then Aslan joyfully invites all who have passed with him through the door to "Come further in! Come further up!"[55] The judgment of those who rejected Aslan is over—now the adventure begins.

There are several ways that Lewis subverts apatheism with the challenge of approaching judgment. Lewis uses translation by showing the cost of rejecting Aslan (translation). He also uses transformation to show

---

50. Lewis, *Last Battle*, 1071.
51. Lewis, *Last Battle*, 1072.
52. Lewis, *Last Battle*, 1073.
53. Lewis, *Last Battle*, 1074.
54. Lewis, *Last Battle*, 1074.
55. Lewis, *Last Battle*, 1077.

the effects of this rejection (transformation, tension). For one, Talking Beasts become less than what they were made to be. For those who fittingly regard Aslan, he is a great treasure. For those who reject him, he is a lost treasure. Lewis also challenges pluralism here. There is one to whom all will give an account, and your response to him will determine your fate (translation, tension, call). These features invite a sobering tension for the apatheist. Once again, Pascal's wager is relevant. The apatheist is already betting.

Lingering in the reader's heart is grief about what could have been. Why did they do this? What if Susan had not turned her heart to short-lived pleasures? What if the Dwarfs had listened like Poggin? Why did some of the Talking Beasts hate someone like Aslan? Aslan's words to Lucy about the Dwarfs echo on: "They have chosen cunning instead of belief."[56]

The Challenge of Heaven

If all one knew of heaven was the caricature of a never-ending life of sitting on a cloud plucking a harp, there is little chance that anyone would exchange even the most basic of temporal pleasures for this. Lewis said it well in his sermon "The Weight of Glory" that "we are half-hearted creatures, fooling about with drink and sex and ambition when infinite joy is offered us."[57] This sentiment is embodied in Susan's life in *The Last Battle*, but this is also a place where Narnia can help. Theologian N. T. Wright makes a related observation: "Here is the challenge, I believe, for the Christian artist, in whatever sphere: 'to tell the story of the new world so that people can taste it and want it, even while acknowledging the reality of the desert in which we presently live.'"[58]

With this in mind, there are three significant ways that Lewis subverts apatheism with this challenge in *The Last Battle*: (1) the joy of discovery, (2) longing for home, and (3) longing for Aslan.

The Joy of Discovery

Lewis describes a world that is both familiar and unexplored. Aslan's Country is more *real* than the Shadowlands, yet similar to what they

56. Lewis, *Last Battle*, 1070.
57. Lewis, *Weight of Glory*, 27.
58. Wright, *Surprised by Scripture*, 203.

all knew and loved in Narnia and England. Lewis's imagined version of heaven as a more real place recalls Plato's forms or ideas.[59] The genre is still fantasy, so there is no need to expect one-to-one correspondence with Christian orthodoxy about bodily resurrection and the new creation. Moreover, a common problem for Christians and non-Christians is imagining an afterlife that is greater than our current one, or one that doesn't involve ethereal cloud living with harps and angel wings.

Lewis powerfully describes the physical world of the new Narnia as being mysteriously more real, deep, and vivid, emphasizing its physicality rather than a disembodied Platonism. Tumnus explains to a bewildered Lucy, "The further up and the further in you go, the bigger everything gets. The inside is larger than the outside."[60] As Lucy looks harder, she sees that the garden, like the stable, is far bigger inside than outside, yet it is not really a garden either, but a whole world, familiar to her.[61]

Longing for Home

Lewis also draws on our longing for home. As we saw in chapter 1, Tolkien described this desire as a "longing for Eden," seeing our nature as "soaked with the sense of 'exile.'"[62] But in contrast to the sense of exile that we often feel in our broken world, the new Narnia feels like home. Jewel the Unicorn cries out: "I have come home at last! This is my real country! I belong here. This is the land I have been looking for all my life, though I never knew it till now."[63] This image is potent. The unicorn is more at home than he has ever been. There is a sense in which we can recognize

---

59. Paul Ford's clarification is helpful: In Christian theology "Plato's ideas, the intelligible blueprints for material realities, become creative thoughts in the mind of God or what he has in mind when creating. Creatures are thus intelligible instances of designs 'thought up' by God. It follows, as Aquinas says, that whatever is of value or excellence in any creature pre-exists in God. Were one able to go 'further up and further in'—into the very mind and being of God—one would find not an utterly new reality but something strangely familiar, something 'like' what one had always known before, only supremely better. . . . Art is able, at times, to capture and represent what is significant in life better than life does. Lewis thought that story was one of the ways in which the eternal might be glimpsed within the temporal." Ford, *Companion to Narnia*, 340.

60. Lewis, *Last Battle*, 1095.

61. Lewis, *Last Battle*, 1095.

62. Carpenter and Tolkien, *Letters of Tolkien*, 110. It is worth noting that Tolkien speaks of Lewis's influence on some of his thought in relation to derived beliefs about Eden, and comments on what is presumed to be Lewis's essay "Myth Became Fact."

63. Lewis, *Last Battle*, 1095.

that while earth is home in a true sense, our hearts also have a restlessness for more. Ford says it well: "The human heart, incited by the limited good and beauties of creation, discovers within itself a restless, piercing desire for the unlimited source of all reality and perfection."[64] The unicorn no longer experiences this limitation, having moved from desire to fulfilment. Furthermore, he invites the reader to recognize this deep-seated desire, because he did not fully recognize it before.

Second, *brokenness and depravity* are absent from this country. Judgment has removed the deceivers and those who reject Aslan, and war is no more. Pretense is no more. Puzzle is now more himself, no longer a confused, manipulated creature, but a gentle, honest, and beautiful one who is embraced by Jill and Lucy.[65]

Bodily decay is also a thing of the past. The stiffness of age and the soreness of hurts are no longer felt. Those who were old and those who were young in the Shadowlands are equals and more alive. As Jewel sets off at "a Unicorn's gallop," all the others follow him and find that they can keep up, running with exhilarating speed, without any tiredness or sense of exertion.[66] Furthermore, in this land, *fear* is no more. Lucy notices that they are unable to feel afraid, even when they try.[67]

Third, in this country, there is *true belonging*—all are in the Inner Ring. In his famous essay by that name, Lewis wrote about the strong desire that we experience to be included in the "Inner Ring," and the fear of being excluded.[68] This fear is absent in Aslan's Country. All belong and are welcome. Familiar and known faces from diverse countries appear and welcome these newcomers as Reepicheep leads them on, including Puddleglum, Caspian, and other old friends. With fresh eyes, Lewis helps us to see the beauty of friendship, belonging, and laughter. The ugliness of marred self-love and fragmentation have vanished (see Jas 4:1–3a). The attraction of oneness in diversity is displayed (see Rev 5:9–10; 7:9–10).

Fourth, in this country, there is a *delightful stay of time*. As the newcomers relish in the fellowship, Lewis makes a passing comment that is quite important: that Lucy and Tumnus might have been talking for half an hour, or half a century, because time works differently there.[69] Time is

64. Ford, *Companion to Narnia*, 333.
65. Lewis, *Last Battle*, 1084.
66. Lewis, *Last Battle*, 1087–88.
67. Lewis, *Last Battle*, 1090.
68. Lewis, *Weight of Glory*, 147.
69. Lewis, *Last Battle*, 1095.

no longer an enemy. Death is no more, and fellowship is not hurried. Our desire in the Shadowlands for the stay of time, the absence of decay, and the desire for peace is satisfied in this country.

Longing for Aslan

Longing for Aslan is another aspect of the challenge of heaven. In the larger context of *The Last Battle*, a prolonged sense of Aslan's absence is compounded by cultural pressure from "the enlightened." Those who do not believe in Aslan are portrayed as the only ones who really know what is going on. Shift has manipulated in Aslan's name, and a graphic and hopeless battle engulfs Narnia. A dark veil of impending death looms over Aslan's people. Contrasted with this numinous world's heavy atmosphere of evil, Lewis depicts Aslan as the object of longing.

In this context of evil, despair over the dwarfs' blindness, and disorientation of entering another world, Aslan appears with a shaking of the earth and a sharp increase of sweetness in the already sweet air.[70] This is also Lewis's language for *Sehnsucht*, the longing that drew him to the Christian faith. Tirian turns around to see him: "There stood his heart's desire, huge and real, the golden Lion, Aslan himself."[71]

Aslan's regal majesty and worth is infectiously conveyed in this scene, in that all kneel at his arrival. Furthermore, Aslan is accessible and visible to those who see. Later, they encounter him again: "Aslan himself was coming, leaping down from cliff to cliff like a living cataract of power and beauty."[72] This conveys Aslan's authority and masculine beauty.

As the throng approaches Aslan, a curious thing occurs. Aslan calls Puzzle to himself, and whispers to him privately.[73] There is a sense in which Puzzle's guilt and shame are first of all made known, but Lewis hints at his forgiveness. Aslan is one who knows, yet forgives. He is a friend of sinners.

As the scene unfolds, Lucy explains that she's afraid of being sent back to their world, and she desperately wants to stay. So many times before, she longed to remain with Aslan in Narnia, but she was sent back to England. But Aslan softly explains that she does not need to fear that.

---

70. Lewis, *Last Battle*, 1069.
71. Lewis, *Last Battle*, 1069.
72. Lewis, *Last Battle*, 1097.
73. Lewis, *Last Battle*, 1097.

As we discussed earlier, Aslan explains to them that they died in a railway accident. They have come to Aslan's Country to stay. Lewis powerfully evokes the hope of eternity in heaven: "Now at last they were beginning Chapter One of the Great Story which no one on earth has read: which goes on forever: in which every chapter is better than the one before."[74]

There are a number of ways that the challenge of heaven undermines apatheism. Lewis translates the concept of God—he is accessible, personal, knowable, and good (translation). Lewis uses transformation both in the lives of those entering the heaven-like country and Puzzle's forgiveness (transformation). He contagiously depicts Aslan and the goodness of heaven (translation, treasure). Moreover, it is our true home. Heaven is a place where friendship is real, sin is forgotten, and a place where adventure is waiting to be had (call).

Lewis also depicts and translates the gathering of the invisible church (translation, call). Michael Ward perceptively notes that the gathering of the 'friends of Narnia' is Lewis's version of Dante's 'Church Triumphant' in Dante's *Paradiso*.[75] Ward explains, "As a literary critic, Lewis knew that, for Dante, the fruit of the planetary Spheres was this 'gathering of the Church Triumphant in heaven' and, as a writer of fiction, he here imitates the great Florentine's example."[76]

CONCLUSION

In this chapter, I have shown how *The Last Battle* advocates Christian theism to apatheists by subverting some of the most common obstacles to faith and advocating faith through narrative apologetics. These include: (1) the challenge of the true story in a place of contested belief, (2) the challenge of mirrored indifference, (3) the challenge of fleeting satisfaction, (4) the challenge of mortality, (5) the challenge of approaching judgment, and (6) the challenge of heaven. Lewis's words are fitting for narrative apologetics to apatheism: "The task of the modern educator is not to cut down jungles but to irrigate deserts. The right defense against false sentiments is to inculcate just sentiments."[77] *The Last Battle* tacitly but powerfully warns of the real consequences of rejecting Jesus,

---

74. Lewis, *Last Battle*, 1098.
75. Ward, "Church in Lewis's Fiction," 88–89.
76. Ward, "Church in Lewis's Fiction," 88.
77. Lewis, *Abolition of Man*, 16.

and contagiously celebrates the living and fixed hope of eternal life in Christ. Lewis cultivates a taste for what is true and challenges what is false. Warning and wooing are both needed.

Cross-Cultural Narrative Apologetics for Moments of Clarity

In *The Silver Chair*, Lewis tells the story of Prince Rilian, who has been missing for ten years because he was kidnapped by a witch who is queen of the Underland. Sadly, the queen bewitched him, causing Rilian to believe that she is good and that the only real life is the life of the Underland. Each night, Rilian's enchantment subsides, and just for a moment, he can think clearly. The problem is that he has come to believe that these are psychotic episodes. In reality, these are his few moments of clarity in a life buried in deceit. Rilian is so enchanted that he does not even try to escape. He willingly submits to the shackles . . . and his enchantment is nearly complete. Rilian needs someone from the outside to help him see for himself that Aslan is real, good, and glorious, and that the world is far greater than the Underland he calls home.

This is much the same in cross-cultural narrative apologetics. Anyone without Jesus Christ is, in a sense, enchanted and shackled (Eph 2:1–3), even if they have momentary glimpses of clarity (Ps 19:1–4; Rom 1:19–20; Acts 17:24–27). The role of narrative apologetics is to graciously and lovingly help to break through the enchantments that keep people from seeing Jesus for all that he is (Rom 10:14–15; 2 Cor 5:20–21; John 3:16; Matt 28:18–20; Rev 21). As we have seen, *The Chronicles of Narnia* provides many natural pathways to the Underworld. More pathways are waiting to be made.

Conclusion

Building Bridges with Story

CLYDE S. KILBY, THE founder of the Marion E. Wade Center at Wheaton College, tells the story of receiving a letter from a teacher in New Jersey who was reading *The Lion, the Witch and the Wardrobe* to her third graders:

> She had come to the point where the lion Aslan allowed himself to be killed by his enemies to save a bad boy's life. "The attitude of the room," said this teacher, "was worship, holiness. The rare impression of that moment will never leave me. When I finished the chapter about Aslan's death the room was stunned in disbelief. Aslan dead! And then a child who had read further said, 'Don't give up—something wonderful is going to happen.' It crept through the room and sighs issued. The little people had caught glimpses of the very real, the miracle of spiritual understanding."[1]

This unknown third grader was a bridge of hope for a class that knew the mythic taste of hopelessness and despair. The child stood between the worlds of Narnia and that New Jersey classroom with a known hope of future resurrection. That same day, a classroom of third graders experienced something like holiness and also became familiar with an untamed lion who was not finally held by death. You could hardly hope for better

---

1. Kilby, *Well of Wonder*, 14; Brian Williams notes this story in his work. See Williams, *Narnia Might Be More Real Than We Think*, 12.

pre-evangelism. All that is required is someone willing to graciously connect the dots. That is narrative apologetics.

WHAT HAVE WE DISCOVERED?

We have explored C. S. Lewis's use of narrative apologetics in *The Chronicles of Narnia*. I have examined how Lewis addresses belief and unbelief to help you enhance your own understanding of how literature can help cultivate and defend Christian belief in engaging with other belief systems. The increase of globalization continues to make cross-cultural apologetics a relevant need. While missiology has for some time recognized the role of Bible storying, which uses oral storytelling to share relevant Bible stories to communicate the gospel cross-culturally, I believe fictional and fantasy stories are an underused pathway for advocating and communicating Christianity cross-culturally.

Narrative apologetics, and *The Chronicles of Narnia* in particular, can contribute to cross-cultural apologetics by helping translate relevant Christian beliefs, advocating Christianity's truth and goodness, subverting the adequacy of non-Christian belief, and helping respond to objections made against Christian belief. We analyzed six of the best works done in narrative apologetics. We considered three classical models: George MacDonald, J. R. R. Tolkien, and C. S. Lewis. Next, we explored three contemporary models: Alister McGrath, Holly Ordway, and Justin Bailey.

After identifying some of the best resources for narrative apologetics, we focused on two cross-cultural apologetic projects, those of Benno van den Toren and Harold Netland. Using these models, we have seen some of the most important needs, barriers, and pathways for cross-cultural apologetic engagement.

We then considered six keys, or narrative motifs, that are especially relevant for cross-cultural apologetics: (1) translation, (2) transformation, (3) treasure, (4) tension, (5) concern, and (6) call. The keys became a tool that allowed me to identify and explore some of the ways that the *Narnia* stories, and those speaking with others about them, might contribute to cross-cultural apologetics.

We then looked at how Narnia can speak to four influential belief systems: Islamic theism, naturalism, Eastern pantheistic monism, and apatheism. We considered the contours of each particular belief system. I then identified some of the essential needs and barriers within each profile for apologetic engagement. Finally, we looked at how *The Chronicles of Narnia* advocates Christian belief to the profile, informed by my six keys.

KEY FINDINGS

There are at least four ways this book helps us better understand cross-cultural and narrative apologetics: first, by analyzing a spectrum of narrative apologetic projects, we have seen a range of resources that exist in narrative apologetics. I have sought to synthesize different models of narrative apologetics, similar to syntheses that have been done for traditional apologetics.[2] Much more could be explored, but we have seen a spectrum of possibilities, projects, and even convictions about the nature of narrative apologetics.

Second, this book has shown how stories, specifically *The Chronicles of Narnia*, can contribute to cross-cultural apologetics. Except for Benno van den Toren, and in different ways Art Lindsley, David Marshall, and John Bowen, few have discussed narrative as a pathway for cross-cultural apologetics using Lewis's work.[3] I identified twenty-six challenges and analyzed them according to my six keys. These challenges are only representative. Much more is possible, both within the specific books of *The Chronicles of Narnia* that I discussed and in other books in the series that I did not develop. Nevertheless, the potential of *The Chronicles of Narnia* for cross-cultural apologetics is significant, compounded by the fact that they has been translated into forty-seven different languages; and the stories themselves continue to grow in influence. This is evident based on movies already produced and in future work, such as the series planned by Netflix.[4]

A NEW WAY OF SEEING

To recognize my need for Jesus, something must displace my unbelief. Those who are committed to a given belief system require motivation to

---

2. See for example, Boa and Bowman, *Faith Has Its Reasons*; Forrest et al., *History of Apologetics*.

3. Marshall, *Case for Aslan*, 166–86. It should be noted that the use of oral storytelling is well known in missiology due in part to the large percentage of the world that communicates orally and in storytelling. Illiteracy is another motivating factor.

4. Halcombe, "Netflix to Develop Series and Films."

leave the false security of that system. This need for impetus is recognized across cross-cultural apologetic models. Another option must be offered, or a person will tend to defend the only model they possess. Thomas Kuhn notes this human need in terms of scientific paradigm shifts, and Benno van den Toren identifies this need with respect to cross-cultural apologetics.

The Chronicles of Narnia invites the reader from any worldview to see through the eyes of something like the Christian worldview, translated into a fantasy world. It woos the reader to Aslan and his kingdom as an alternative paradigm, through which one can see the world anew. Lewis memorably said, "I believe in Christianity as I believe that the Sun has risen, not only because I see it, but because by it I see everything else."[5] Christianity *became* the model through which Lewis could finally see the world. *The Chronicles of Narnia* introduces a new way of seeing, through the medium of story.

When we have friends and neighbors who share the common story of *The Chronicles of Narnia* as a point of reference, we can help connect the dots from Narnia to Christianity, using worldview-relevant points of contact that I have identified in my six keys.

THE POWER OF NARNIA

A third area we have explored is *The Chronicles of Narnia*'s effectiveness as a work of narrative apologetics. For example, as detailed earlier, the testimonies of Dr. Holly Ordway (a former atheist) and Dr. Fong Choon Sam (a former Buddhist) demonstrate the ability of *The Chronicles of Narnia* to help some readers (treasure) Aslan and (translate) doctrines like the incarnation.[6]

I also shared how *The Chronicles of Narnia* contributed to my cross-cultural university class (translation, treasure), and in sharing the gospel with my daughter, Zoe (translation, call). Similarly, Clyde Kilby's letter from a third-grade teacher affirms the potency of *The Chronicles of Narnia*. As Kilby records, "The little people caught glimpses of the very real, the miracle of spiritual understanding" (translation, treasure).[7]

5. Lewis, "Is Theology Poetry?" 165.

6. Dr. Holly Ordway's story is found in chapter 2 in the section "Imagination and Incarnation" (p. 54); Dr. Fong Choon Sam's story is found in chapter 5 on Islam in the section "The Challenge of Aslan" (p. 125).

7. Kilby, *Well of Wonder*, 14.

Other testimonies corroborate the ability of *The Chronicles of Narnia* to cultivate "favorable conditions" for belief. For example, Lewis scholar Dr. Brian Williams tells how his heart was stirred as a second-grade boy when his teacher read *The Lion, the Witch and the Wardrobe*. Williams says he was usually a very fidgety child, but when this story was read in class, it gripped him. Williams recalls, "This story captured my imagination and produced in my heart a longing so intense that I would have given anything in my possession to be granted real, rather than merely imaginary access through the wardrobe into Narnia" (treasure, call).[8] In seminary, while reading Lewis's *Surprised by Joy*, Williams understood from Lewis that the longing he experienced in *The Lion, the Witch and the Wardrobe* was pointing to something beyond the world. By then, he was already a Christian. Nevertheless, Williams says looking back: "Joy was calling me to Him who is absolute truth, goodness, and beauty, the fountain of all legitimate pleasure in whose presence alone our hearts find rest. This One is none other than Christ the Lord."[9] *The Lion, the Witch and the Wardrobe* was a *praeparatio evangelica* for Williams.

Another example is found in the correspondence between Lewis and a concerned mother on May 6, 1955. Her nine-year-old son, Laurence, was concerned that he somehow *loved Aslan more than Jesus*. Lewis's reply is helpful: "Laurence can't *really* love Aslan more than Jesus, even if he feels that's what he is doing. For the things he loves Aslan for doing or saying are simply the things Jesus really did and said. So that when Laurence thinks he is loving Aslan, he is really loving Jesus: and perhaps loving Him more than he ever did before" (treasure, translation).[10]

Yet another example is from Dr. John Bowen, retired professor of evangelism at Wycliffe College, Ontario. Bowen describes Narnia's impact based on theological conversations he had with a woman in her thirties through email correspondence. With her permission, Bowen shares the kinds of questions that were evoked for her after reading *The Chronicles of Narnia*: (1) Moved by the creation story in *The Magician's Nephew*, she asked herself, as a created being with purpose, "Who am I meant to be?" (translation, call). (2) Inspired by the Dwarfs' love for making crowns and Bowen's observation that "it was what they were made to do . . . thus what they do well," the woman was challenged vocationally.

---

8. Williams, *Why Narnia Might Be More Real Than We Think*, 12.
9. Williams, *Why Narnia Might Be More Real Than We Think*, 13.
10. Lewis, *Letters to Children*, 52.

She wondered, "'What is it that I have been made to do well?'" (treasure, translation, tension). (3) After reading *Prince Caspian* and seeing Susan's hesitation to follow Aslan, even though she believed, the woman wondered, "What are the things that stop me following Aslan even though I believe in him (like Susan in *Prince Caspian*)? This is one I *really* need to work on" (treasure, translation, tension).[11] Bowen concludes, "I cannot imagine that (humanly speaking) any amount of preaching would have caused her to ask such questions [tension, treasure]. But Narnia has reached very deep into her soul, and drew her closer to Aslan almost by the day. The watchful dragons were indeed driven back."[12]

A final example is one told by Christian author Christin Ditchfield. She tells the story of a woman who came to faith because of her exposure to *The Chronicles of Narnia*. Ditchfield explains that she was doing a book signing at a Christian bookstore when this woman approached her. Ditchfield recounts, "She told me she had come into this Christian bookstore some time earlier with her kids on a hot day."[13] She had come into the store's air conditioning to escape the heat and to get a break with her kids. The woman continues:

> And as she looked around, she realized there was nothing in the store that was familiar to her. And then her eyes landed on a copy of *A Family Guide to Narnia*, and she thought "Narnia, Narnia. I think I read that series when I was in school. What's it doing in a religious bookstore?" She didn't know it had any spiritual parallels or principles or anything. But it was the one thing that looked familiar, so she picked it up, and she bought it. She said to me, in this letter, "I went home, and I read that, and I pulled out *The Chronicles of Narnia*, and we started reading it together as a family. And then I would read what you had written about the Scriptures there."[14]

The woman continues, "I went back to the bookstore to get a Bible, so that I could look it up for myself, so that we could share those truths together. . . . I told my husband, I think we need to be in a church."[15] Ditchfield writes, "And they started visiting and found a local church

---

11. Bowen, "Evangelistic Text?" paras. 44–48.
12. Bowen, "Evangelistic Text?" para. 51.
13. Ditchfield, "Biblical Truths," 15.
14. Ditchfield, "Biblical Truths," 15.
15. Ditchfield, "Biblical Truths," 15.

that felt like home to them."[16] The woman told Ditchfield, "I want you to know that my husband and I and all of my kids, we've been baptized. We've made a profession of faith. We found Jesus through *The Chronicles of Narnia*, and we are walking with Him and serving Him as a result" (translation, treasure).[17] By the woman's own account, *The Chronicles of Narnia* prepared the way for her whole family to meet Jesus. Ditchfield's book *A Family Guide to Narnia* does something like narrative apologetics as I have described it. Ditchfield takes the stories and points to parallels and principles in Scripture, to include biblical doctrines like the destiny of the wicked (translation, tension, treasure, call).

Each of these examples suggest that *The Chronicles of Narnia* has great potential to contribute to narrative apologetics. Other examples also exist in print.[18] The fact that there are forty-seven translations of *The Chronicles of Narnia* strongly suggests that their potential for cross-cultural apologetics is a door that is already open and they can be used for more.

THE SIX KEYS

A fourth advancement is that my study has identified and highlighted some of narrative's most critical targets for cross-cultural apologetics, and created a Six Keys Model that can be used for analysis or creativity. First, *translation* is needed to understand basic Christianity because some fundamental understanding is required for salvation. Following the Reformers, *notitia*, *assensus*, and *fiducia* are needed for saving faith. *Noticia* is the content of faith—namely, the object of faith, Jesus Christ. *Assensus* requires that the content be affirmed and believed to be true. Finally, *fiducia* means to entrust ourselves to Jesus.[19] Narrative can afford something like a devotional experiment for the reader. Moreover, translation is needed to understand the actual content of the Christian faith.

Second, *transformation* is a needed target because it reflects the impact that Aslan (and Christ) has on individuals and societies. Many harbor false beliefs about what Christianity is, and this is an actual obstacle for them. Imaginative transformation shows the positive impact of Aslan

16. Ditchfield, "Biblical Truths," 15.
17. Ditchfield, "Biblical Truths," 16.
18. See Phemister and Lazo, *Mere Christians*.
19. Sproul, *Justified by Faith Alone*, 48–49.

and his kingdom values. It is a kind of pre-evangelism in that it shows the kind of impact that Jesus has on individuals and societies, contrary to caricatures and misrepresentations.

Third, *treasure* is another important narrative target. It highlights the goodness of Jesus and Christian truths. It also cultivates sentiments and points to the One who satisfies our deep longings. Treasure is also effective in a way that recalls Lewis's desire to go past watchful dragons. Lewis felt that being told one must care about certain things froze one's feelings. By celebrating the goodness of Jesus and Christian truths through narrative, treasure cultivates favorable conditions for belief.

Fourth, *tension* is vital because it engages the existential pressures of a given belief system. Tensions include cosmic security, questions of immortality and life after death, fulfillment and unfulfilled meaning and purpose, forgiveness and guilt, truth and living against the truth, and love. It also includes known problems in a given worldview. These targets are natural places for narrative engagement. The narrative tensions trade on what Francis Schaeffer termed the "mannishness of man"—that God has made the world and man for it. To live at odds with God's design is to live in tension.

Fifth, *concern* is needed because true obstacles hinder belief for the non-Christian. By addressing concerns and offering preliminary responses, the narrative contributes to apologetics. Furthermore, concerns are even obstacles for the believer. Headlines of prominent people leaving the faith or "deconstructing" suggest that concern is also a needed target for professing believers.

Sixth, *call* is an essential target because it is a narrative appeal to belief. I have shown how *The Chronicles of Narnia* call the reader to see with fresh eyes. Recall that the children were brought to Narnia to know Aslan for a little while, but they will know him by another name in England. Thoughtful readers are invited to know the Aslan of England. In addition, arguments like Lewis's argument from desire and the living object of its satisfaction are presented in narrative form. Other potent images that call include the need and source of forgiveness as presented in Eustace's un-dragoning and Edmund's redemption.

Finally, the targets I have identified are also enhanced by the specific needs and tensions within individual worldview profiles. The specificity of potential targets for engagement is informed by cross-cultural apologetic research and missiological studies. Future writers across worldviews who, like Lewis, allow "the man" in them to have a turn can seek to bypass precise barriers through literary art. Moreover, writers can be informed by the obstacles that exist across worldviews.

THREE GROUPS WHO MAY BENEFIT

I believe this book can especially help you if you are in any of the following three groups: first, it can help *normal Christians* who are looking for natural paths to discuss the truth, goodness, and beauty of Christianity in a pluralistic world. *The Chronicles of Narnia* and other stories offer a common ground for narrative apologetic discussions across worldviews. A few examples will help illustrate some of the ways this could work. I know of a literature student from the UK who held a reading of *The Lion, the Witch and the Wardrobe* over food on two consecutive Sundays with fellow literature students. He found that it was an enjoyable way to connect with people, and it also opened the door to spiritual conversations. The six keys we discussed in the book, translation, transformation, treasure, tension, concern, and call, can be applied in similar contexts by helping identify some of the most fruitful points of discussion. The challenges I explained in the specific worldview discussions furthermore show some of the ways narrative can bridge into cross-cultural apologetic conversations.

Consider several of the six keys based on Edmund's life in *The Lion, the Witch and the Wardrobe*. Think about these six questions:

- In what ways are even the nicest people tempted like Edmund? (Translation)
- Do you remember the cost of Edmund's betrayal of his family? (Translation)
- Could Edmund free himself? Why or why not? (Translation)
- Do you remember what it took to set him free? (Translation, treasure)
- What was Aslan willing to do for Edmund? (Translation, treasure)
- What kind of changes occurred in Edmund's life after meeting Aslan? (Transformation, translation, treasure)

Based on a perfectly natural discussion about Edmund, it is easy to explain how Christians are similar to Edmund. All Christians begin with recognizing that they are not morally innocent. Furthermore, the transformation and forgiveness we need come from the outside. Aslan gave his life for Edmund, and this is very similar to what Jesus did on the cross.

The six keys also apply outside of *The Chronicles of Narnia*. Consider the movie *Schindler's List*. In the film, the director poignantly conveys the horrors of the Holocaust by filming a young Jewish girl in a red coat as she walks through the Jewish ghetto. Her fear and innocence strongly contrast with the senseless evil surrounding her, as people are murdered in cold blood just feet from her when she walks home. The senselessness of evil is further emphasized because her red coat is the only color in the entire movie, and it is later pictured among the pile of victims' clothes.

Consider some of the six keys based on this story. Reflect on these six questions that relate to cross-cultural apologetics:

- How does this movie convey the evil of the Holocaust? (Translation)
- Why do you think we are so outraged by what happened in the Holocaust? Do we have the right to judge other cultural beliefs? (Concern, tension)
- Based on this film, do you think that evil is real or merely an illusion? Why? (Tension)
- Based on your worldview, is there any hope for justice for Hitler and those behind the Holocaust? (Concern, tension)
- Based on your worldview, is there any hope for those who died beyond the grave? Why? (Tension, concern)
- If there really is hope beyond death, would you want to know about it? Why or why not? (Call, tension, treasure).

A second group that may benefit from my research is *Christians living in closed countries, missionaries, or missiologists*. If you are in this group, I hope this book might help you communicate or advocate Christianity using the stories of *The Chronicles of Narnia*, if they are available. Three representative contexts come to mind. First, *The Chronicles of Narnia* are available in forty-seven languages, so, where contextually appropriate, you can create book clubs similar to the literature student from the UK. Using the six keys and the representative challenges I have identified, you can create custom questions based on the dominant worldview of your context. Alternatively, English clubs or English classes at schools and universities worldwide are natural places to discuss *The Chronicles of Narnia* in ways that I have illustrated in this book. Because *The Chronicles of Narnia* is children's literature, the vocabulary is more accessible. For true beginners, a student could have copies in English and their primary language.

Another application is to use film adaptations of *The Chronicles of Narnia* to discuss and compare worldviews or introduce Christian themes for dialogue. I have done this in English clubs in minority Christian contexts and Christian university contexts. This should not be heavy-handed; it should be an actual conversation about important ideas, and with compassionate hearts for fellow image bearers. Films like *The Lion, the Witch and the Wardrobe* afford natural dialogue and worldview comparison. The six keys I have identified are particularly relevant for truth-seekers like Lewis himself, who found that the Christian story does indeed explain the world better than every alternative.

Alternatively, the six keys might help you as a missionary or missiologist to recognize and analyze stories that already exist in a given context for existentially relevant talking points.

The apostle Paul did something like this in Athens (Acts 17:22–34). Paul analyzed two Athenian artifacts. One, an idol with the words "To the unknown god" (translation, treasure, tension): You are very religious. You do acknowledge something beyond yourself. You are concerned about covering your bases. You don't know God. Second, Paul notes and analyzes the words of a known poet: "For we are indeed his offspring" (translation, tension): Roughly, you don't know the One who gives you life, but even your poet knows that we are from him. Paul then used these bridges as talking points for the gospel (translation, treasure, tension, call). Paul interpreted their unspoken void: "What therefore you worship as unknown, this I proclaim to you" (Acts 17:23). This would be possible in more obvious works in Russian such as Fyodor Dostoevsky's *The Brothers Karamazov*, *The Idiot*, *Crime and Punishment*, and *The Adolescent*. However, the six keys can be used to identify and engage in dialogue about most stories that explore themes related to life, whether in literature or film.[20]

---

20. The publisher Bloomsbury has a series called Perspectives on Children's Literature that includes volumes on metaphysics in children's literature and, notably, a volume that explores the role of British children's literature in Japanese culture. Another fruitful place to explore is a series called The Gospel in Great Writers, published by Plough Publishing House, which features works by Fyodor Dostoyevsky, Leo Tolstoy, Dorothy Sayers, George MacDonald, and Gerard Manley Hopkins, and promises to add future writers as well.

A third group that may benefit from this book is *story makers* in any cultural context. If you are a writer, I would encourage you to think about how you can deploy the six keys in your own creative writing where artistically appropriate. I have identified themes that are both naturally relevant because of their existential significance and important because they are dividing lines among worldviews. What Lewis termed supposal is one possible way for these kinds of themes and arguments to be embodied in stories and myths. The power of supposal is that the laws of sub-creation and creative possibilities they create can avoid feeling contrived.

For Lewis, all *The Chronicles of Narnia* and his science fiction books began with images that came to him.[21] His inspiration was mysterious. Lewis once described an author's inspiration as "the golden moments of unimpeded composition."[22] Nevertheless, Lewis's excellence, power, and creativity were not lost when "the man" in him began "to have his turn."[23] While intentional in revision, his work was not artificial. The continued power of the *Narnia* books to capture imaginations of new generations, and continuing book sales, prove their success in resonating as good stories, as well as containing Christian truth.

Even fellow Inkling J. R. R. Tolkien, who was especially quiet about his faith in association with his stories, acknowledges his *conscious* "revision" of *Lord of the Rings* in private correspondence with Robert Murray.[24] These authors show that intention is not automatically at odds with creative excellence. The key point for story makers is this: the themes need to fit the literature in a natural way. Both of these writers included this aspect in revision.

MOVING FORWARD

So, what's next? What else can be done to explore narrative apologetics, cross-cultural engagement, and the *Narnia* books more deeply? There are at least five significant ways to reflect further on these themes in ways I think could be fruitful.

One way is to look at all the books of *The Chronicles of Narnia* and how they address more worldviews than those I have considered. What

---

21. Lewis, "It All Began with a Picture," 67.
22. Lewis, "Vision of John Bunyan," 207.
23. See Lewis, "Sometimes Fairy Stories," 57–59.
24. Carpenter and Tolkien, *Letters of Tolkien*, 172.

I have developed is intended to show what is possible, but a much more complete project is feasible, done book by book. I didn't analyze *The Horse and His Boy* or *Prince Caspian*, and there are many more worldviews that could be brought into dialogue with the *Chronicles*. Sire's work includes nine models, not including apatheism, and there are many different religions, philosophies, and varieties of belief in the world.

Second, because each religious context differs in needs, obstacles, and points of interest, one could build on what I have done for a specific religious context. It would be fruitful to consider how *The Chronicles of Narnia* engage a specific group and how narrative insights like what I have included could help advocate belief in that context. For example, there are different schools of thought within Islam, Hinduism, and Buddhism.

Third, research into how *The Chronicles of Narnia* can apologetically reinforce Christian belief among Christians is also a worthy consideration. There are many pressures that contest traditional doctrines for Christians, and narrative apologetics may help reinforce Christian belief and deepen our own understanding and spiritual growth as much as it provokes cross-cultural faith.

Fourth, it would be fascinating to see research into the impact of *The Chronicles of Narnia* based on readers who ascribe to non-Christian belief systems but still read the *Chronicles*. Data already exists in books and writings of non-Christians and skeptics from across worldviews. This would reveal a fuller picture of Narnia's impact and further inform narrative apologetics.

A final place for further exploration is the role of myth and myth-making in cross-cultural apologetics. Here is why: in his introduction to *George MacDonald: An Anthology*, Lewis says something curious for a writer to say. When contemplating the greatness of the story of the Balder myth, Lewis says his attraction is *not* about the words themselves. Lewis writes,

> If the story is anywhere embodied in words, that is almost an accident. What really delights and nourishes me is *a particular pattern of events*, which would *equally delight and nourish if it had reached me by some medium which involved no words at all*—say by a mime, or a film.... But in a myth—in a story where the mere pattern of events is all that matters—this is not so. Any means of communication whatever which succeeds in lodging those events in our imagination has, as we say, "done the trick."[25]

---

25. Lewis, *George MacDonald*, xxx; emphasis added.

Not just narrative apologetics, but *mythic* apologetics, could be very important for communicating Christian truths across cultures, especially if they are divided by language. Lewis appears to suggest that mythic stories do not depend on language as much as patterns of events. Starr wonders, "Perhaps as a pattern, though, myth is a kind or mode of [*languaging* (my term)] itself, a language not of words but of images."[26] Language is often a significant obstacle to translation and communication. What if myth could bridge the gap and cultivate longing or more?

SOME FINAL THOUGHTS

Seeing something for the first time can be a striking experience. I still remember the day my youngest daughter, as a toddler, first opened the doors of a TV cabinet in our house. The cabinet was large enough to put a medium-sized TV inside and close the doors. To my eyes, she was looking into a TV cabinet, and there wasn't even a TV inside at the time. But she had never looked behind those doors. As she looked, her eyes opened wide with wonder, as though she was seeing into another world. Her amazement made me look at the cabinet differently.

Her delight reminded me that things can become dulled with familiarity. The psalmist wrote, "The heavens declare the glory of God" (Ps 19:1), but sometimes we barely notice. Our homes are presently traveling around the sun at over sixty-seven thousand miles per hour, thirty kilometers every second, "the speed of traveling from Rio de Janeiro to Cape Town (or alternatively London to New York) in about 3 minutes."[27] Yet many are bored.[28] In his essay "Tremendous Trifles," G. K. Chesterton memorably wrote, "The world will never starve for want of wonders; but only for want of wonder."[29] Stories and imagination, as Lewis, Tolkien, and others understood, can help us to see the familiar with awe.

Sometimes stories allow us to gain a first-time understanding as well. I will also never forget the day I watched a film version of *The Lion, the Witch and the Wardrobe* with a cross-cultural English club where Christianity was the clear minority. When Aslan died, the packed room

---

26. Starr, "Meaning, Meanings, and Epistemology," 169.

27. Urritia and Howell, "How Fast Is Earth Moving?"

28. N. D. Wilson helpfully and creatively commented on our lack of wonder at the movement of the earth in a similar way. See Wilson, *Notes from the Tilt-A-Whirl*.

29. Chesterton, "Tremendous Trifles," 7.

audibly gasped at losing someone so great. In that moment, I knew the college students had briefly grasped something of the cost of redemption through Edmund's life. They had also witnessed something like the love of God, and the price Jesus paid to deliver rebel hearts (John 3:16; Rom 5:8; 2 Cor 5:21). I was further reminded of the price of redemption for my own life through their wonder, not unlike watching my daughter look inside our TV cabinet for the first time. In a happy coincidence, our TV cabinet was shaped like a wardrobe. On that day in the English club, Lewis's stories traveled over six thousand miles from his home in England, past the watchful dragons guarding the minds of fellow image bearers who had never heard of Jesus. It was only a beginning, but Lewis made the unfamiliar story of Jesus unforgettably familiar to people who had never heard the gospel. Many great conversations followed, involving three of the keys: translation, transformation, and treasure.

In *The Silver Chair*, a desperately thirsty and terrified Jill Pole found herself in a new land, face to face with a lion inviting her to drink. The stream looked fresh and sounded lively, but it was with the lion. There was no other place to drink. Similarly, a very thirsty Samaritan woman once found herself talking to a Jewish man promising living water that she had never tasted. Neither of these ladies would ever be the same. My hope is that this book will help you discover some of the ways that narrative can build previously unknown bridges to those who have never tasted and seen what they are missing in Jesus, the wellspring of living water.

Appendix

Key Terms and Explanations

Advocate

To advocate means to "publicly recommend or support."[1] As I use the term in this project, it is generally understood as the way a narrative helps to commend, communicate, or support Christian belief. This effort may be conscious or unconscious because of the nature of supposal. Moreover, a given narrative could be used in conversation to more explicitly advance Christian truth claims (see *Supposal*).

Aesthetic Experience

Aesthetic experience may be defined as "our sense of morality, the longing for joy, and the love of beauty."[2] Joseph Loconte notes its importance for Lewis in relation to Owen Barfield's spiritualism: "[Barfield's spiritualism,] for all its eccentricities, appeared to offer a better explanation for these experiences than that of the materialist. He helped Lewis to consider the possibility that our moral intuitions, our aesthetic experiences, could lead us to objective truth: imagination might be as good a guide to reality as rational argument."[3]

---

1. Soanes and Stevenson, *Concise Oxford English Dictionary*, s.v. "advocate."
2. Loconte, *Hobbit, a Wardrobe*, 128.
3. Loconte, *Hobbit, a Wardrobe*, 127.

Beauty

Beauty may be defined as "a combination of qualities that delights the aesthetic senses."[4] For Lewis, beauty is an attribute of God. Adam Barkman notes, "Because of Lewis's Neoplatonic Christian theory of Beauty—i.e., God is Beauty, Creation participates in Beauty, and man has a heavenly desire for, among other things, God *qua* Beauty."[5] Peter Kreeft says it well: "Our wills want not only some good and some evil, but all good, without limit. Our desires, imaginations, feelings or hearts want not just some beauty and some ugliness, but all beauty, without limit."[6] Like truth and goodness, Kreeft explains, beauty is an attribute of God.[7]

Christian Apologetics

Christian apologetics is broadly understood as an effort to defend or advocate the truth and goodness of the Christian faith. When effective, apologetics commends Christianity and/or removes obstacles that impede Christian belief.

Imagination

Imagination is understood in the historic sense as "the power to create or form mental images."[8] Charles Taliaferro and Jill Evans explain: "'Imagination' does not refer to a thing or object or event, but a power possessed by subjects that can either be cultivated or suppressed for good or ill."[9]

For Lewis, the imagination can be distinguished in several ways. One is fantasy or daydreaming, which is often foolish or unproductive. A second way he understands imagination is *invention*, creating stories and art.[10] A third way that he uses imagination is in what Lewis considers

---

4. Soanes and Stevenson, *Concise Oxford English Dictionary*, s.v. "beauty."
5. Barkman, *C. S. Lewis & Philosophy*, 550.
6. Kreeft, "Truth, Goodness, and Beauty," 11.
7. Kreeft, "Truth, Goodness, and Beauty," 11.
8. Taliaferro and Evans, *Image in Mind*, 12.
9. Taliaferro and Evans, *Image in Mind*, 12; elsewhere they note that imagination enables us to "fill our worldviews, or understandings of nature, that can be assessed evidentially." Taliaferro and Evans, *Image in Mind*, 30.
10. Lewis, *Surprised by Joy*, 16.

the highest, spiritual sense.¹¹ It is the "spiritual significance" (Charlie Starr's language) that Lewis believed is revealed in his experience with *Sehnsucht*.¹²

Moreover, for Lewis, imagination is "the organ of meaning," or what Starr calls "seen connection" or "signification."¹³ Lewis writes, "Imagination, producing new metaphors or revivifying old, is not the cause of truth, but its condition" (see *Meaning*).¹⁴

Longing

Longing, as Lewis understood it, is something that he also calls *Joy* or *Sehnsucht*. In *Surprised by Joy*, he defines longing as "an unsatisfied desire which is itself more desirable than any other satisfaction." Lewis distinguishes it from happiness and pleasure, as it is a more profound desire that lies beyond our power to control.¹⁵

If Lewis is correct, this longing points to God, even if it is found in other contexts. In *Mere Christianity* Lewis writes, "If I find in myself a desire which no experience in this world can satisfy, the most probable explanation is that I was made for another world."¹⁶

Meaning

A dictionary definition of meaning is "what is meant by a word, text, concept, or action."¹⁷ This is primarily how I use it in this work. For Lewis, meaning "is the antecedent condition both of truth and falsehood, whose antithesis is not error but nonsense."¹⁸ Lewis explains, "For me, reason is the natural organ of truth; but imagination is the organ of meaning. Imagination, producing new metaphors or revivifying old, is not the cause of truth, but its condition."¹⁹ Drawing on Lewis's concrete versus

---

11. Lewis, *Surprised by Joy*, 16.
12. Lewis, *Surprised by Joy*, 16–18; also see Starr, *Faun's Bookshelf*, 103–4.
13. Starr, "Meaning, Meanings, and Epistemology," 177.
14. Lewis, "Bluespels and Flalansferes," 354.
15. Lewis, *Surprised by Joy*, 19.
16. Lewis, *Mere Christianity*, 136–37.
17. Soanes and Stevenson, *Concise Oxford English Dictionary*, s.v. "meaning."
18. Lewis, "Bluespels and Flalansferes," 354.
19. Lewis, "Bluespels and Flalansferes," 354.

abstract knowing, Starr explains meaning as "a product of imaginative connection through metaphor. The opposite of meaning is simply non-meaning, or 'nonsense.'"[20] Meaning, he continues, is "seen connection, . . . [it] begins in the imagination. Perceived relations occur as imaginative perceptions of metaphor" (see *Imagination*).[21]

Myth

Lewis believes that myth bridges the gap between concrete (experiential) knowing and abstract (reasoned) knowing. Charlie Starr explains,

> Myth solves the problem of knowing by removing abstraction from the equation. In myth the object is not external to the subject once the story pattern is perceived. The myth is a real object of thought, a sub-created, concrete reality, intended not to represent reality outside itself (though such representations occur when we allegorize from myth), but to be simply what it is, a pattern of the reality *behind* (not a pattern *about* that reality but an actual taste of the reality itself).[22]

Starr also notes that "when we find truth in myth, we are not reading it as myth but are allegorizing the myth. . . . Though this is not the *best* way to read myth, that Lewis believes myth contains truth shows that it is a *valid* way to read myth."[23]

Narrative Apologetics

Narrative apologetics, in its various forms and expressions, uses the resources of narrative and the imagination to defend or advocate the truth and goodness of the Christian faith. More than simply the creation of narrative, narrative apologetics can draw on the final form of literature or story for apologetic ends. It uses story or metaphor to teach or advocate the truth. Understood in this way, Jesus used narrative apologetics in parables, and the prophet Nathan used narrative apologetics to convict King David of his sin (2 Sam 12:1–9).

---

20. Starr, "Meaning, Meanings, and Epistemology," 177.
21. Starr, "Meaning, Meanings, and Epistemology," 178–79.
22. Starr, "Meaning, Meanings, and Epistemology," 176.
23. Starr, "Meaning, Meanings, and Epistemology," 171.

Reason

The dictionary definition of reason is the mental capacity to think, understand, and form logical judgments.[24] Charlie Starr explains the act of reasoning in Lewis's thought: "Whether or not a meaning corresponds to reality (whether or not it is true) is something that must be determined by reason."[25] He continues,

> First, language is metaphorical, that is, language functions by making *meaningful* connections between a sign and a signified. Second, reasoning to truth consists of arriving at *language* statements which correspond with reality. Therefore, if reason always depends on language (even the language of mathematics) in order to function, it will always depend on meaning which is central to the function of language.[26]

Supposal (or Supposing)

Lewis's letter to Anne Jenkins on March 5, 1961, explains what Lewis meant by narrative "supposing."[27] Rather than Aslan being an allegory for Christ, Lewis *supposes* how the Son might become incarnate in a world of Talking Beasts. It is imaginative speculation about what might happen in another world, rather than directly symbolizing Christian truths.

Translation

Translation is broadly defined as the communication of Christian beliefs, concepts, terms, or practices in a manner that is, in some sense, understandable to a reader (or a conversation partner, if discussing the stories). *The Chronicles of Narnia* present the reader with a world that embodies images that recall various Christian doctrines and beliefs, such as the resurrection, the existence of true moral guilt and accountability, forgiveness, the incarnation, theism, creation, and the virtue of having faith in a way that is concrete and conceivable.

---

24. Soanes and Stevenson, *Concise Oxford English Dictionary*, s.v. "reason."
25. Starr, "Meaning, Meanings, and Epistemology," 177.
26. Starr, "Meaning, Meanings, and Epistemology," 177.
27. Lewis, *Collected Letters*, 3:1244–45.

Translation, as I define it, can be intentional or unintentional. We can know translation is purposeful in *The Chronicles of Narnia* when Lewis confirms his intent. For example, in his letter to Anne Jenkins, Lewis explains what he means by "supposing" (see *Supposal*). Alister McGrath's explanation is helpful concerning narrative apologetics—see the discussion of key one, translation, in chapter 4, pp. 93–94.

Truth

Truth, as I use it here and as Lewis understands it, is consistent with the correspondence theory of truth: truth is that which corresponds with reality. In Lewis's essay "Myth Became Fact" he writes, "Truth is always about something, but reality is that about which truth is."[28] In this context, Lewis distinguishes between abstract, reasoned knowing and concrete, experiential knowing.

---

28. Lewis, "Myth Became Fact," 66.

Bibliography

Aeschliman, Michael. *The Restitution of Man: C. S. Lewis and the Case Against Scientism*. 2nd ed. Grand Rapids: Eerdmans, 1998.

Ahmad, Imran. "Narnia in the Eyes of a Young Muslim Reader." HuffPost, April 4, 2012. Updated June 4, 2012. https://www.huffpost.com/entry/narnia_b_1400025.

Alderman, Matthew. "Whatever Happened to Susan Pevensie?" *First Things*, February 17, 2009. https://www.firstthings.com/web-exclusives/2009/02/whatever-happened-to-susan-pevensie.

Alexander, Joy. "The Whole Art and Joy of Words: Aslan's Speech in *The Chronicles of Narnia*." *Mythlore* 91 (2003) 37–48.

Alighieri, Dante. *The Divine Comedy*. Translated by Allen Mandelbaum. Everyman's Library 183. New York: Knopf, 1995.

Alston, William P. "The Inductive Argument from Evil and the Human Cognitive Condition." *Philosophical Perspectives* 5 (1991) 29–67.

———. *The Reliability of Sense Perception*. New York: Cornell University Press, 1996.

Anacker, Gayne. "Narnia and the Moral Imagination." In *"The Chronicles of Narnia" and Philosophy: The Lion, the Witch, and the Worldview*, edited by Gregory Bassham and Jerry L. Walls, 130–42. Popular Culture and Philosophy 15. Chicago: Open Court, 2005.

Anderson, Tawa J. *Why Believe: Christian Apologetics for a Skeptical Age*. Edited by Heath A. Thomas. Nashville: B&H Academic, 2021.

Anderson, Tawa J., et al. *An Introduction to Christian Worldview: Pursuing God's Perspective in a Pluralistic World*. Downers Grove, IL: IVP Academic, 2017.

Anselm. *Complete Philosophical and Theological Treatises of Anselm of Canterbury*. Translated by Jasper Hopkins and Herbert Richardson. Minneapolis: Banning, 2000.

Armstrong, Chris R. *Medieval Wisdom for Modern Christians: Finding Authentic Faith in a Forgotten Age with C. S. Lewis*. Grand Rapids: Brazos, 2016.

Arnell, Carla A. "On Beauty, Justice and the Sublime in C. S. Lewis's *Till We Have Faces*." *Christianity and Literature* 52 (2002) 23–34.

Aslan, Reza. *No god but God: The Origins, Evolution, and Future of Islam*. New York: Random House, 2011.

Baggett, David, and Jerry Walls. *God and Cosmos: Moral Truth and Human Meaning*. New York: Oxford University Press, 2016.

Baggett, David, et al. *C. S. Lewis as Philosopher: Truth, Goodness, and Beauty*. 2nd ed. Lynchburg, VA: Liberty University Press, 2017.

Bailey, Justin. *Reimagining Apologetics: The Beauty of Faith in a Secular Age.* Downers Grove, IL: IVP Academic, 2020.
Barbour, Ian G. *When Science Meets Religion: Enemies, Strangers, or Partners?* San Francisco: HarperOne, 2000.
Barkman, Adam. "Aristotelian Ethics in C. S. Lewis's Philosophy." *CSL Bulletin* 38 (2007) 1–9.
———. "Augustinian Will and Aristotelian *Phronesis* in C. S. Lewis's Theory of Moral Action." *Inklings: Jahrbuch für Literatur und Ästhetik* 24 (2006) 117–42.
———. *C. S. Lewis & Philosophy as a Way of Life: A Comprehensive Historical Examination of His Philosophical Thoughts.* Wayne, PA: Zossima, 2009.
———. "C. S. Lewis and the Concept of an 'Old Western Man.'" *Inklings: Jahrbuch für Literatur und Ästhetik* 25 (2007) 253–68.
———. "'First to Aslan and Truth': Images of Christ in *The Last Battle*." *Pilgrimage* 13 (2006) 12–15.
———. "The Philosophical Christianity of C. S. Lewis: Its Sources, Content and Formation." PhD diss., Free University of Amsterdam, 2009.
Bassham, Gregory. "Con: Quenching the Argument from Desire." In *C. S. Lewis's Christian Apologetics: Pro and Con*, edited by Gregory Bassham, 45–55. Leiden: Brill, 2015.
Bassham, Gregory, and Jerry L. Walls. *"The Chronicles of Narnia" and Philosophy: The Lion, the Witch, and the Worldview.* Popular Culture and Philosophy 15. Chicago: Open Court, 2005.
Bennett, Matthew. *40 Questions About Islam.* 40 Questions Series. Grand Rapids: Kregel Academic, 2020.
Berger, Peter L. *The Heretical Imperative: Contemporary Possibilities of Religious Affirmation.* Garden City, NY: Doubleday, 1979.
———. *The Many Altars of Modernity: Toward a Paradigm for Religion in a Pluralist Age.* New York: De Gruyter, 2014.
———. *The Sacred Canopy: Elements of a Sociological Theory of Religion.* New York: Anchor, 1990.
Berger, Peter L., and Thomas Luckmann. *The Social Construction of Reality: A Treatise in the Sociology of Knowledge.* Garden City, NY: Doubleday, 1967.
Beshears, Kyle. *Apatheism: How We Share When They Don't Care.* Nashville: B&H Academic, 2021.
———. "Athens Without a Statue to the Unknown God." *Themelios* 44 (2019) 517–29. https://www.thegospelcoalition.org/themelios/article/athens-without-a-statue-to-the-unknown-god/.
———. "Sharing the Gospel with Apatheist Friends and Neighbors." Lifeway Voices, March 17, 2021. https://voices.lifeway.com/discipleship-evangelism/sharing-the-gospel-with-apatheist-friends-and-neighbors/.
Beversluis, John. *C. S. Lewis and the Search for Rational Religion.* Amherst, MA: Prometheus, 2007.
Bilbro, Jeffrey. "The Taste of Strawberries: Tolkien's Imagination of the Good." The Imaginative Conservative, August 25, 2014. http://www.theimaginativeconservative.org/2014/08/the-taste-of-strawberries-tolkiens-imagination-of-the-good.html.
Billy, Dennis J. *C. S. Lewis and the Fullness of Life: Longing for Deep Heaven.* Boston: Paulist, 2009.

Biola University. "Holly Ordway: Imagination in Service to Truth—Literature as a Mode of Apologetics." YouTube, September 14, 2013. https://www.youtube.com/watch?v=DcEshjUB4zo.

Blamires, Harry. "Teaching the Universal Truth: C. S. Lewis Among the Intellectuals." In *The Pilgrim's Guide: C. S. Lewis and the Art of Witness*, edited by David Mills, 15–26. Grand Rapids: Eerdmans, 1998.

Boa, Kenneth D., and Robert M. Bowman Jr. *Faith Has Its Reasons: An Integrative Approach to Defending Christianity*. Colorado Springs: NavPress, 2001.

Bowen, John. "Are *The Chronicles of Narnia* an Evangelistic Text?" Wycliffe College Institute of Evangelism, March 10, 2005. Lecture transcript. https://institute.wycliffecollege.ca/2005/03/are-the-chronicles-of-narnia-an-evangelistic-text/.

Bowman, Mary R. "A Darker Ignorance: C. S. Lewis and the Nature of the Fall." *Mythlore* 91 (2003) 64–80.

Bowman, Robert M., Jr., and J. Ed Komoszewski. *The Incarnate Christ and His Critics: A Biblical Defense*. Grand Rapids: Kregel Academic, 2024.

———. *Putting Jesus in His Place: The Case for the Deity of Christ*. Grand Rapids: Kregel, 2007.

Brawley, Chris. "The Ideal and the Shadow: George MacDonald's *Phantasies*." *North Wind* 25 (2006) 91–112.

Bray, Suzanne. "La dialectique du désir chez C. S. Lewis." *La conversion religieuse* (2000) 237–46.

———. "Ecrivains et apologistes en Grande-Bretagne, 1900–1963: G. K. Chesterton, Dorothy L. Sayers, T. S. Eliot et C. S. Lewis." PhD diss., Université Lille-III (Charles-de-Gaulle), 1999.

Brazier, P. H. "C. S. Lewis: A Doctrine of Transposition." *Heythrop Journal* (2009) 669–88.

———. *C. S. Lewis—An Annotated Bibliography and Resource*. C. S. Lewis: Revelation and the Christ 4. Eugene, OR: Pickwick, 2012.

———. *C. S. Lewis—Revelation, Conversion, and Apologetics*. C. S. Lewis: Revelation and the Christ 1. Eugene, OR: Pickwick, 2012.

———. "'God . . . Or a Bad, or Mad, Man': C. S. Lewis's Argument for Christ—A Systematic Theological, Historical and Philosophical Analysis of *Aut Deus Aut Malus Homo*." *Heythrop Journal* 51 (2010) 1–30.

———. "Why Father Christmas Appears in Narnia." *Sehnsucht* 3 (2009) 61–77.

Brown, Devin. *Inside Narnia: A Guide to Exploring "The Lion, the Witch, and the Wardrobe."* Grand Rapids: Baker, 2005.

Budimir, Milenko. "Apatheism: The New Face of Religion?" *Philosophy of Religion* 45 (2008) 88–93.

Bundy, Murray Wright. *The Theory of Imagination in Classical and Medieval Thought*. Urbana: University of Illinois Press, 1927.

Burnand, Eugène. *The Disciples Peter and John Running to the Tomb on the Morning of the Resurrection*. 1898. Oil on canvas. Musée d'Orsay, Paris. https://commons.wikimedia.org/wiki/File:Disciples_running_by_EB.jpg.

Burson, Scott R., and Jerry L. Walls. *C. S. Lewis and Francis Schaeffer: Lessons for a New Century from the Most Influential Apologists of Our Time*. Grand Rapids: InterVarsity, 1998.

Carnell, Corbin Scott. *Bright Shadow of Reality: Spiritual Longing in C. S. Lewis*. Grand Rapids: Eerdmans, 1999.

———. "The Dialectic of Desire: C. S. Lewis' Interpretation of *Sehnsucht*." PhD diss., University of Florida, 1960.

———. "Longing, Reason, and the Moral Law in C. S. Lewis's Search." In *C. S. Lewis: Lightbearer in the Shadowlands; The Evangelistic Vision of C. S. Lewis*, edited by Angus J. L. Menuge, 103–15. Wheaton, IL: Crossway, 1997.

Carpenter, Humphrey, and Christopher Tolkien. *The Letters of J. R. R. Tolkien*. London: HarperCollins, 2012. Kindle.

Carretero González, Margarita, and Encarnación Hidalgo Tenorio, eds. *Behind the Veil of Familiarity: C. S. Lewis (1898–1998)*. Bern: Lang, 2001.

Carroll, Lewis. *Alice's Adventures in Wonderland*. Illustrated by John Tenniel. London: Macmillan, 1865. Transcribed by Arthur DiBianca and David Widger. Project Gutenberg, 2008. Last updated June 26, 2025. https://www.gutenberg.org/ebooks/11.

Caughey, Shanna. *Revisiting Narnia: Fantasy, Myth, and Religion in C. S. Lewis's "Chronicles."* Dallas: Benbella, 2005.

Chafe, Wallace L. "Cognitive Constraints on Information Flow." In *Coherence and Grounding in Discourse*, edited by Russell S. Tomlin, 21–52. Typological Studies in Language. Amsterdam: Benjamins, 1987.

Chatterjee, Amita. "Naturalism in Classical Indian Philosophy." Stanford Encyclopedia of Philosophy (Winter 2021 ed.), last revised November 9, 2021. https://plato.stanford.edu/archives/win2021/entries/naturalism-india/.

Chaves, Mark A. A., and David Voas. "Is the United States a Counterexample to the Secularization Thesis?" *American Journal of Sociology* 121 (2016) 1517–56.

Chesterton, G. K. Introduction to *George MacDonald and His Wife*. By Greville MacDonald, 9–15. London: Allen & Unwin, 1924.

———. "Tremendous Trifles." In *Tremendous Trifles*, 3–7. Mineola, NY: Dover, 2007.

Chittenden-Bascon, C. "Expressions of Religious Experience in the Fiction of C. S. Lewis." MA thesis, University of Exeter, 1990.

Cobble, William J. "C. S. Lewis's Understanding of God's Work in Paganism." *Journal of Theta Alpha Kappa* 25 (Fall 2001) 16–28.

Coleridge, Samuel Taylor. *Biographia Literaria*. Edited by Adam Roberts. New ed. Edinburgh: Edinburgh University Press, 2014.

Connolly, Sean. *Inklings of Heaven: C. S. Lewis and Eschatology*. Leominster, UK: Gracewing, 2007.

Copan, Paul. "Apatheism and the Unexamined Life: Part 1." Worldview Bulletin Newsletter, April 22, 2019. https://worldviewbulletin.substack.com/p/apatheism-and-the-unexamined-life.

———. *Loving Wisdom: A Guide to Philosophy and Christian Faith*. 2nd ed. Grand Rapids: Eerdmans, 2020.

Copan, Paul, and Paul K. Moser, eds. *The Rationality of Theism*. London: Routledge, 2003.

Corduan, Winfried. *Neighboring Faiths*. Downers Grove, IL: IVP Academic, 2012.

———. "Islamic Theism." In *The Universe Next Door*, by James W. Sire, 234–66. 6th ed. Downers Grove, IL: IVP Academic, 2020.

Craig, William Lane. *Reasonable Faith: Christian Truth and Apologetics*. 3rd ed. Wheaton, IL: Crossway, 2008.

Crawford, Matthew David. "C. S. Lewis's Concept of *Sehnsucht*: Philosophical Foundations, Aesthetic Analysis, and Implications for Evangelism and Apologetics." PhD diss., Southern Baptist Theological Seminary, 2015.

Crossan, John Dominic. *Jesus: A Revolutionary Biography*. San Francisco: HarperCollins, 1991.

Csapo, Eric. *Theories of Mythology*. Oxford: Blackwell, 2005.

Daigle, Marsha A. "Dante's *Divine Comedy* and C. S. Lewis's *Narnia Chronicles*." *Christianity and Literature* 34 (1985) 42–46.

Dalferth, Ingolf U. "Post-Secular Society: Christianity and the Dialectics of the Secular." *Journal of the American Academy of Religion Studies* 78 (2010) 339.

Davis, Stephen T. *God, Reason, and Theistic Proofs*. Edinburgh: Edinburgh University Press, 1997.

———. "The Ontological Argument." In *The Rationality of Theism*, edited by Paul Copan and Paul K. Moser, 93–110. London: Routledge, 2003.

Dawkins, Richard. *The Blind Watchmaker: Why the Evidence of Evolution Reveals a Universe without Design*. New York: Norton, 2015.

———. *The God Delusion*. Boston: Mariner, 2008.

———. *River Out of Eden: A Darwinist's View of Life*. New York: Basic, 1995.

Demy, Timothy James. "Technology, Progress, and the Human Condition in the Life and Thought of C. S. Lewis." PhD diss., Salve Regina University, 2004.

Detzler, Wayne, and Douglas Potter. *Cross-Cultural Apologetics: Bridging Culture to Defend the Faith*. CreateSpace, 2011.

De Wit, Willem J. *On the Way to the Living God: A Cathartic Reading of Herman Bavinck and an Invitation to Overcome the Plausibility Crisis of Christianity*. Amsterdam: VU University Press, 2011.

DeWitt, Richard. *Worldviews: An Introduction to the History and Philosophy of Science*. 3rd ed. Hoboken, NJ: Wiley-Blackwell, 2018.

Ditchfield, Christin. "Biblical Truths in C. S. Lewis's *The Chronicles of Narnia*." *Broadcast Talks* 8 (2023) 1–19.

Donne, John. "Batter my heart, three-person'd God." Poetry Foundation. https://www.poetryfoundation.org/poems/44106/holy-sonnets-batter-my-heart-three-person'd-god.

Dooyeweerd, Herman. "La secularisation de la science." *La revue réformée* 5 (1954) 138–155.

Dorsett, Lyle W., ed. *The Essential Lewis*. New York: Scribner, 1996.

———. *And God Came In: The Extraordinary Story of Joy Davidman*. New York: Ballantine, 1983.

Downing, David. *Into the Region of Awe: Mysticism in C. S. Lewis*. Downers Grove, IL: InterVarsity, 2005.

———. *Into the Wardrobe: C. S. Lewis and "The Narnia Chronicles."* San Francisco: Wiley & Sons, 2005.

———. *The Most Reluctant Convert: C. S. Lewis's Journey to Faith*. Downers Grove, IL: InterVarsity, 2002.

Dreher, Rod. *The Benedict Option*. New York: Penguin Random House, 2017.

Dronke, Peter. *Fabula: Explorations into the Uses of Myth in Medieval Platonism*. Leiden: Brill, 1974.

Dumsday, Travis. "C. S. Lewis on the Problem of Divine Hiddenness." *Anglican Theological Review* 97 (2015) 33–51. http://www.anglicantheologicalreview.org/read/article/1798/.

Edwards, Bruce L., ed. *C. S. Lewis: Life, Works, and Legacy*. 4 vols. Westport, CT: Praeger, 2007.

Edwards, L. Clifton. *Creation's Beauty as Revelation: Toward a Creational Theology of Natural Beauty*. Eugene, OR: Pickwick, 2014.

Evans, C. Stephen. *Natural Signs and the Knowledge of God*. Oxford: Oxford University Press, 2012.

Feddes, David. *Missional Apologetics: Cultural Diagnosis and Gospel Plausibility in C. S. Lewis and Lesslie Newbigin*. Monee, IL: Christian Leaders, 2012.

Feinberg, John S. *The Many Faces of Evil: Theological Systems and the Problems of Evil*. Rev. ed. Wheaton, IL: Crossway, 2004.

Feinendegen, Norbert. "Denk-Weg zu Christus: C. S. Lewis als kritischer Denker der Moderne." PhD diss., University of Bonn, 2008.

Ferrar, Austin. "The Christian Apologist." In *Light on C. S. Lewis*, edited by Jocelyn Gibb, 23–43. New York: Harcourt Brace Jovanovich, 1976.

Flew, Antony, et al. "Theology & Falsification: A Symposium." In *The Philosophy of Religion*, edited by Basil Mitchell, 13–22. London: Oxford University Press, 1991.

Flieger, Verlyn, and Douglas A. Anderson. Editors commentary in *On Fairy-Stories*. By J. R. R. Tolkien, edited by Verlyn Flieger and Douglas A. Anderson, 85–121. Exp. ed. London: HarperCollins, 2014.

———. Introduction to *On Fairy-Stories*. By J. R. R. Tolkien, edited by Verlyn Flieger and Douglas A. Anderson, 9–23. Exp. ed. London: HarperCollins, 2014.

Ford, Paul D. *Companion to Narnia: A Complete Guide to the Magical World of C. S. Lewis's "The Chronicles of Narnia."* Rev. ed. New York: HarperCollins, 2005.

Forrest, Benjamin K., et al., eds. *The History of Apologetics: A Biographical and Methodological Introduction*. Grand Rapids: Zondervan Academic, 2020.

Freeman, Austin M. *Tolkien Dogmatics: Theology Through Mythology with the Maker of Middle-Earth*. Bellingham, WA: Lexham, 2022.

Freshwater, Mark. *C. S. Lewis and the Truth of Myth*. Lanham, MD: University Press of America, 1988.

Fujimura, Makoto. *Culture Care: Reconnecting with Beauty for Our Common Life*. Downers Grove, IL: InterVarsity, 2017.

Gannon, Kathy. "Each Year, 1,000 Pakistani Girls Forcibly Converted to Islam." AP, December 28, 2020. https://apnews.com/article/karachi-pakistan-coronavirus-pandemic-christianity-marriage-2d335f305278348540db41b593a9a2a9.

Gehring, Michael J. *The Oxbridge Evangelist: Motivations, Practices, and Legacy of C. S. Lewis*. Eugene, OR: Cascade, 2017.

Geisler, Normal L. *Miracles and the Modern Mind: A Biblical Defense of Biblical Miracles*. Grand Rapids: Zondervan, 1992.

Geivett, R. Douglas. "Is Jesus the Only Way?" In *Jesus Under Fire: Modern Scholarship Reinvents the Historical Jesus*, edited by Michael J. Wilkins and J. P. Moreland, 231–69. Grand Rapids: Zondervan, 1995.

Geivett, R. Douglas, and Gary R. Habermas, eds. *In Defense of Miracles: A Comprehensive Case for God's Action in History*. Downers Grove, IL: InterVarsity, 1997.

Gibson, Evan K. *C. S. Lewis, Spinner of Tales: A Guide to His Fiction*. Grand Rapids: Eerdmans, 1980.

Gillespie, Michael Allen. *The Theological Origins of Modernity*. Chicago: University of Chicago Press, 2008.

Glymour, Clark. *Theory and Evidence*. Princeton: Princeton University Press, 1980.

Goetz, Stewart. *C. S. Lewis*. Malden, MA: Wiley-Blackwell, 2018.

González, Luis Daniel. *Una guía de Narnia: 100 preguntas sobre las "Crónicas de Narnia"; "El leon, la bruja, y el armario."* Madrid: Palabra, 2006.

———. *Una magia profunda: Guía de las "Crónicas de Narnia."* Madrid: Palabra, 2005.

Gorski, Philip S. "The Ongoing Plausibility of Peter Berger: Sociological Thoughts on *The Sacred Canopy* at Fifty." *Journal of the American Academy of Religion* 85 (2017) 1118–31.

Gould, Paul. *Cultural Apologetics: Renewing the Christian Voice, Conscience, and Imagination in a Disenchanted World*. Grand Rapids: Zondervan, 2019.

Gray, William. "Death, Myth and Reality in C. S. Lewis." *Journal of Beliefs and Values* 18 (1997) 147–54.

Green, William. Initium omnis peccati superbia: *Augustine on Pride as the First Sin*. Berkeley: University of California Press, 1949.

Greggersen, Gabriele. "C. S. Lewis and the Rejection of the Tao." *Dialog* 42 (2003) 120–25.

Grewell, Cory Lowell. "'It's All One': Medievalist Synthesis and Christian Apology in Owen Garfield's Studies of Meaning." *Journal of Inklings Studies* 3 (2013) 11–40.

———. "Medievalist Fantasies of Christendom." *Journal of Inklings Studies* 3 (2013) 3–10.

Groothuis, Douglas R. *Christian Apologetics: A Comprehensive Case for Biblical Faith*. 2nd ed. Downers Grove, IL: IVP Academic, 2022.

Gruenler, Curtis. "C. S. Lewis and René Girard on Desire, Conversion, and Myth: The Case of *Till We Have Faces*." *Christianity and Literature* 60 (2011) 247–65.

Guinness, Os. *Fool's Talk: Recovering the Art of Christian Persuasion*. Downers Grove, IL: InterVarsity, 2015.

Guite, Malcolm. "Telling the Truth Through Imaginative Fiction." In *C. S. Lewis at Poets' Corner*, edited by Michael Ward and Peter S. Williams, 15–24. Eugene, OR: Cascade, 2017.

Hackett, Conrad, and Brian J. Grim, researchers. *The Global Religious Landscape: A Report on the Size and Distribution of the World's Major Religious Groups as of 2010*. Pew-Templeton Global Religious Futures Project. Washington, DC: Pew Forum on Religion & Public Life, 2012. https://www.pewresearch.org/religion/2012/12/18/global-religious-landscape-exec.

Hadot, Pierre. *Philosophy as a Way of Life: Spiritual Exercises from Socrates to Foucault*. Edited by Arnold I. Davidson, translated by Michael Chase. Oxford: Blackwell, 1995.

———. *The Veil of Isis: An Essay on the History of the Idea of Nature*. Translated by Michael Chase. Cambridge: Belknap, 2006.

———. *What Is Ancient Philosophy?* Translated by Michael Chase. Cambridge: Belknap, 2004.

Halcombe, Don. "Netflix to Develop Series and Films Based on C. S. Lewis's Beloved *The Chronicles of Narnia*." Netflix, October 3, 2018. https://media.netflix.com/en/press-releases/netflix-to-develop-series-and-films-based-on-c-s-lewis-beloved-the-chronicles-of-narnia.

Haldane, John. "Philosophy, the Restless Heart and the Meaning of Theism." *Ratio* 19 (2006) 421–40.
Halverson, Dean. *The Compact Guide to World Religions*. Minneapolis: Bethany House, 1996.
Hardy, Dean. *Waking the Dead: George MacDonald as Philosopher, Mystic, and Apologist*. Hamden, CT: Winged Lion, 2020.
Harrold, Philip. "Stealing Past the Watchful Dragons: C. S. Lewis's Incarnational Aesthetics and Today's Emerging Imagination." In *Apologist, Philosopher, & Theologian*, edited by Bruce L. Edwards, 183–208. Vol. 3 of *C. S. Lewis: Life, Works, and Legacy*. Westport, CT: Praeger, 2007.
Hartley, Gregory P. "Lower Sacraments: Theological Eating in the Fiction of C. S. Lewis." PhD diss., University of South Florida, 2012.
Hazen, Craig J. *Five Sacred Crossings*. Los Angeles: Contend, 2012.
Heck, Joel. "The Liberal Arts, Antidote for Atheism: A Partial Theological Justification for the Liberal Arts." *Lingaculture* 2 (2014) 67–78.
Hedberg, Trevor, and Jordan Huzarevich. "Appraising Objections to Practical Apatheism." *Philosophia* 45 (2017) 257–76.
Hegner, Ian von. "Gods and Dictatorships: A Defense of Heroical Apatheism." *Science, Religion and Culture* 3 (2016) 31–48.
Hein, Rolland. *Christian Mythmakers: C. S. Lewis, Madeleine L'Engle, J. R. R. Tolkien, George MacDonald, G. K. Chesterton, Charles Williams, Dante Alighieri, John Bunyan, Walter Wangerin, Robert Siegel, and Hannah Hurnard*. 2nd ed. Eugene, OR: Wipf & Stock, 2014.
Hess, Jared, dir. *Nacho Libre*. Paramount Pictures, Nickelodeon Movies, and Black & White Productions, 2006.
Hesselgrave, David J. *Communicating Christ Cross-Culturally: An Introduction to Missionary Communication*. 2nd ed. Grand Rapids: Zondervan, 1991.
Hick, John. *Evil and the God of Love*. Basingstoke, UK: Palgrave Macmillan, 2010.
Hiebert, Paul. *Transforming Worldviews: An Anthropological Understanding of How People Change*. Grand Rapids: Baker Academic, 2009.
Higgins, Sørina. "Double Affirmation: Medievalism as Christian Apologetic in the Arthurian Poetry of Charles Williams." *Journal of Inklings Studies* 3 (2013) 59–96.
Hilderbrand, K. Michael. *God the Evangelist: Partnering with God in Making Disciples; Application and Commentary on Research into the Reasons Thai Theravada Buddhists Became Christian*. Bangkok: BaanRao, 2021.
Holland, Tom. *Dominion: How the Christian Revolution Remade the World*. New York: Basic, 2019.
Holmer, Paul L. *C. S. Lewis: The Shape of His Faith and Thought*. New York: Harper & Row, 1976.
Holyer, Robert. "The Argument from Desire." *Faith and Philosophy* 5 (1988) 61–71.
Honda, Mineko. *The Imaginative World of C. S. Lewis: A Way to Participate in Reality*. Lanham, MD: University Press of America, 2000.
Hooper, Walter. *C. S. Lewis, A Companion and Guide*. London: HarperCollins, 1996.
———. *Past Watchful Dragons: A Guide to C. S. Lewis's "Chronicles of Narnia."* London: Collins, 1980.
Hunter, James Davison. *To Change the World: The Irony, Tragedy, & Possibility of Christianity in the Late Modern World*. Oxford: Oxford University Press, 2010.

Hyatt, Douglas T. "Joy, the Call of God in Man: A Critical Appraisal of Lewis's Argument from Desire." In *C. S. Lewis: Lightbearer in the Shadowlands; The Evangelistic Vision of C. S. Lewis*, edited by Angus J. L. Menuge, 305–28. Wheaton, IL: Crossway, 1997.

International Network of Creatives. "Art Transforms: Dr. Jerry Root." Facebook, July 3, 2018. https://fb.watch/gQ5uMbwxay/.

Jackson, Liz. "Pascal's Wager for Christianity." In *The Wiley-Blackwell Companion to Christian Apologetics*, edited by Robert Stewart and Timothy McGrew. Hoboken, NJ: Wiley-Blackwell, forthcoming.

Jackson, Peter, dir. *The Lord of the Rings: The Return of the King*. Los Angeles: New Line Cinema, 2003.

Jacobs, Alan. *The Narnian: The Life and Imagination of C. S. Lewis*. London: SPCK, 2005.

Janosik, Daniel. *The Guide to Answering Islam: What Every Christian Needs to Know About Islam and the Rise of Radical Islam*. Cambridge: Christian Publishing House, 2019. Kindle.

Joanou, Phil, dir. *U2: Rattle and Hum*. Hollywood: Paramount Pictures, 1988.

Johns, Morris, et al. *Abductions, Forced Conversions, and Forced Marriages of Religious Minority Women and Girls in Pakistan*. London: APPG, 2021. https://appgfreedomofreligionorbelief.org/media/APPG-Pakistan-Minorities-Report.pdf.

Johnson, Kirstin Jeffrey. "Rooted in All Its Story, More Is Meaning than Meets the Ear: A Study of the Relational and Revelational Nature of George MacDonald's Mythopoeic Art." PhD diss., University of St. Andrews, 2011.

Jones, Clay. *Immortal*. Eugene, OR: Harvest House, 2019.

Jones, Julie. "APPG for Pakistani Minorities: Abductions, Forced Conversions, and Forced Marriages of Religious Minority Women and Girls in Pakistan." APPGFoRB, November, 26, 2021. https://appgfreedomofreligionorbelief.org/appg-for-the-pakistani-minorities-abductions-forced-conversions-and-forced-marriages-of-religious-minority-women-and-girls-in-pakistan.

Kant, Immanuel. *The Critique of Pure Reason*. Edited and translated by Paul Guyer and Allen W. Wood. Cambridge Edition of the Works of Immanuel Kant. Cambridge: Cambridge University Press, 1998.

Kehl, D. G. "Writing the Long Desire: The Function of *Sehnsucht* in *The Great Gatsby* and *Look Homeward, Angel*." *Journal of Modern Literature* 24 (2000–2001) 309–19.

Khalil, Mohammad Hassan, and Mucahit Bilici. "Conversion Out of Islam: A Study of Conversion Narratives of Former Muslims." *Muslim World* 91 (2007) 111–24.

Khoddam, Salwa, et al., eds. *C. S. Lewis and the Inklings: Reflections on Faith, Imagination, and Modern Technology*. Cambridge: Cambridge Scholars, 2015.

Kilby, Clyde S. *The Christian World of C. S. Lewis*. Grand Rapids: Eerdmans, 1964.

———. *A Well of Wonder: Essays on C. S. Lewis, J. R. R. Tolkien, and the Inklings*. Edited by Loren Wilkinson and Keith Call. Brewster, MA: Paraclete, 2018.

Kintsch, Walter. *Comprehension: A Paradigm for Cognition*. Cambridge: Cambridge University Press, 1998.

Knuuttila, Simo. *Emotions in Ancient and Medieval Philosophy*. Oxford: Oxford University Press, 2006.

Kreeft, Peter. *C. S. Lewis for the Third Millennium: Six Essays on "The Abolition of Man."* San Francisco: Ignatius, 1994.

———. "C. S. Lewis's Argument from Desire." In *The Riddle of Joy: G. K. Chesterton and C. S. Lewis*, edited by Michael H. MacDonald and Andrew A. Tadie, 249–72. Grand Rapids: Eerdmans, 1989.

———. *Heaven, the Heart's Deepest Longing*. Exp. ed. San Francisco: Ignatius, 1989.

———. "Lewis's Philosophy of Truth, Goodness, and Beauty." In *C. S. Lewis as Philosopher: Truth, Goodness, and Beauty*, edited by David Baggett et al., 11–28. 3rd ed. High Bridge Books, 2024.

———. *The Philosophy of Tolkien: The Worldview Behind "The Lord of the Rings."* San Francisco: Ignatius, 2005.

Kreeft, Peter, and Ronald K. Tacelli. *Handbook of Christian Apologetics*. Downers Grove, IL: InterVarsity, 2004.

Kuhn, Robert Lawrence, creator. "Why Believe in God?" Season 11, episode 3 of *Closer to Truth*. Originally aired 2013. YouTube, July 1, 2020. https://youtu.be/UFJ_Yeb_2RY.

Kuhn, Thomas S. *The Structure of Scientific Revolutions*. 2nd ed. Chicago: University of Chicago Press, 1970.

Lee, Jong-Tae. "Into the Region of Awe: C. S. Lewis, Wonder and the Re-Enchantment of the World." PhD diss., Graduate Theological Union, 2015.

Lee, Seung Chun. "C. S. Lewis's Mythopoeia of Heaven and Earth: Implications for the Ethical and Spiritual Formation of Multicultural Young Learners." *International Journal of Children's Spirituality* 20 (2015) 15–28.

Levelt, W. J. M. "The Speaker's Linearization Problem." *Philosophical Transactions of the Royal Society B* 295 (1981) 305–15.

Lewis, C. S. *The Abolition of Man*. San Francisco: HarperOne, 2009.

———. *All My Road Before Me: The Diary of C. S. Lewis, 1922–1927*. Edited by Walter Hooper. London: HarperCollins, 1991.

———. "Bluespels and Flalansferes: A Semantic Nightmare." In *Selected Literary Essays*, edited by Walter Hooper, 335–55. New York: Cambridge University Press, 2013.

———. "Christianity and Culture." In *Christian Reflections*, 12–36. Grand Rapids: Eerdmans, 1982.

———. *Collected Letters of C. S. Lewis*. 3 vols. San Francisco: HarperOne, 2000–2007.

———. "The Decline of Religion." In *God in the Dock: Essays on Theology and Ethics*, edited by Walter Hooper, 218–23. Grand Rapids: Eerdmans, 1970.

———. "De Descriptione Temporum." In *They Asked for a Paper: Papers and Addresses*, 9–25. London: Bles, 1962.

———. *The Discarded Image: An Introduction to Medieval and Renaissance Literature*. Cambridge: Cambridge University Press, 2012.

———. "'Early Prose Joy': C. S. Lewis's Early Draft of an Autobiographical Manuscript." *VII: Journal of the Marion E. Wade Center* 30 (2013) 13–50.

———. *English Literature in the Sixteenth Century, Excluding Drama*. Oxford: Clarendon, 1954.

———. *An Experiment in Criticism*. Cambridge: Cambridge University Press, 1961.

———. *George MacDonald: An Anthology*. New York: HarperCollins, 2015.

———. *God in the Dock: Essays on Theology and Ethics*, edited by Walter Hooper. Grand Rapids: Eerdmans, 1970.

———. *The Great Divorce: A Dream*. London: Collins, 2015.

———. *A Grief Observed*. London: Faber & Faber, 1966.

———. *The Horse and His Boy*. In *The Chronicles of Narnia Complete 7-Book Collection*, 294–452. New York: HarperCollins, 2013. Kindle.

———. *Image and Imagination*, edited by Walter Hooper. New York: Cambridge University Press, 2013.

———. "Is Theology Poetry?" In *They Asked for a Paper: Papers and Addresses*, 150–65. London: Bles, 1962.

———. "It All Began with a Picture." In *Of Other Worlds: Essays and Stories*, 67–68. San Francisco: HarperOne, 2017. Kindle.

———. *The Last Battle*. In *The Chronicles of Narnia Complete 7-Book Collection*, 954–1100. New York: HarperCollins, 2013. Kindle.

———. *Letters of C. S. Lewis*. Edited by W. H. Lewis and Walter Hooper. San Francisco: HarperOne, 2017.

———. *Letters to Children*. Edited by Lyle W. Dorsett and Marjorie Lamp Mead. New York: Simon and Schuster, 1995.

———. *The Lion, the Witch and the Wardrobe*. In *The Chronicles of Narnia Complete 7-Book Collection*, 161–293. New York: HarperCollins, 2013. Kindle.

———. *The Magician's Nephew*. In *The Chronicles of Narnia Complete 7-Book Collection*, 20–159. New York: HarperCollins, 2013. Kindle.

———. "Man or Rabbit." In *God in the Dock: Essays on Theology and Ethics*, edited by Walter Hooper, 108–13. Grand Rapids: Eerdmans, 1970.

———. "Meditation in a Toolshed." In *God in the Dock: Essays on Theology and Ethics*, edited by Walter Hooper, 230–35. Grand Rapids: Eerdmans, 1970.

———. *Mere Christianity*. Rev. ed. San Francisco: HarperOne, 2015. Kindle.

———. *Miracles*. San Francisco: HarperSanFrancisco, 2001.

———. "Myth Became Fact." In *God in the Dock: Essays on Theology and Ethics*, edited by Walter Hooper, 63–67. Grand Rapids: Eerdmans, 1970.

———. "On Obstinacy in Belief." In *The World's Last Night and Other Essays*, 93–113. New York: Harcourt, Brace & World, 1960.

———. "On Stories." In *Of Other Worlds: Essays and Stories*, 3–31. San Francisco: HarperOne, 2017. Kindle.

———. "On Three Ways of Writing for Children." In *Of Other Worlds: Essays and Stories*, 33–53. San Francisco: HarperOne, 2017. Kindle.

———. *Out of the Silent Planet*. In *The Space Trilogy*, 1–158. New York: Scribner, 2011.

———. *The Pilgrim's Regress*. Edited by David C. Downing. Wade annotated ed. Grand Rapids: Eerdmans, 2014.

———. *A Preface to "Paradise Lost."* San Francisco: HarperOne, 2022. Kindle.

———. *Prince Caspian*. In *The Chronicles of Narnia Complete 7-Book Collection*, 454–607. New York: HarperCollins, 2013. Kindle.

———. *The Problem of Pain*. Rev. ed. San Francisco: HarperOne, 2015.

———. *The Silver Chair*. In *The Chronicles of Narnia Complete 7-Book Collection*, 783–953. New York: HarperCollins, 2013. Kindle.

———. "Sometimes Fairy Stories May Say Best What's to Be Said." In *Of Other Worlds: Essays and Stories*, 55–60. San Francisco: HarperOne, 2017. Kindle.

———. *Surprised by Joy: The Shape of My Early Life*. San Francisco: HarperOne, 2017. Kindle.

———. "Tolkien's *The Lord of the Rings*." In *On Stories: And Other Essays On Literature*, 127–38. San Francisco: HarperOne, 2017. Kindle.

———. "The Vision of John Bunyan." In *Selected Literary Essays*, edited by Walter Hooper, 206–15. New York: Cambridge University Press, 2013. Kindle.

———. *The Voyage of the Dawn Treader*. In *The Chronicles of Narnia Complete 7-Book Collection*, 608–782. New York: HarperCollins, 2013. Kindle.

———. *The Weight of Glory*. San Francisco: HarperOne, 2009.

Lindsley, Art. *C. S. Lewis's Case for Christ: Insights from Reason, Imagination and Faith*. Downers Grove, IL: InterVarsity, 2005.

Lindvall, Terry. *Surprised by Laughter*. Rev. ed. Nashville: Nelson, 2012.

Loconte, Joseph. *A Hobbit, a Wardrobe, and a Great War: How J. R. R. Tolkien and C. S. Lewis Rediscovered Faith, Friendship, and Heroism in the Cataclysm of 1914–18*. Nashville: Nelson, 2015.

Loke, Andrew Ter Ern. "A New Moral Argument for the Existence of God." *International Journal of Philosophy and Religion* 93 (2023) 25–38. https://doi.org/10.1007/s11153-022-09842-1.

Lovell, Steven. "Breaking the Spell of Skepticism: Puddleglum Versus the Green Witch." In *"The Chronicles of Narnia" and Philosophy: The Lion, the Witch, and the Worldview*, edited by Gregory Bassham and Jerry L. Walls, 41–52. Popular Culture and Philosophy 15. Chicago: Open Court, 2005.

MacDonald, George. "The Fantastic Imagination." In *The Complete Works of George MacDonald*, 18741–47. Ill. ed. Musaicum, 2017. Kindle.

———. "The Imagination: Its Functions and Its Culture." In *The Complete Works of George MacDonald*, 18474–509. Ill. ed. Musaicum, 2017. Kindle.

———. *Phantastes*. In *The Complete Works of George MacDonald*, 402–659. Ill. ed. Musaicum, 2017. Kindle.

———. Preface to *For the Right*, by Karl Emil Franzos, 1–54. Translated by Julie Sutter. New York: Harper & Brothers, 1888. Kindle.

———. *There and Back*. In *The Complete Works of George MacDonald*, 14906–15450. Ill. ed. Musaicum, 2017. Kindle.

———. *Wilfrid Cumbermede*. In *The Complete Works of George MacDonald*, 5539–6091. Ill. ed. Musaicum, 2017. Kindle.

———. "Wordsworth's Poetry." In *The Complete Works of George MacDonald*, 18682–99. Ill. ed. Musaicum, 2017. Kindle.

Maharaj, Rabi R. *Death of a Guru: A Remarkable True Story of One Man's Search for Truth*. Eugene, OR: Harvest House, 1984.

Mangalwadi, Vishal. *The Book that Made Your World: How the Bible Created the Soul of Western Civilization*. Nashville: Nelson, 2011.

Markos, Louis. *The Myth Made Fact: Reading Greek and Roman Mythology Through Christian Eyes*. Camp Hill, PA: Classical Academic, 2020.

Marshall, David. *The Case for Aslan: Evidence for Jesus in the Land of Narnia*. Tampa: DeWard, 2022.

Martin, Michael. *Atheism: A Philosophical Justification*. Philadelphia: Temple University Press, 1990.

Mathis, David, and John Piper, eds. *The Romantic Rationalist: God, Life, and Imagination in the Work of C. S. Lewis*. Wheaton, IL: Crossway, 2014.

McCarty, Emily L. "The Chronicles of Narnia and the Philosophy of Religion: Lessons from C. S. Lewis." In *Philosophy of Religion and Art*, edited by Gregory E. Trickett and John R. Gilhooly, 107–31. Newcastle upon Tyne, UK: Cambridge Scholars, 2021.

McGilchrist, Iain. *The Master and His Emissary: The Divided Brain and the Making of the Western World*. New Haven: Yale University Press, 2009.

McGrath, Alister. *C. S. Lewis—A Life: Eccentric Genius, Reluctant Prophet*. Repr. ed. Carol Stream, IL: Tyndale House, 2016.

———. "An Enhanced Vision of Rationality: C. S. Lewis on the Reasonableness of Christian Faith." *Theology* 6 (2013) 410–17.

———. *The Intellectual World of C. S. Lewis*. Chichester, UK: Wiley-Blackwell, 2013.

———. *Mere Apologetics: How to Help Seekers and Skeptics Find Faith*. Grand Rapids: Baker, 2012.

———. *Narrative Apologetics: Sharing the Relevance, Joy, and Wonder of the Christian Faith*. Grand Rapids: Baker, 2019.

———. *The Twilight of Atheism*. Oxford: Oxford University Press, 2004.

McGuire, W. J. "Input and Output Variables Currently Promising for Constructing Persuasive Communications." In *Public Communication Campaigns*, edited by Ronald E. Rice and Charles K. Atkin, 22–48. 3rd ed. Thousand Oaks, CA: SAGE, 2001.

McSporran, Cathy. "Daughters of Lilith: Witches and Wicked Women in *The Chronicles of Narnia*." In *Revisiting Narnia: Fantasy, Myth and Religion in C. S. Lewis's "Chronicles,"* edited by Shanna Caughey, 191–204. Dallas: Benbella, 2005.

Menuge, Angus J. L., ed. *C. S. Lewis: Lightbearer in the Shadowlands; The Evangelistic Vision of C. S. Lewis*. Wheaton, IL: Crossway, 1997.

———. "Why Eustace Almost Deserved His Name." In *"The Chronicles of Narnia" and Philosophy: The Lion, the Witch, and the Worldview*, edited by Gregory Bassham and Jerry L. Walls, 193–203. Popular Culture and Philosophy 15. Chicago: Open Court, 2005.

Miller, Duane. "The Secret World of God: Aesthetics, Relationships, and the Conversion of 'Frances' from Shi'a Islam to Christianity." *Global Missiology* 9 (2012) 1–14.

Miller, Michael Matheson. "C. S. Lewis, Scientism, and Moral Imagination." In *The Magician's Twin: C. S. Lewis on Science, Scientism, and Society*, edited by John G. West, 309–38. Seattle: Discover Institute, 2012.

Moon, W. Jay, and W. Bud Simon. *Effective Intercultural Evangelism: Good News in a Diverse World*. Downers Grove, IL: InterVarsity, 2021.

Moreland, J. P. *Scaling the Secular City: A Defense of Christianity*. Grand Rapids: Baker Book House, 1987.

———. *Scientism and Secularism: Learning to Respond to a Dangerous Ideology*. Wheaton, IL: Crossway, 2018.

Moreland, J. P., and Tim Muehlhoff. *The God Conversation: Using Stories and Illustrations to Explain Your Faith*. Westmont, IL: InterVarsity, 2017.

Moreland, J. P., and William Lane Craig. "Christian Doctrines I: The Trinity." In *Philosophical Foundations of a Christian Worldview*, 575–94. 2nd ed. Downers Grove, IL: InterVarsity, 2017.

Moreland, J. P., et al., eds. *Debating Christian Theism*. New York: Oxford University Press, 2013.

Morris, Thomas, *Making Sense of It All*. Grand Rapids: Eerdmans, 1992.

Most, Glenn. "From Logos to Mythos." In *From Myth to Reason? Studies in the Development of Greek Thought*, edited by Richard Buxton, 25–50. Oxford: Oxford University Press, 2005.

Mosteller, Timothy M. "The Tao of Narnia." In *"The Chronicles of Narnia" and Philosophy: The Lion, the Witch, and the Worldview*, edited by Gregory Bassham and Jerry L. Walls, 94–105. Popular Culture and Philosophy 15. Chicago: Open Court, 2005.

Mosteller, Timothy M., and Gayne J. Anacker, eds. *Contemporary Perspectives on C. S. Lewis's "The Abolition of Man": History, Philosophy, Education, and Science*. London: Bloomsbury Academic, 2017.

Muck, Terry, and Frances S. Adeney. *Christianity Encountering World Religions: The Practice of Mission in the Twenty-First Century*. Grand Rapids: Baker Academic, 2009.

Muck, Terry, et al., eds. *Handbook of Religion: A Christian Engagement with Traditions, Teachings, and Practices*. Grand Rapids: Baker Academic, 2014.

Murray, Penelope. "What Is a *Muthos* for Plato?" In *From Myth to Reason? Studies in the Development of Greek Thought*, edited by Richard Buxton, 251–62. Oxford: Oxford University Press, 2005.

Muth, Michael P. "Beastly Metaphysics: The Beasts of Narnia and Lewis's Reclamation of Medieval Sacramental Metaphysics." In *C. S. Lewis as Philosopher: Truth, Goodness, and Beauty*, edited by David Baggett et al., 281–98. 2nd ed. Lynchburg, VA: Liberty University Press, 2017.

Myers, Doris. *C. S. Lewis in Context*. Kent, OH: Kent State University Press, 1994.

Nagasawa, Yujin. *Maximal God: A New Defence of Perfect Being Theism*. Oxford: Oxford University Press, 2017.

Nash, Robert. *Religious Pluralism in the Academy: Opening the Dialogue*. New York: Lang, 2001.

Nash, Ronald. *Faith and Reason: Searching for a Rational Faith*. Grand Rapids: Academie, 1988.

Nelson, Michael. "One Mythology Among Many: The Spiritual Odyssey of C. S. Lewis." *Virginia Quarterly Review* 72 (1996) 619–33.

Netland, Harold A. "A Christian Theology of Religions." In *Handbook of Religion: A Christian Engagement with Traditions, Teachings, and Practices*, edited by Terry Muck et al., 19–26. Grand Rapids: Baker Academic, 2014.

———. *Christianity and Religious Diversity*. Grand Rapids: Baker Academic, 2015.

———. *Encountering Pluralism: The Challenge to Christian Faith Mission*. Downers Grove, IL: IVP Academic, 2001.

———. "Harold A. Netland." Trinity Evangelical Divinity School. https://www.tiu.edu/divinity/faculty/harold-a-netland/.

———. "Toward Contextualized Apologetics." *Missiology, An International Review* 16 (1988) 289–303.

Newbigin, Lesslie. *Foolishness to the Greeks: The Gospel and Western Culture*. Grand Rapids: Eerdmans, 1988.

Nicholi, Armand M. *The Question of God: C. S. Lewis and Sigmund Freud Debate God, Love, Sex, and the Meaning of Life*. New York: Free Press, 2002.

Noble, Alan. *Disruptive Witness: Speaking Truth in a Distracted Age*. Downers Grove, IL: InterVarsity, 2018.

Odero, Jose Miguel, and Maria Dolores Odero. *C. S. Lewis y la imagen del hombre*. Pamplona, Spain: Eunsa, 1993.

Olson, Richard. *Science Deified and Science Defied*. 2 vols. Berkeley: University of California Press, 1995.

Ordway, Holly. *Apologetics and the Christian Imagination: An Integrated Approach to Defending the Faith*. Steubenville, OH: Emmaus Road, 2017.

———. "'Further Up and Further In': Representations of Heaven in Tolkien and Lewis." *Journal of Inklings Studies* 3 (2013) 5–23.

Otto, Rudolf. *The Idea of the Holy: An Inquiry into the Non-Rational Factor in the Idea of the Divine and Its Relation to the Rational*. Translated by John W. Harvey. Oxford: Oxford University Press, 1958.

Paivio, Allan, and Ian Begg. *Psychology of Language*. Englewood Cliffs, NJ: Prentice-Hall, 1981.

Papineau, David. "Naturalism." The Stanford Encyclopedia of Philosophy (Winter 2016 ed.), edited by Edward N. Zalta, last revised September 15, 2015. https://plato.stanford.edu/archives/win2016/entries/naturalism/.

Patrick, James. "The Heart's Desire and the Landlord's Rules: C. S. Lewis as a Moral Philosopher." In *The Pilgrim's Guide: C. S. Lewis and the Art of Witness*, edited by David Mills, 70–85. Grand Rapids: Eerdmans, 1998.

Payne, Leanne. *Real Presence: The Christian Worldview of C. S. Lewis as Incarnational Reality*. Westchester, IL: Crossway, 1988.

Pearce, Joseph. *Beauteous Truth: Faith, Reason, Literature, and Culture*. South Bend: Saint Augustine's, 2014.

Pearcey, Nancy. *Total Truth: Liberating Christianity from Its Cultural Captivity*. Wheaton, IL: Crossway, 2004.

Pelser, Adam C. "Irrigating Deserts: Thinking with C. S. Lewis About Education for Emotional Formation." *Christian Scholar's Review* 44 (2014) 27–43.

———. "Philosophy in *The Abolition of Man*." In *Contemporary Perspectives on C. S. Lewis's "The Abolition of Man": History, Philosophy, Education, and Science*, edited by Timothy M. Mosteller and Gayne J. Anacker, 5–24. London: Bloomsbury Academic, 2017.

Pérez Díez, María del Carmen. *Por siempre jamás: C. S. Lewis y la tierra de Narnia*. León: Publicaciones Universidad de León, 2004.

Pertler, Nicolas R. "C. S. Lewis and the Premodern Rhetorical Tradition: *The Abolition of Man* as Rhetoric and Philosophy of Education." PhD diss., Duquesne University, 2014.

Peters, Thomas C. "The War of the Worldviews: H. G. Wells and Scientism Versus C. S. Lewis and Christianity." In *The Pilgrim's Guide: C. S. Lewis and the Art of Witness*, edited by David Mills, 203–20. Grand Rapids: Eerdmans, 1998.

Peterson, Michael. *C. S. Lewis and the Christian Worldview*. New York: Oxford University Press, 2020.

———. "C. S. Lewis on the Necessity of Gratuitous Evil." In *C. S. Lewis as Philosopher: Truth, Goodness, and Beauty*, edited by David Baggett et al., 211–27. 2nd ed. Lynchburg, VA: Liberty University Press, 2017.

———. *God And Evil: An Introduction To The Issues*. Boulder: Routledge, 1998.

Peterson, Michael, and Adam Peterson. "Time Keeps on Ticking, or Does It? The Significance of Time in *The Chronicles of Narnia*." In *"The Chronicles of Narnia" and Philosophy: The Lion, the Witch, and the Worldview*, edited by Gregory Bassham and Jerry L. Walls, 204–17. Popular Culture and Philosophy 15. Chicago: Open Court, 2005.

Peterson, Michael, et al., eds. "The Upanishads: 'Atman Is Brahman.'" In *Philosophy of Religion: Selected Readings*, 266–68. 5th ed. New York: Oxford University Press, 2014.
Phemister, Mary Anne, and Andre Lazo, eds. *Mere Christians: Inspiring Stories of Encounters with C. S. Lewis*. Grand Rapids: Baker, 2009.
Phillips, Timothy R., and Dennis Okholm. *Christian Apologetics in the Postmodern World*. Downers Grove, IL: InterVarsity, 1995.
Pike, Mark. "Ethical English Teaching: Learning Democratic Values or Living by the Tao?" *Changing English: Studies in Culture and Education* 18 (2011) 351–59.
Pike, Mark, et al. "Narnian Virtues: C. S. Lewis as Character Educator." *Journal of Character Education* 11 (2015) 71–86.
Plantinga, Alvin. *God, Freedom, and Evil*. Grand Rapids: Eerdmans, 1989.
———. "Is Naturalism Irrational?" In *The Analytical Theist: An Alvin Plantinga Reader*, edited by James Sennett, 72–96. Grand Rapids: Eerdmans, 1998.
———. *Where the Conflict Really Lies: Science, Religion, and Naturalism*. New York: Oxford University Press, 2011.
Plato. *The Republic*. Translated by Desmond Lee. 2nd ed. Penguin Classics. London: Penguin, 2007.
Poe, Harry Lee. "The Book C. S. Lewis Never Wrote: On Imagination and the Knowledge of God." *Sewanee Theological Review* 57 (2014) 465–79.
Proper, Jennifer Rains. "C. S. Lewis's Animal Images in *The Chronicles of Narnia*." PhD diss., Drew University, 2006.
Puckett, Joe, Jr. *The Apologetics of Joy: A Case for the Existence of God from C. S. Lewis's Argument from Desire*. Eugene, OR: Wipf & Stock, 2012.
Purtill, Richard L. *C. S. Lewis's Case for the Christian Faith*. San Francisco: Ignatius, 2004.
Qureshi, Nabeel. *Seeking Allah, Finding Jesus: A Devout Muslim Encounters Christianity*. Grand Rapids: Zondervan, 2016.
Qutub, Sarmad, and Musa Qutub. "Islam: Adherent Essay." In *Handbook of Religion: A Christian Engagement with Traditions, Teachings, and Practices*, edited by Gerald R. McDermott et al., 177–80. Grand Rapids: Baker Academic, 2014.
Rauch, Jonathan. "Let It Be." *Atlantic Monthly* (May 2003) 34–35. https://www.theatlantic.com/magazine/archive/2003/05/let-it-be/302726/.
Rea, Michael. *World Without Design: The Ontological Consequences of Naturalism*. New York: Oxford University Press, 2004.
Reichenbach, Bruce R. "At Any Rate There's No Humbug Here: Truth and Perspective." In *"The Chronicles of Narnia" and Philosophy: The Lion, the Witch, and the Worldview*, edited by Gregory Bassham and Jerry L. Walls, 53–64. Popular Culture and Philosophy 15. Chicago: Open Court, 2005.
Reilly, R. J. *Romantic Religion: A Study of Owen Barfield, C. S. Lewis, Charles Williams and J. R. R. Tolkien*. Great Barrington, MA: Lindisfarne, 2006.
Reppert, Victor. *C. S. Lewis's Dangerous Idea: In Defense of the Argument from Reason*. Downers Grove, IL: InterVarsity, 2003.
———. "*Miracles*: C. S. Lewis's Critique of Naturalism." In *Apologist, Philosopher, & Theologian*, edited by Bruce L. Edwards, 153–82. Vol. 3 of *C. S. Lewis: Life, Works, and Legacy*. Westport, CT: Praeger, 2007.
Rogers, Jonathan. *The World According to Narnia: Christian Meaning in C. S. Lewis's Beloved Chronicles*. New York: Time Warner, 2005.
Rookmaaker, Hans. *Art Needs No Justification*. Vancouver, Can.: Regent College, 2010.

———. *Modern Art and the Death of a Culture*. Downers Grove, IL: IVP, 1970.
Root, Jerry. "Tools Inadequate and Incomplete: C. S. Lewis and the Great Religions." In *The Pilgrim's Guide: C. S. Lewis and the Art of Witness*, edited by David Mills, 221–35. Grand Rapids: Eerdmans, 1998.
Root, Jerry, and Mark Hall. *The Surprising Imagination of C. S. Lewis: An Introduction*. Nashville: Abingdon, 2015.
Rowe, William L., et al. "Evil, Evidence, and Skeptical Theism—A Debate." In *The Problem of Evil: Selected Readings*, edited by Michael L. Peterson, 130–65. 2nd ed. Notre Dame, IN: University of Notre Dame Press, 2016. Kindle.
Ryken, Leland, and Marjorie Lamp Mead. *A Reader's Guide Through the Wardrobe: Exploring C. S. Lewis's Classic Story*. Downers Grove, IL: InterVarsity, 2005.
Sagan, Carl. *Cosmos*. New York: Ballantine, 2013.
Sam, Fong Choon. "A Narnia Inspired Imagination in Calling and Missions." Lecture given during the Inklings Week in Oxford, July 17, 2013. https://www.uu.edu/societies/inklings/recordings.cfm.
Sarapura Sarapura, Mercedes. "Jane Austen y C. S. Lewis: De la literatura al cine; Análisis de transposición." *Correspondencia & análisis* 6 (2016) 289–322.
Sayer, George. *Jack: C. S. Lewis and His Times*. San Francisco: Harper & Row, 1988.
Schaeffer, Francis A. *The Complete Works of Francis A. Schaeffer: A Christian Worldview*. Vol. 1. Westchester, IL: Crossway, 1982.
Schakel, Peter J. *Imagination and the Arts in C. S. Lewis: Journeying to Narnia and Other Worlds*. Columbia: University of Missouri Press, 2002.
———. "Irrigating Deserts with Moral Imagination." *Christian Reflection* 11 (2004) 21–29. https://ifl.web.baylor.edu/sites/g/files/ecbvkj771/files/2023-02/inklingsarticleschakel.pdf.
———. *Reading with the Heart: The Way into Narnia*. Grand Rapids: Eerdmans, 1979.
———. *Reason and Imagination in C. S. Lewis: A Study of "Till We Have Faces."* Grand Rapids: Eerdmans, 1984.
———. *The Way into Narnia*. Grand Rapids: Eerdmans, 2005.
Schindler, D. C. *Plato's Critique of Impure Reason: On Goodness and Truth in the Republic*. Washington, DC: Catholic University of America Press, 2008.
Schwartz, Sanford. "Paradise Reframed: Lewis, Bergson, and Changing Times on *Perelandra*." *Christianity and Literature* 51 (2002) 569–602.
Scruton, Roger. *Beauty: A Very Short Introduction*. Oxford: Oxford University Press, 2011.
Seachris, Joshua, and Linda Zagzebski. "Weighing Evils: The C. S. Lewis Approach." *International Journey for Philosophy of Religion* 62 (2007) 81–88.
Seckler, Thomas W. *Experiencing the Gospel: An Examination of Muslim Conversion to Christianity in Cambodia*. Eugene, OR: Pickwick, 2020.
Sellars, J. T. *Reasoning Beyond Reason: Imagination as a Theological Source in the Work of C. S. Lewis*. Eugene, OR: Pickwick, 2010.
Shen, Hsiang Yen. "Cross-Cultural Effectiveness of Christian Message Films: Taiwanese Responses to the Concepts of God and Christianity in the Film *Bruce Almighty*." PhD diss., Regent University, 2010.
Sidlo, Katarzyna. "'Coming Out' or 'Staying in the Closet'—Deconversion Narratives of Muslim Apostates in Jordan." *Marburg Journal of Religion* 18 (2016). https://doi.org/10.17192/mjr.2016.18.4572.
Sijuwade, Joshua R. *The Rational Ontological Argument: Modality, Ontology and God*. London: Bloomsbury Academic, 2025.

Sire, James W. *Apologetics Beyond Reason: Why Seeing Really Is Believing*. Downers Grove, IL: IVP Academic, 2014.

———. *Habits of the Mind: Intellectual Life as a Christian Calling*. Downers Grove, IL: InterVarsity, 2000.

———. *Naming the Elephant*. 2nd ed. Downers Grove, IL: IVP Academic, 2015.

———. *The Universe Next Door*. 6th ed. Downers Grove, IL: IVP Academic, 2020.

Sloan, Robert Lee. "As If Swallowing Light Itself: C. S. Lewis's Argument from Desire, Part I." In *C. S. Lewis as Philosopher: Truth, Goodness, and Beauty*, edited by David Baggett et al., 315–26. 2nd ed. Lynchburg, VA: Liberty University Press, 2017.

Smilde, Arend. "Horrid Red Herrings: A New Look at the 'Lewisian Argument from Desire'—and Beyond." *Journal of Inklings Studies* 4 (2014) 33–92.

Smith, James K. A. *How (Not) to Be Secular: Reading Charles Taylor*. Grand Rapids: Eerdmans, 2014.

Smith, Stephen M. "Awakening from the Enchantment of Worldliness: The Chronicles of Narnia as Pre-Apologetics." In *The Pilgrim's Guide: C. S. Lewis and the Art of Witness*, edited by David Mills, 168–81. Grand Rapids: Eerdmans, 1998.

Soanes, Catherine, and Angus Stevenson, eds. *Concise Oxford English Dictionary*. 11th ed. Oxford: Oxford University Press, 2004.

Soto Sapriza, Erwin. "El 'mito verdadero' y las metáforas doctrinales de C. S. Lewis." PhD diss., Universidad de Navarra (Spain), 2004.

Spielberg, Steven, dir. *Schindler's List*. Universal Pictures, Amblin Entertainment, 1993.

Sproul, R. C. *If There Is a God, Why Are There Atheists? A Surprising Look at the Psychology of Atheism*. Minneapolis: Bethany Fellowship, 1978.

———. *Justified by Faith Alone*. Wheaton, IL: Crossway, 2010.

Sproul, R. C., et al. *Classical Apologetics: A Rational Defense of the Christian Faith and a Critique of Presuppositional Apologetics*. Grand Rapids: Baker, 1984.

Stackhouse, John. *Humble Apologetics*. Oxford: Oxford University Press, 2006.

Stafford, Tim. "New Theologians." *Christianity Today*, February 1999, 30–49.

Starr, Charlie W. "Aesthetics vs. Anesthesia: C. S. Lewis on the Purpose of Art." In *C. S. Lewis and the Arts: Creativity in the Shadowlands*, edited by Rod Miller, 115–31. Baltimore: Square Halo, 2013.

———. *The Faun's Bookshelf: C. S. Lewis on Why Myth Matters*. Kent, OH: Kent State University Press, 2018.

———. "Meaning, Meanings, and Epistemology in C. S. Lewis." *Mythlore* 25 (2007) 161–82.

———. "So How *Should* We Teach English?" In *Contemporary Perspectives on C. S. Lewis's "The Abolition of Man": History, Philosophy, Education, and Science*. Edited by Timothy M. Mosteller and Gayne J. Anacker, 63–81. London: Bloomsbury Academic, 2017.

Svensson, Manfred. *Ética y política: Una mirada desde C. S. Lewis*. Barcelona: Editorial Clie, 2005.

———. *Más allá de la sensatez: El pensamiento de C. S. Lewis*. Barcelona: Editorial Clie, 2011.

Taliaferro, Charles. "A Narnian Theory of the Atonement." *Scottish Journal of Theology* 41 (1988) 75–92.

Taliaferro, Charles, and Jill Evans. *The Image in Mind: Theism, Naturalism, and the Imagination*. New York: Bloomsbury Academic, 2013.

Taylor, Charles. *A Secular Age*. Cambridge: Harvard University Press, 2007.

Tennent, Timothy. *Christianity at the Religious Roundtable: Evangelicalism in Conversation with Hinduism, Buddhism, and Islam*. Grand Rapids: Baker Academic, 2002.

Tolkien, J. R. R. *The Lord of the Rings*. 50th anniv. ed. Boston: Houghton Mifflin Harcourt, 2005.

———. *On Fairy-Stories*. Edited by Verlyn Flieger and Douglas A. Anderson. Exp. ed. London: HarperCollins, 2014.

———. *Tales from the Perilous Realm*. Boston: Houghton Mifflin Harcourt, 2008.

Tollefsen, Christopher. "The Tao of Enchantment." *National Review* 65 (2013) 50–51.

Travers, Michael. "The Abolition of Man: C. S. Lewis's Philosophy of History." In *Apologist, Philosopher, & Theologian*, edited by Bruce L. Edwards, 107–31. Vol. 3 of *C. S. Lewis: Life, Works, and Legacy*. Westport, CT: Praeger, 2007.

Trueman, Carl R. *The Rise and Triumph of the Modern Self: Cultural Amnesia, Expressive Individualism, and the Road to Sexual Revolution*. Wheaton, IL: Crossway, 2020.

Tyson, Paul. *Returning to Reality*. Eugene, OR: Cascade, 2014.

Urrutia, Doris Elin, and Elizabeth Howell. "How Fast Is Earth Moving?" Space, last updated February 27, 2025. https://www.space.com/33527-how-fast-is-earth-moving.html.

Van den Toren, Benno. "Challenges and Possibilities of Inter-Religious and Cross-Cultural Apologetic Persuasion." *Evangelical Quarterly* 82 (2010) 42–64.

———. *Christian Apologetics as Cross-Cultural Dialogue*. London: T&T Clark, 2011.

———. "Prof. Dr. B. van den Toren." Protestantse Theologische Universiteit. https://www.pthu.nl/en/about-us/people/b.vandentoren/.

———. "Why Inter-Religious Dialogue Needs Apologetics: Intrinsic to Bearing Witness to Christ Is Making Truth Claims." *IFES Word & World* 4 (2017) 19–26. https://ifesworld.org/en/journal/why-inter-religious-dialogue-needs-apologetics-benno-van-den-toren/.

Vanhoozer, Kevin J. "In Bright Shadow: C. S. Lewis on the Imagination for Theology and Discipleship." In *The Romantic Rationalist: God, Life, and Imagination in the Work of C. S. Lewis*, edited by John Piper and David Mathis, 81–104. Wheaton, IL: Crossway, 2014.

Van Inwagen, Peter. *Metaphysics*. Boulder: Westview, 2015.

Vaus, Will, and Douglas Gresham. *Mere Theology: A Guide to the Thought of C. S. Lewis*. Downers Grove, IL: IVP Academic, 2004.

Walsh, Chad. *C. S. Lewis: Apostle to the Skeptics*. New York: Macmillan, 1949. Repr., Eugene, OR: Wipf & Stock, 2008.

Ward, Michael. *After Humanity: A Guide to C. S. Lewis's "The Abolition of Man."* Des Plaines, IL: Word on Fire Academic, 2021.

———. "The Church in C. S. Lewis's Fiction." In *C. S. Lewis and the Church: Essays in Honour of Walter Hooper*, edited by Judith Wolfe and B. N. Wolfe, 67–89. London: Bloomsbury, 2012.

———. "Escape to Wallaby Wood: C. S. Lewis's Depictions of Conversion." In *C. S. Lewis: Lightbearer in the Shadowlands; The Evangelistic Vision of C. S. Lewis*, edited by Angus J. L. Menuge, 143–68. Wheaton, IL: Crossway, 1997.

———. "The Good Serves the Better and Both the Best: C. S. Lewis on Imagination and Reason in Apologetics." In *Imaginative Apologetics: Theology, Philosophy, and the Catholic Tradition*, edited by Andrew Davison, 59–78. Grand Rapids: Baker Academic, 2012.

———. *Planet Narnia: The Seven Heavens in the Imagination of C. S. Lewis.* New York: Oxford University Press, 2010.

———. "Science and Religion in the Writings of C. S. Lewis." *Science & Christian Belief* 25 (2013) 3–16.

Watson, Micah J. "Natural Law in *The Abolition of Man.*" In *Contemporary Perspectives on C. S. Lewis's "The Abolition of Man": History, Philosophy, Education, and Science,* edited by Timothy M. Mosteller and Gayne J. Anacker, 25–46. London: Bloomsbury Academic, 2017.

Weaver, Richard. *Ideas Have Consequences.* Chicago: University of Chicago Press, 1948.

Webb, Stephen. "Aslan's Voice." In *"The Chronicles of Narnia" and Philosophy: The Lion, the Witch, and the Worldview,* edited by Gregory Bassham and Jerry L. Walls, 3–14. Popular Culture and Philosophy 15. Chicago: Open Court, 2005.

White, William Luther. *The Image of Man in C. S. Lewis.* Nashville: Abingdon, 1969.

Wilkens, Steve, and Mark L. Sanford. *Hidden Worldviews: Eight Cultural Stories That Shape Our Lives.* Downers Grove, IL: IVP Academic, 2017.

Willard, Timothy. "C. S. Lewis's Language of Beauty." Timothy Willard, April 22, 2014. https://web.archive.org/web/20191222044151/http://www.timothywillard.com/blog/2014/4/22/cs-lewiss-language-of-beauty.

———. "Endless Twilight: A Study of C. S. Lewis's Language of Beauty." PhD diss., King's College London, 2016.

Williams, Brian. *C. S. Lewis' Pre-Evangelism for a Post-Christian World: Why Narnia Might Be More Real Than We Think.* Cambridge: Christian Publishing House, 2021. Kindle.

Williams, Clifford. *Existential Reasons for Belief in God: A Defense of Desires & Emotions for Faith.* Downers Grove, IL: IVP Academic, 2011.

Williams, Donald. "Anselm and Aslan: C. S. Lewis and the Ontological Argument." *Touchstone* 27 (2014) 36–39.

———. *An Encouraging Thought: The Christian Worldview in the Writings of J. R. R. Tolkien.* Cambridge: Christian Publishing House, 2018. Kindle.

Williams, Paul. *The Unexpected Way: On Converting from Buddhism to Catholicism.* Edinburgh: T&T Clark, 2002.

Williams, Peter S. *C. S. Lewis vs. the New Atheists.* Colorado Springs: Paternoster, 2013.

———. "Pro: A Defense of C. S. Lewis's Argument from Desire." In *C. S. Lewis's Christian Apologetics: Pro and Con,* edited by Gregory Bassham, 45–55. Leiden: Brill, 2015.

Williams, Rowan, and Monica Capoferri. *The Lion's World: A Journey into the Heart of Narnia.* New York: Oxford University Press, 2013.

Williams, Thomas M. *The Heart of "The Chronicles of Narnia": Knowing God Here by Finding Him There.* Nashville: Nelson, 2006.

Wilson, N. D. *Notes from the Tilt-a-Whirl: Wide-Eyed Wonder in God's Spoken World.* Nashville: Nelson, 2009.

Wolfe, Gregory. *Beauty Will Save the World: Recovering the Human in an Ideological Age.* Wilmington, DE: ISI, 2014.

Wolterstorff, Nicholas. *Reason Within the Bounds of Revelation.* Grand Rapids: Eerdmans, 1976.

Wood, Ralph C. *The Gospel According to Tolkien.* Louisville: Westminster John Knox, 2003.

Wooddell, Joseph D. *The Beauty of the Faith: Using Aesthetics for Christian Apologetics.* Eugene, OR: Wipf & Stock, 2011.

Wright, N. T. *Evil and the Justice of God.* Westmont, IL: InterVarsity, 2013.

———. *Surprised by Scripture: Engaging Contemporary Issues.* New York: HarperCollins, 2015.

Wykstra, Stephen J. "The Humean Obstacle to Evidential Arguments from Suffering: On Avoiding the Evils of 'Appearance.'" *International Journal for Philosophy of Religion* 16 (1984) 73–93.

Yandell, Keith E. *Philosophy of Religion: A Contemporary Introduction.* Routledge Contemporary Introductions to Philosophy. New York: Routledge, 1999.

Yandell, Keith E., and Harold Netland. *Buddhism: A Christian Exploration and Appraisal.* Downers Grove, IL: IVP Academic, 2009.

Index

The Abolition of Man, 39, 45, 200
afterlife, 78, 112, 196, 212
affection(s), 24, 39–40, 44, 130, 200
agnosticism, 195
allegory, 15, 28, 41, 141, 237
Anselm, 6, 154, 155–57, 161–66, 200
antichrist, 94
An Experiment in Criticism, 3–6, 40
apatheism, 10, 97, 99, 100, 194–202,
    205, 207–8, 210–11, 215, 218,
    229
argument from desire, 10, 98, 162,
    164–65, 188, 224
art, 5, 6, 8, 16–20, 22, 27, 29, 33–34, 40,
    44–45, 59, 70, 143, 225, 234
Aslan, 1, 9, 11, 42, 51, 54, 91, 93–98,
    103, 110, 114–15, 117, 120,
    123–32, 144, 147–51, 153–54,
    156–64, 168, 176, 179–90, 192,
    194, 203–11, 213–17, 219–26,
    230, 237
assensus, 223
atheism, 3, 21, 134, 151, 195
atheist(s), 40, 54, 60, 116, 132, 134,
    140–41, 143, 150, 152, 166, 183,
    195, 220
authority, 61, 69, 110–11, 115, 121, 126,
    142, 148, 158–59, 176, 182–83,
    186, 188, 214
Augustine, 52, 67

Bailey, Justin, 8, 47, 61–71, 218
    Contemporary Narrative Apologetics
    (Bailey), 47, 61–71

    Thick Authenticity and the Theater
    of God's Glory, 61–62
    The Apologetics of Hope, 62–64
    Three Elements for Reimagining
    Apologetics, 64–68
    Everyday and Extended Imaginative
    Apologetics, 68–69
    Helpful Insights, 69–70
baptism, 38, 142
Barfield, Owen, 16, 54, 199, 233
Barkman, Adam, 5, 234
beauty, 3, 7, 19–23, 25, 31, 34, 42,
    46, 53, 58–60, 63, 65, 68, 70,
    115, 158, 168, 183, 185, 189,
    197, 200–1, 213–14, 221, 225,
    233–34
Berger, Peter, 75, 138, 139, 197
Beshears, Kyle, 198, 201, 202
Bible, 1, 110, 173, 218, 222–23
body of belief, 37
Bowen, John, 219, 221, 222
Buddha, 87, 180, 184
Buddhism, 79, 87, 91, 172–75, 182, 229

Call, (See Six Keys for Cross-Cultural
    Narrative Apologetics)
Chesterton, G. K., 16, 26, 31, 230
Christ, 33, 41, 43, 50, 54, 56, 60, 62,
    65–66, 73, 75–77, 80–81,
    84–85, 89, 93–94, 110, 116, 119,
    122, 131, 158,175, 185, 198,
    203, 216, 221, 223
Christian Theism, 88, 104, 112, 198,
    215

INDEX

The Chronicles of Narnia, ix, 1, 6–7, 9–10, 16, 27, 32, 37–38, 40, 53–54, 60, 72, 90–91, 93–97, 99–100, 132, 141, 158–59, 176, 180, 190, 195, 216, 218–29, 237–38
chronological snobbery, 199
church, 24, 58, 64, 74, 132, 138, 215, 222
Classic Narrative Apologetics, 15, 44–45, 91
    Lewis, C. S., (*See* Lewis, C. S., Classic Narrative Apologetics)
    MacDonald, George, (*See* MacDonald, George, Classic Narrative Apologetics)
    Tolkien, J.R.R., (*See* Tolkien, J.R.R., Classic Narrative Apologetics)
Concern, (*See* Six Keys for Cross-Cultural Narrative Apologetics)
conscience, 16, 20, 116–17, 183
Contemporary Narrative Apologetics, 45–47, 70
    Bailey, Justin, (*See* Bailey, Justin, Contemporary Narrative Apologetics)
    McGrath, Alister, (*See* McGrath, Alister, Contemporary Narrative Apologetics)
    Ordway, Holly, (*See* Ordway, Holly, Contemporary Narrative Apologetics)
Conversion, 3–4, 9, 27, 54, 56, 74, 80, 84, 89, 100, 117, 128, 137–38, 140–41, 143, 145, 174
Correspondence theory of truth, 238
Cosmological argument, 25
Corduan, Winfried, 104–9
Creation, 4, 23, 34, 49, 63, 65–67, 85, 93, 106, 134, 176, 182, 184, 186, 189, 212–13, 221, 234, 237
    ex nihilo, 25, 83, 105, 159
    sub-creation, 4, 27–30, 33–34, 36, 165, 228
Creator, 18, 34, 90, 105, 116, 168, 175–76, 180–83, 185, 188, 190, 192–93
Cross-Cultural Apologetics, 6, 7, 9, 46, 72–73, 77, 79–83, 88–89, 91–93, 100, 104, 109, 136–37, 173, 195, 218–20, 223, 226, 229
Netland, Harold, (*See* Netland, Harold, Cross-Cultural Apologetics)
Van den Toren, Benno, (*See* Van den Toren, Benno, Cross Cultural Apologetics)
Crucifixion, 111
Culture, 3–6, 39, 50, 58, 70, 73, 78, 81–83, 86, 89, 94, 116, 137, 139, 174, 197–99,

Dawkins, Richard, 134–35
death, 10, 32, 56, 68–69, 71, 79, 83, 85, 93–94, 96–97, 99, 103–4, 107, 110, 116–17, 122–24, 130–31, 135, 143, 151, 159, 171–72, 179, 181, 186–88, 191, 195, 197, 206–9, 214, 217, 224, 226
death and resurrection, 83, 85, 93–94, 103, 159
delight, 4, 20, 23, 25, 103, 107, 121–22, 127, 184, 229–30
Descartes, René, 6, 155

Eastern Mysticism, (*See* Eastern Pantheistic Monism)
Eastern Pantheistic Monism, 10, 99–100, 168–69, 172, 176, 192, 218
elves, 35
epistemology, 4–5
eternity, 186, 215
Eustace (Scrubb), 51, 133, 142–48, 150, 153–54, 157–58, 206, 208–9
evangelism, ix, 55, 84
Evans, C. Stephen, 88
evil, 10, 78–79, 83–85, 90–91, 95–97, 105, 107–8, 116, 135, 159, 168, 171, 175–80, 185–86, 188, 192–93, 214, 226, 234

fantasy, 1, 16, 26, 28, 30–31, 34, 38–39, 43, 45, 58, 151, 157, 159, 212, 218, 220, 234
fiducia, 223
Freud, Sigmund, 50

Gandalf, 36
God as artist, 27
gods, 3, 116, 134, 175, 194,
gospel, ix, 2, 10, 33, 46, 48, 50, 53, 58, 64–65, 73, 76, 80, 82–3, 86–87, 90, 108, 117, 119, 125, 128, 131, 173–74, 180–81, 197, 203, 218, 220, 227, 231
Gollum, 35
grace, 1, 2, 7, 25, 28, 32, 35, 51, 55, 67, 85, 87, 96, 103, 125, 127–28, 140, 143, 173, 179, 185, 192, 200
Groothuis, Douglas R., 156, 161, 165, 167

Hardy, Dean, 22, 24
heaven, 24, 38, 55, 107, 117, 150, 187–88, 202, 209, 211–12, 214–15
hell, 25, 55, 107
Hinduism, 168–69, 172–75, 181, 190, 229
holiness, 39, 127, 147, 183, 189, 210, 217
home, 31, 35, 57–58, 115, 138, 140, 146, 164, 189, 211–13, 215–16, 223
humanity, 35–36, 77, 95, 170

image of God, 4, 6
imagination, 2–3, 5, 15–18, 20, 22, 27, 32, 37–38, 42–43, 47, 53–55, 58, 60–62, 65–67, 72, 77, 125, 131–132, 138, 140–41, 150, 152, 162, 221, 229–30, 233–36
immortality, 9, 32, 96, 135, 224
Incarnation, 33, 50, 52, 54, 93, 103, 105, 109, 110, 112, 132, 141, 220, 237
Inklings, 8, 15, 27, 228
Islam, 10, 103–12, 115, 117–18, 127–28, 132

Jadis, 179–81, 190
Janosik, Daniel, x, 111–12
Jesus, 1, 7, 31, 49, 55, 58, 73–78, 80, 82–83, 85, 90–91, 96, 108–11, 116, 123, 125–26, 130–32, 140, 151, 173–75, 180, 183–84, 190, 193, 215–16, 219, 221–24, 226, 231, 236
Johnson, Kirstin, 17

joy, 3, 25, 32–33, 37, 42, 46, 59, 115, 150, 174, 187–89, 203, 206, 211, 221, 233, 235
judge, 35, 55, 127, 156, 191, 226
judgment, 107, 110, 117, 160, 194–95, 202, 209–10, 213, 215
just sentiments, 39, 215

Kilby, Clyde, 35, 220
King, 95, 116, 121–22, 126, 142, 158, 180, 189–90, 203–4, 206–7, 210, 236
Kingdom, 9, 40, 60, 94–96, 121, 127, 154, 160, 176, 187–90, 192, 194, 207, 220, 224
Kreeft, Peter, 34, 234
Kuhn, Robert Lawrence, 68–69, 71, 137
Kuhn, Thomas S., 137–39, 220

Lewis, C. S.
    Classic Narrative Apologetics (Lewis), 15–16, 20–21, 25–28, 32, 34, 37–46
    conversion, 3–4, 27, 140, 143
    conversion, metaphors for, 56, 145
    culture and making, 3–6, 39
    familiarization, 37–38, 40–41, 44
    Joy, 3, 21, 46, 59, 149–50, 187–88, 204, 206, 211, 221, 233, 235
    "the man" vs. "the artist," 7–8, 224
    longing, 235, (*See Sehnsucht*)
    meaning, 236
    myth, 5, 37–38, 49–50, 113–14, 116, 229–30, 236
    Ontological argument, 154–55, 157, 163–64
    true myth, 27, 50
    Sehnsucht, 3, 41, 91, 124, 150–51, 214, 235
    supposal, 40–41, 44–45, 94, 96, 141, 164–65, 228, 233, 237–38
    past watchful dragons, 7, 37, 40–41, 43, 90, 112, 140–41, 222, 224, 231
Lindsley, Art, 219
Lindvall, Terry, 184
logic, 24, 65, 77, 90, 120
Loke, Andrew Ter Ern, 180

longing, 3, 9, 33, 35–36, 41, 45–46, 59, 68, 70, 91, 96, 98, 115, 124–25, 146, 149–52, 183, 211–12, 214, 221, 230, 233, 235
love, 1, 10, 21, 25, 53, 59–60, 64–66, 69, 96–97, 119, 131, 140, 168, 173, 176, 179–80, 182, 187, 190, 192–93, 200–1, 209–10, 213, 221, 224, 231, 233

MacDonald, George, 8, 15–27, 29, 37, 39, 44–47, 64–65, 140, 218, 229
    Classic Narrative Apologetics (MacDonald),
    argumentation, 24–25
    communicates what is difficult to define, 18–19
    creates atmosphere for belief, 18–20
    wakes the reader, 18, 20
    transformation, 18, 20–21
    encountered beauty, 21–23
Maharaj, Rabi R., 175, 183, 188
Mangalwadi, Vishal, 190–92
Marshall, David, 219
Martyr, Justin, 49
materialism, 43, 133, 145
maya, 170
McGrath, Alister, 8, 47–52, 61, 218
    Contemporary Narrative Apologetics (McGrath), 47–52, 61
    The Seed of Story, 48–50
    The Potential of Narrative Apologetics, 50–52
    Helpful Insights, 52–53
meaning, 10, 19–20, 22, 48–49, 52, 54–57, 59–60, 63, 65, 67, 70, 93, 96, 99, 106, 110, 136, 199, 201, 208, 224, 235–37
Mere Christianity, 27, 56–57, 111, 117, 120, 151, 235
metaphor, 56, 87, 97, 201, 236
metaphysics, 36
Middle-earth, 33, 35, 58
miracle, 115, 196, 217, 220
monism, (*See* Eastern Pantheistic Monism)
monotheism, 104
moral argument, 10, 98, 165

moral evil, 96
moral law, 4, 39, 95–96, 117–18, 180, 207
morality, 135, 137, 145, 199, 233
Muhammad, 87, 108, 126
myth, 5, 27, 37–38, 49–50, 52, 113–14, 116, 229–30, 236, 238
myth became fact, 114
Myth Became Fact, 238
mythology, 3
    Eastern Mysticism, (*See* monism)

natural law, 91
naturalism, 10, 99–100, 133–34, 136–37, 139, 141–42, 145–46, 151–53, 164, 199, 218
Netland, Harold, 9, 81–91, 95, 174, 182, 218
    Cross-Cultural Apologetics (Netland), 81–91, 95
    What Is Contextualized Apologetics?, 81–82
    Six Needs for Cross-Cultural Apologetics, 82–83
    Four Barriers to Cross-Cultural Apologetics, 83–85
    Six Topics for Cross-Cultural Engagement, 85–88
Newbigin, Lesslie, 139
northernness, 42
nostalgia, 115, 146
notitia, 223
numinous experience, 42, 150, 214

Ontological argument, 6, 10, 93, 98, 100, 153–57, 159, 163–64, 166
Ordway, Holly, 8, 47, 53–61, 132, 141, 218, 220
    Contemporary Narrative Apologetics (Ordway), 47, 53–61
    Imagination and Incarnation, 54
    Reason, Imagination, and Meaning, 54–60
    Helpful Insights, 60
Out of the Silent Planet, 37

pain, 24, 27, 59, 147, 186
pantheism, 169

INDEX

Pascal, Blaise, 62
Pascal's wager, 163, 207, 209, 211
Pelser, Adam, 200
Phantastes, 3, 21, 38–39, 41, 44, 140, 142, 150, 152
philosophy, 34–35, 134, 200
Plato, 153–55, 164
plausibility structure (plausibility), 73, 120, 138–39, 141, 144–45, 149, 152, 155–56, 163, 197
pre-evangelism, 2, 42, 218, 224
pride, 168, 178, 184, 205
Prince Caspian, 95, 222, 229
problem of evil, 83–85, 186, 188
providence, 45, 146, 148, 158

Qur'an, 105–12

reincarnation, 57, 78, 171
relativism, 80, 83–84, 87, 89
resurrection, 33, 36, 83, 85, 93–94, 103, 117, 131, 159, 212, 217, 237
revelation, 17, 85, 105, 108, 116, 139
ring, 28, 32, 34–36, 65, 168, 177
Rowling, J. K., 32

Sagan, Carl, 133–34
salvation, 4, 51, 91, 94, 104, 107, 109, 128, 130, 138, 140, 170, 173, 223
Sam, Fong Choon, 125, 220
Sayer, George, 38, 95
Schaeffer, Francis A., 2, 96, 145, 198, 201, 224
science, 24, 31, 64–65, 76, 78, 83–84, 133, 135, 137, 144, 178, 197, 228
scripture, 48–50, 53, 85, 223
sin, 1, 35, 51, 55, 58, 84, 94, 104–6, 109–11, 116–17, 122, 126, 128, 175–76, 184–86, 189, 215, 236
Sire, James, 99, 134–36, 169–73, 185
Six Keys for Cross-Cultural Narrative Apologetics
    Call, 9–10, 93, 97–98, 100, 116–20, 123–28, 130–31, 143, 145–49, 151, 153, 180, 183, 188, 205, 207, 209, 211, 215, 218, 220–21, 223–27
    Concern, 9–10, 82, 93, 96–97, 100, 114, 116, 126, 132, 148–49, 153, 178, 180, 183, 186, 188, 190, 204–5, 218, 224–26
    Tension, 9–10, 78–80, 93, 95–98, 100, 114, 116–19, 122–23, 125–28, 130–31, 143, 145–46, 148–49, 153, 171, 174, 178, 180–81, 183, 187, 190, 201, 205, 207–9, 211, 218, 222–27
    Transformation, 9–10, 20–21, 91, 93–96, 98, 100, 115, 126, 147–49, 188, 207, 209–11, 215, 218, 223, 225–26, 231
    Translation, 9–10, 50, 66, 93–94, 98, 100, 103, 114–24, 126–28, 130–31, 143, 145–49, 151, 178–80, 182–86, 188, 190, 204, 207, 209–11, 215, 218, 220–23, 225–27, 230–31, 237–38
    Treasure, 9–10, 93, 96, 98, 100, 114–16, 118–19, 124, 126–28, 130–31, 146–47, 149, 151, 153, 178, 180–81, 183–86, 188, 190, 205, 207, 209, 211, 215, 218, 220–27, 231
skepticism, 10, 97, 120, 157, 162
Smith, James K. A., 197
Socrates, 155
The Space Trilogy, 37, 40
Starr, Charlie, 4, 113, 152, 230, 235–37
stock responses, 39–40
story, 1–2, 4–8, 10, 17, 28–38, 42–43, 47–53, 65–66, 68, 70, 72, 76–77, 80, 91, 94–100, 103, 106, 113–14, 117, 119–21, 123–24, 127, 129, 134, 142, 146, 149, 154–55, 164, 166, 168, 173, 176, 180–82, 185–86, 190–92, 194, 202–3, 211, 215–17, 220–22, 226–29, 231, 236
sub-creation, 4, 27–30, 33–34, 36, 165, 228
suffering, 32, 59, 97, 107, 111, 175–76, 186, 188
supposal, (See Lewis, C. S.) 40–41, 44–45, 94, 96, 141, 164–65, 228, 233, 237–38

supposing, 43, 93, 164–65, 237–38
Surprised by Joy, 21, 143, 221, 235

Tao, 95, 200
Taylor, Charles, 61, 139, 197
temptation, 108, 177, 179, 187–88
Tension, (*See* Six Keys for Cross-Cultural Narrative Apologetics)
The Chronicles of Narnia, 1, 6–7, 9–10, 16, 27, 32, 37–38, 40, 53–54, 60, 72, 90–91, 93–97, 99–100, 132, 141, 158–59, 176, 180, 190, 195, 216, 218–29, 237–38
The Fellowship of the Ring, 34
The Golden Key (MacDonald), 28
Theism, Christian, 88, 104, 112, 198, 215
The Last Battle, 10, 94, 97, 100, 194–95, 202–5, 208–9, 211, 214–15
The Lion, the Witch, and the Wardrobe, 1, 7, 10, 50–51, 94–95, 100, 103–4, 112–13, 120, 123, 125, 132, 159, 217, 221, 225, 227, 230
The Magician's Nephew, 10, 100, 159, 168–69, 176, 181, 186, 188–90, 192, 221
theodicy, 176
The Problem of Pain, 27
The Silver Chair, 6, 10, 50, 100, 153–54, 156, 165, 216, 231
The Voyage of the Dawn Treader, 10, 51, 100, 126, 133–34, 142, 148, 150–52
The Weight of Glory (Lewis), 151, 211
Tolkien, J. R. R., 8, 15–16, 27, 47, 54, 116, 218, 228
  Classic Narrative Apologetics (Tolkien)
  consolation, 32–33
  escape, 31–32
  eucatastrophe, 32–33
  recovery, 30–31, 36–37, 45
  sub-creation, 34–36
Transformation, (*See* Six Keys for Cross-Cultural Narrative Apologetics)
Translation, (*See* Six Keys for Cross-Cultural Narrative Apologetics)
Treasure, (*See* Six Keys for Cross-Cultural Narrative Apologetics)

Trinity, 110, 112
truth, 2, 6–7, 10, 15–16, 19–21, 27, 39, 47, 49–50, 53, 56–60, 63, 65, 68, 72–73, 83–85, 87, 89, 96–97, 108, 117, 119–21, 123, 127, 132, 135, 138–39, 154–55, 160, 171, 183–85, 195, 197, 199, 201, 204–5, 218, 221, 224–25, 227–28, 233–38

unbelief, 66, 69, 108, 122–23, 132, 143–44, 218–19
Uncle Andrew, 177–79, 181, 183

Van den Toren, Benno, 9, 72–80, 88–90, 97, 112, 143, 218–20
  Cross-Cultural Apologetics (Van den Toren), 72–80, 88–90
  What Is Cross-Cultural Apologetics?, 73
  Barriers to Cross-Cultural Persuasion, 73–75
  Possibilities for Cross-Cultural Persuasion, 75–80
  Helpful Insights for Cross-Cultural Apologetics, 80–81

Ward, Michael, 41–42, 57, 215
Weight of Glory, 151, 211
Willard, Timothy, 42
Williams, Brian, 221
Williams, Donald, 34, 159
Williams, Paul, 182
wonder, 23–25, 30–31, 42–43, 45, 47, 51, 57, 66, 88, 115, 119–20, 132, 142, 158, 168, 177, 181, 183, 200, 230–31
worldview, 10, 15, 27, 30, 34–35, 57, 59, 74–80, 83, 87, 89–90, 96–100, 103–4, 121, 123, 127, 132–34, 136, 141, 143, 146, 152–55, 168–69, 173–76, 182, 190–92, 195, 199, 201, 220, 224–27
worship, 4, 24, 217, 227
Wright, N. T., 211

Yandell, Keith, 184
yoga, 175

www.ingramcontent.com/pod-product-compliance
Lightning Source LLC
Chambersburg PA
CBHW050842230426

43667CB00012B/2111